SECOND EDITION

The 200 Best Home Businesses

Easy to Start • Fun to Run • Highly Profitable

Katina Z. Jones

A
ADAMS MEDIA
Avon, Massachusetts

For Howard Lund, a master entrepreneur.

Originally published as *Easy to Start, Fun to Run &*
Highly Profitable Home Businesses, copyright © 1998 Adams Media.

Published by Adams Media, an F+W Publications Company
57 Littlefield Street
Avon, MA 02322. U.S.A.
www.adamsmedia.com

ISBN: 1-59337-296-5

Printed in Canada.
J I H G F E D C B A

Library of Congress Cataloging-in-Publication Data

Jones, Katina Z.
The 200 best home businesses / Katina Z. Jones.—2nd ed.
p.   cm.
Rev. ed. of: Easy to start, fun to run & highly profitable home businesses. ©1998.
Includes index.
ISBN 1-59337-296-5
1. Home-based businesses—Management. 2. New business enterprises. I. Title: Two
hundred best home businesses. II. Jones, Katina Z. Easy to start, fun to run & highly
profitable home businesses. III. Title.

HD62.38.J66 2005
658'.0412—dc22
2005009559

Composition and interior design by Electronic Publishing Services, Tennessee

This book is available at quantity discounts for bulk purchases.
For information, call 1-800-872-5627.

Contents

Introduction

There has never been a more exciting time to start your own business. New businesses are springing up every day across the country, and the majority of them are started right at home. Whether these new ventures are inspired by stay-at-home moms looking to earn extra cash, young people starting their careers with their own businesses, previously employed middle managers, or just regular folks looking to increase their monthly income, many are finding themselves caught in the entrepreneurial spirit.

As companies are learning to be leaner and meaner, career-minded individuals are learning that the only place to find true job security is right in their own home. They already know that the best way to prevent a layoff is to open up shop for themselves. Changes in government programs and tax benefits for these entrepreneurs have created a market situation for which it has never been easier to start—and operate—a new business. It's almost as if you'd be foolish not to try your hand at running your own show.

New technology in both the communications and computer industries has made home offices the norm, instead of the exception. Many entrepreneurs have been able to start their own home ventures while still employed, thus increasing their capital and minimizing their day-to-day financial risk.

This book, revised and updated with twenty-four new business opportunities, emphasizes the potential for many businesses that might start out as hobbies, personal interests, or an expansion of a particular skill you might already have. Take time to read through all of the business opportunities included here. You'll find that there is a balanced mix of part-time and full-time opportunities. Many jobs listed are considered white collar, but there are plenty of businesses listed that require a more hands-on approach and specific technical skills.

As you read each business description, you'll notice some specific statistical information at the beginning of each entry. It is organized as follows:

Start-up costs: Start-up costs can include everything from outfitting your home office with furniture, computer equipment, and business cards, to advertising campaigns and staffing. We've calculated these costs by adding together all potential equipment, advertising, and operating capital estimates (such as payroll, benefits, and utilities). We considered every possible cost, and then asked the question: "What's the least amount of money you would need to start this business the right way?"

Potential earnings: For most businesses listed in this book, this range is calculated by multiplying typical fees by a forty-hour work week. However, the market for some of these jobs is such that, while they would provide great extra or part-time income, they are not likely to provide forty hours of pay per week, year round. Obviously, your potential earnings will change dramatically if you are only considering starting any new business part-time. Please note: Potential earnings do not take into consideration the costs incurred during startup.

Typical fees: Each business idea has been thoroughly researched to find out what people who are actually in the business are charging their clients. For many entries, you will see a range instead of one flat fee, since pricing strategies often vary depending on geographic location.

Advertising: Here we have listed all the possible ways you could promote your business, from methods that cost nothing, such as networking, to developing actual media campaigns that might cost thousands of dollars a year. These expenses have been figured into initial start-up costs.

Qualifications: This category contains everything you need to know about professional certifications, licenses, and other information pertinent to what it takes to work at home in a particular field.

Equipment needed: The equipment purchases you are likely to make to run your business efficiently.

Staff required: A high percentage of these businesses won't require anyone but yourself, but those needing additional staff are identified, often with a suggested number of employees.

Hidden costs: This is probably the most important element of each entry. The costs that you don't think about are often the ones that drive your business into the ground. They include insurance coverage, workers' compensation, and even fluctuating material costs. Many of these are expenses that you simply can't predict or that you might not have realized are incurred by state and federal government requirements. Some may be as simple as the cost of additional gasoline.

The rest of each entry provides detailed descriptions of what the job entails and what you would need to be effective in your new venture. With each job, you'll get a total picture of what's involved in successfully running the kind of business that matches your skills and interests.

What You Do: This section supplies the details of exactly what each business demands of its owner, what your daily activities would be, and who your customers would be. This section also includes information on specific marketing opportunities.

What You Need: Here you'll find an in-depth breakdown of your start-up costs, including office furniture, computer equipment, and advertising costs. You will also find valuable information on how to arrive at specific income goals for each business.

Keys to Success: This section points out the positive and negative aspects of each business, so you'll know exactly what you're in for. Remember, there are positives and negatives for every opportunity.

In 1992, I started my own home business, a resume service, with about $500, a laptop computer, and some specialty paper that I bought from catalogs. Today, this business is still thriving and still a home-based business. In the interim, I've written seventeen books, got married, gave birth to a beautiful new daughter, adopted two more children from China, and have had at least two other "full-time" jobs. No matter what life brings me, this small business keeps going, profitably.

I can tell you that there is no greater reward than working for yourself at home (often without even getting fully dressed!). This book certainly will not provide all the answers, but it will help you think about the most crucial issues as you determine whether your business idea matches your current ideals and whether an entrepreneur's lifestyle really is for you. Plan for the future. Keep a watchful eye on emerging trends and allow yourself to dream. Good luck as you embark on what may become one of the most interesting journeys of your life!

Katina Z. Jones
June 2005

Accountant

Start-up cost:	$3,000–$6,000
Potential earnings:	$20,000–$80,000
Typical fees:	$35 and up per hour
Advertising:	Membership and active participation in community groups, ads in newspapers and publications for local fundraisers, referrals, possibly your own Web site with tax preparation tips on it as a resource for potential new clients
Qualifications:	CPA and some experience with services on which you choose to focus
Equipment needed:	Office area, furniture, computer, suite software, printer, business cards, letterhead, envelopes, cell phone is optional but handy
Staff required:	No
Hidden costs:	Errors and omissions insurance, subscriptions and membership dues, continuing education

What You Do

This is a service that virtually everyone needs. The challenge is to show potential clients how you can improve their lives by helping them manage their financial affairs better. The two major approaches chosen by solo accountants are (1) to work with individuals on tax issues and personal financial planning and (2) to serve the burgeoning small business market with bookkeeping setup, payroll, tax planning, and all the other financial activities that an enterprise requires. You will need to be creative in distinguishing yourself from this rather crowded field. How are your accounting services better than those of the other accountants in town? How can you show an individual that you can serve him better than the big storefront operations that prepare taxes for low fees during the winter and early spring?

What You Need

Will you meet clients in your office, or will you travel to their homes or businesses? These decisions will control your start-up costs (which could be as little as $3,000).

Keys to Success

Being an excellent accountant and being able to create a profitable business are two different things. The people skills required have probably been completely neglected in your education and possibly in your experience if you have worked for a large firm. Gaining the confidence of potential clients is far more than simply having excellent accounting skills up your sleeve, which is why an informative company Web site might be advantageous for business-building, especially in the beginning. You'll need to find a way to present your services in a way that appeals to people who want your help but don't really understand how you can best help them find ways to save money. On the downside, your services will be particularly needed during peak tax preparation seasons; you'll be busiest in December and March/April.

EXPERT ADVICE

What sets your business apart from others like it?

Personalized service and affordable rates are what set apart Kelly M. Zimmerman's accounting business in Cuyahoga Falls, Ohio. "I take a genuine interest in my clients' businesses. I really care about whether or not they succeed."

Things you couldn't do without

Zimmerman says she couldn't do without a computer, telephone, and calculator.

Marketing tips

"Get involved in an organization that you believe in personally and where you can also promote your business. Marketing for accountants is basically word-of-mouth, so be sure to do everything you can to keep your current clients happy. They'll send you more clients if they know you've gone out of your way for them."

If you had to do it all over again . . .

"I would try to be more organized and focused on the types of clients I really want to serve."

Adoption Agency

Start-up cost:	$5,000–$125,000
Potential earnings:	$200,000–$600,000+
Typical fees:	$12,000–$30,000 for each local and international adoption

Advertising:	Local family publications, adoption magazines, Web site with photo-listing of Waiting Children and plenty of adoption resources, banner ads on related Web sites of interest, registration with search engines, referrals
Qualifications:	Must be licensed by state and/or county
Equipment needed:	Office furniture, phone, computers with Internet access, letterhead
Staff required:	Yes—will need at least one licensed social worker to do home studies and possibly a team of folks to handle and review adoption paperwork
Hidden costs:	Notary services; postage; long-distance phone calls, particularly to foreign countries

What You Do

For some, the dream of having a child in their family would never be realized without the services of a qualified adoption agency. You can specialize in private, local adoptions or include international adoptions from a list of specific countries from which you've received permission to help place children in need of homes. Whether the child is from China, Korea, India, Russia, or your home state here in the United States, you will have to scrutinize potential parents through the required home study process, match them with children who are the best fit, then offer counseling and support as the parents and child are united. You can also help children born with special needs find the good homes they so deserve. This is a business in which the blessings far exceed any financial benefits. Many adoption agencies carry high overhead, so what seems like a fortune in potential earnings can actually be offset a bit by the costs of staffing and running a busy agency. Still, there are plenty of good reasons to choose this line of work, such as the more than four million children currently residing in orphanages worldwide.

What You Need

You will need to staff an office with everything from people to computers, since few hopeful parents would be willing to pay huge fees to someone who's a sole proprietor running an adoption agency out of his or her home. You need to instill confidence in your abilities and qualifications from the outset, and then work hard to keep your reputation intact in what can be a volatile business. It's not unusual for a birth mother in the United States to decide to keep her baby at the last minute, leaving you and your client family back at square one.

Keys to Success

Reputation is everything in this business. You need to be honest and upfront with your clients about all costs so that they don't feel you are taking advantage of their emotional distress over not having a child. Keep posting new testimonials on your Web site as you receive them—and don't be afraid to ask for more. Better yet, create a database of satisfied parents you've helped and who are willing to speak to your prospects about how wonderful you are. Such a list is worth its weight in gold!

☞ Advertising Agency

Start-up cost:	$7,000–$20,000
Potential earnings:	$35,000–$75,000
Typical fees:	$75–$150 per hour, a monthly retainer, or a per-job basis
Advertising:	Networking, ads in trade publications, participation in local chamber of commerce, and a Web site that is a true showcase of your company's talents
Qualifications:	Knowledge of design, layout, and typography; writing skills; experience working with businesses on brand and identity development
Equipment needed:	Cell phone (with or without hands-free accessories); computer with Internet access and full suite of presentation and design software; high-resolution color printer, scanner; digital camera; fax; copy machine; business cards; letterhead; envelopes
Staff required:	No
Hidden costs:	Your high-end Web site will definitely cost you some money to design and host, but it's worth its weight in gold for helping you quickly secure a high profile in the marketplace

What You Do

You're probably not going to be doing the Cadillac ads for General Motors in the beginning, but if you are motivated and highly skilled you can build up a home-based ad agency serving clients in a specialized area. To get a foothold, you'll need to have at least some experience from a larger agency or a list of potential clients who already know you and your work. Your participation in activities such as indoor soccer or squash, etc., could be your lead-in to a small but profitable market. Or you could specialize in one type of store, one product, or a type of service. You will get to know your client organizations well, and you will draw on all of your creativity, both written and graphic. New ways of getting a commercial message out to the public, including targeted e-messaging, high-end Web sites with e-commerce and exciting new brand-building capabilities are revolutionizing the advertising field, so creativity extends into the nature of the business itself as well. Very few businesses can succeed without advertising in one way or another, so your creativity and awareness of market needs has many possible customers. You'll need to educate your clients about the value of advertising, even when things don't seem to be going very well for the company. In fact, that's when they need you the most.

What You Need
High-end computers with the graphics and print-production software now available enable small agencies to produce outstanding ads that once required an entire art department. Setting up this equipment is expensive, though, and could cost from $3,000–$5,000. Bill out between $75–$150 per hour, or determine your rates on a per-job basis that takes into account how much work is actually involved in the project. Many ad agencies also work on monthly retainers of $500 or more; again, look at the workload and the time and expertise involved in each project. For presentations, you might also find a laptop especially helpful, which could cost another $2,000–$3,000.

Keys to Success
Advertising is a rewarding occupation because it relies so heavily on ideas and inspiration, connected directly to business results. Successful ad agency personnel (in this case, you) develop close relationships with their clients. You'll be serving an area or group that you know about and enjoy, and you'll be using all of your talents to do so. As a one-man (or one-woman) band, you must be able to do all the facets of the advertising process, from sales to writing, design, and promotion. But remember that it may also be very wise to partner with a good Web design firm to add to your portfolio of services without adding a regular, full-time staff. While this is a fun and always challenging business, its one downside is that the pressure never lets up because the competition for clients can be shark-like.

Expert Advice

What sets your business apart from others like it?
For Carol Wilkerson, owner of Wilkerson Ltd., in Portland, Oregon, it's experience that sets her business apart: "I have over twenty-three years of experience in advertising and public relations, and I have dealt from the bottom up with any kind of promotional effort there is. Also, I'm small and selective about who I work with, because I want to make sure I can really provide the top-notch service the client's looking for, turning things around quickly enough to keep them coming back for more."

Things you couldn't do without

Wilkerson's business depends on a computer, laser printer, fax, telephone, and overnight delivery services.

Marketing tips

"Before you start, determine what your strengths are and identify them for your clients. You really run into problems when you start promising things you really can't do . . . you can't fake knowledge and experience. Farm out what you can't do to others who can, and you'll gain a lot more respect."

If you had to do it all over again . . .

"Oddly enough, I didn't promote myself well enough in the beginning . . . I wasn't a big enough cheerleader for my own business. It's so ironic!"

Advertising Sales Representative

Start-up cost:	$2,500 and up
Potential earnings:	$40,000–$150,000
Typical fees:	Commission-only is standard and ranges from 5 to 25 percent
Advertising:	Direct mail, small ads or classifieds in trade journals, networking
Qualifications:	Experience with an advertising agency or as a periodical sales rep
Equipment needed:	Basic office equipment, business cards, letterhead, envelopes, laptop computer, cell phone (with or without hands-free accessories)
Staff required:	No
Hidden costs:	Expect high phone bills and mileage expenses

What You Do

This business must be built on extensive experience in the field. Your expertise lies in matching the need to the availability. If you know how, you can sell advertising space in all publications to the advertisers who need it. Your job is to find a buyer at a good price that might never have discovered this advertising venue unaided. You'll need contacts and experience to make a success of this enterprise, but room exists for the independent rep and many earn $100,000 or more. Much depends on the type of publication for which you're selling ad space; for instance, if you're selling ads in a trade journal or well-known national publication, your income will be quite high. However, if you're selling ads for a community newspaper, your income may reach its peak at $35,000.

What You Need
The telephone is your major tool, and you may discover a great need for a cell phone, particularly one with hands-free accessories (a necessity while driving in some states). You'll need access to reference books listing periodicals, rates, and dates.

Keys to Success
If you love selling, this is selling in its purest form. No limitations bind you to one focus, one time, or one perspective. Businesses need to advertise, and finding space for their commercial messages can be a real challenge. Your services are the perfect answer to their needs. Businesses' penchant for doing the same things the same old ways will be your biggest hindrance to getting new customers. Established agencies are your competitors, and you will need to market your services vigorously. Your best bet is to find a few really good "anchor" customers who will advertise on a long-term contract, then go after the smaller fish.

Animal Breeder

Start-up cost:	$10,000–$15,000
Potential earnings:	$45,000–$80,000
Typical fees:	Often $200–$600 per animal
Advertising:	Breeding magazines and shows, newspaper ads, networking, Web site
Qualifications:	Knowledge of specific animal breed, familiarity with breed standards; a permit will likely be necessary as well (check with your local zoning board)
Equipment needed:	Cell phone (with or without hands-free accessories), computer with Internet access, fax, printer, business cards, letterhead, envelopes
Staff required:	No
Hidden costs:	Home kennel and breeding area (check with your local zoning board for permit fees)

What You Do

Dog and cat shows are more popular than ever. All you need is cable television to witness the craze. But where, besides the highly undesirable "puppy mills," do the most beautiful breeds come from? If you have a passion for purebreds, becoming an animal breeder might be just what the veterinarian ordered! Once you pick a breed in which to specialize, you will need to build a small kennel and breeding ground and find your prize-winning bitch or stud. Then you will advertise your breeding service. You may also decide to find a suitable breed match for your initial animal and sell their offspring to smaller pet shops or directly to the new pet owners. Once you become known as a breeder, you will be able to quickly and easily connect with breed lovers via shows and the Internet.

What You Need

A cell phone will probably be your most important piece of office equipment, along with e-mail for communicating with distant customers and contacts. A good computer with a high-resolution digital camera will also help you showcase the animals you are offering for sale.

Keys to Success

The most important asset you have is your breed. You will constantly need to protect the integrity of the breed characteristics, so your animals cannot be bred with just any other of its species. What will help you the most to grow your business is for your animals to win major show titles, so that their offspring become more valuable due to their lineage. Like the many animals you'll breed, this business will take time to grow.

⌂ Antiques Dealer

Start-up cost:	$1,000–$40,000 (depending on how large you would like your inventory to be)
Potential earnings:	$35,000–$150,000
Typical fees:	Varied; your pieces will sell anywhere from $10–$10,000
Advertising:	Yellow Pages, community newspapers, direct mail, show participation, a Web site of your own, possibly listing on sites like Antiques.com, a large sign to advertise on outside of home
Qualifications:	Should be knowledgeable about antiques and pricing
Equipment needed:	Credit card processing equipment, computer with high-quality digital camera and Internet access, printer, fax

Staff required: No

Hidden costs: Insurance, warehousing, packaging and shipping

What You Do

The lure of the old and priceless draws many a sentimental customer into an antique store, and you could start such a business with a dozen or so nice pieces of furniture, some antique china, and lots of old books and toys. All of these items tend to sell well, as they are collectible and worth increasingly more with each passing year. You'll need to develop a sizable stock or inventory of pieces to sell, which can best be accomplished by combing thrift shops, flea markets, estate sales, and Internet auctions on eBay, Yahoo!, and Antiques.com for the best and most interesting old items you can find. Watch the newspaper for garage sales, too. Sometimes people will unknowingly unload a fabulous antique at a steal of a price.

Basically, you should keep in mind that your business will need to be run just like any other retail establishment, which means you'll need to price yourself well enough to cover your operating expenses in addition to building a profit. Folks will want to barter with you on price, so you'll need to hold firm with your price or raise your price enough to compensate for allowing customers to talk you down the typical 10–15 percent. You can also choose to conduct online auctions to automatically generate competitive bidding.

What You Need

It all depends on how you plan on growing your business. You can start off with just a few pieces for under $2,000, and then add more accordingly. To really turn a profit, you'll want to start with significant inventory that will run you upwards of $20,000. Look to earn $35,000–$150,000, depending on three things: location, quality of product line, and price. Obviously, if you're in a quaint New England town, you might fare better than an antique shop in the middle of Kentucky. But if you have antique items in high demand around the country, location won't even be an issue—and the sky's the limit.

Keys to Success

It's a competitive market, and too many well-intended entrepreneurs make the mistake of thinking this will be an easy ride. If you are focused on high-end antiques and have sufficient working capital to buy the kinds of pieces that will build your reputation for the finer things, then you'll have little problem making a living. If, on the other hand, you choose to specialize in less-expensive antiques and collectibles, you'll need to round up lots of inventory because you'll likely be turning it around very quickly.

Apartment Preparation Service

Start-up cost:	$500
Potential earnings:	$20,000–$30,000
Typical fees:	$50 and up per apartment
Advertising:	Yellow Pages, direct contact with apartment owners, banner ads at Web sites such as Apartments.com or ApartmentFinder.com
Qualifications:	Knowledge of cleaning procedures and painting skills
Equipment needed:	Cleaning supplies, sweeper, mops, buckets, painting equipment, cell phone
Staff required:	No
Hidden costs:	Insurance, equipment maintenance

What You Do

You add the finishing touches to apartment buildings before the next tenant moves in. To increase your marketability, offer several services, including carpet cleaning, wall washing, painting, wallpaper repair, and overall cleaning services. Set fee schedules appropriately depending on individual services (or offer an all-inclusive package price). Advertise your services to many apartment complexes. To cut down on driving, try to get a contract with a multiunit apartment complex that offers short-term lease options.

What You Need

Invest in good-quality cleaning equipment, including a sweeper and carpet cleaner. Start-up costs can be as low or as high as you want, depending on what services you are going to offer and the quality of equipment you purchase. This business can be started for a relatively low cost with high return on investment. Keep a cell phone with you so that you can easily respond to your next customer.

Keys to Success

This business is not for someone who is afraid of using good, hard elbow grease. Be prepared to encounter some messy situations. An apartment preparer might spend quite a bit of time on their hands and knees cleaning baseboards and floors. Consider the health of your back and always wear a back brace. In addition, invest in a good pair of kneepads and rubber gloves.

Artists'/Photographers' Agent

Start-up cost:	$5,000–$15,000
Potential earnings:	$25,000–$50,000
Typical fees:	20 percent commission on each sale
Advertising:	Trade publications for artists and photographers, a listing in the annual *Photographer's Market* and *Guide to Literary Agents/Art Photo Reps* (Writer's Digest Books), direct mail to related associations, a Web site with an online portfolio of your clients' work
Qualifications:	Ideally, an artistic and/or sales background
Equipment needed:	Computer with Internet access, printer, fax, copier, phone
Staff required:	No
Hidden costs:	Insurance, bad risks (representing artists because you care about them rather than because they are marketable)

What You Do

Behind every successful artist or photographer is an agent who carts around resumes and slides from market to market, seeking the best opportunity to sell works of art to everyone from gallery owners to art catalog publishers and distributors. As an agent, you can also sell your clients' work by using a well-designed, easily accessible Web site that you promote through e-messaging, blogging, and by hooking your clients into cash cows like GettyImages.com. The key is to juggle several artists and/or photographers at once and market them as widely as possible. To grow your stable of clients to represent, advertise in the publications that artistic types generally read. Invite them to send a detailed resume and plenty of slides. When you decide to represent someone, provide a contract that clearly spells out what services your client can expect from you and what commission per sale you expect from your client.

What You Need

You'll need to promote your services in each of the respective professional trade publications, and that will likely cost you in the neighborhood of $3,000–$5,000 (some directories, however, allow you a free listing). Next, you'll need to have a set of dynamic, yet professional-looking promotional materials of your own (including an impressive Web site) and a basic office set-up to keep it all running smoothly. With a commission of 20 percent on each sale you make, you should be able to earn an annual paycheck between $25,000–$50,000, depending on where you live and how many successful artists you represent.

Keys to Success

The art world is extremely tight-knit. Cliques abound, and if your name isn't known as one of the "chosen few," you may not succeed as much as you'd like. Work the art show openings and other functions and attend trade shows and the like if you really want to get your name out there fast. Above all else, be knowledgeable about art. If you're not, it will definitely show. There are far more talented artists than there are folks to represent them, so the potential to develop your client base quickly is quite high. Be choosy about whom you represent and offer a wide range of artwork for sale to increase your chances of success.

Arts Festival Promoter

Start-up cost:	$1,500–$5,000
Potential earnings:	$20,000–$45,000+
Typical fees:	40 percent of registration fees from artists and, in most cases, a commission from each ticket sold (typically 3–5 percent)
Advertising:	Networking, ads in artists' newsletters and publications, direct mail to artists, newspaper/billboard ads for the event itself, a promotional Web site that includes a "Call for Artists" and a volunteer sign-up area
Qualifications:	Strong organizational and event-planning skills
Equipment needed:	Cell phone (with or without hands-free accessories), computer with desktop publishing software, laser printer
Staff required:	No, but local volunteers are often needed
Hidden costs:	Insurance and low attendance due to poor advertising or inclement weather; try to have a backup plan for each event

What You Do

Annual arts festivals abound in nearly every community, and you could cash in on the public's interest in the arts by sponsoring or promoting your own group of arts festivals. Give your events a flashy name so that you can win instant recognition with your buying public and among artists (who get barraged with requests to appear in shows all over the country). You'll need to promote your festivals two ways: first, to artists who might like to participate; second, to folks who might like to attend. Your advertising budget must be split to reach both. Set your festivals apart by inviting only particular types of artists/craftsmen. You can also set them apart by attaching your festivals to some sort of theme, such as an Oktoberfest arts festival. That way, you've set an annual time for the show to be expected to recur. You can build your mailing list for the following year by requiring everyone to sign in (or, better yet, by offering a drawing for an exquisite work of art).

What You Need

You'll need $1,500–$5,000 to launch this interesting and artistic enterprise. This seed money will primarily cover your computer and printer costs and a little advertising until you have one or two shows under your belt. Once you've established your business, you could have annual repeat business in certain areas and begin to make more than $45,000 per year doing something you truly enjoy.

Keys to Success

You love the arts and know that others like artsy events. So what's the downside? The only real negative is that sometimes the weather rains on your parade of artists. You could avoid such mishaps if you hold all of your events indoors. Even though it may raise your space rental cost, the payoff might be worth it. Or, you could secure some tents and charge each artist a small rental fee so that you're "covered."

Association Management Services

Start-up cost:	$2,000–$9,000
Potential earnings:	$20,000–$50,000
Typical fees:	Monthly retainers of $1,000–$5,000 are not uncommon (directly dependent upon the association's size)
Advertising:	Network with professional and trade associations, advertise in related publications, link to your own Web site from the Web sites you manage for your client associations
Qualifications:	Good organizational, writing, marketing, communication, and motivation skills; an eye for detail; possibly management or administrative experience
Equipment needed:	Cell phone (with or without hands-free accessories), computer with Internet access and Web-hosting capabilities, phone, fax, copier, business cards, letterhead, supplies
Staff required:	No
Hidden costs:	Membership in associations, subscriptions to related publications, Web server space to host your clients' Web sites

What You Do

From the Association for Association Management (yes, there really is an association for everyone) to the Association for Children for Enforcement of Support, most organizations need help in managing their operations. Especially well suited to a management service are groups too big to rely solely on volunteers but not big enough to justify hiring someone to do it on a full-time basis. Your services for each client may vary, but may include maintaining membership lists, publishing a newsletter, mailing out information about the organization, keeping records, collecting dues, and handling meetings, events, and fundraising activities. Not only can you work for an existing organization, you could also start an association of your own if you base it on your own profession or something else with which you have personal experience.

What You Need

Office and computer equipment are your biggest expenses (about $2,000). You may be able to get the organization(s) you represent to pay for some supplies (but don't rely on this when creating your business plan). Charge a monthly retainer of $1,000–$5,000 for your services to make sure you cover all of your expenses. Since many of these associations work with volunteers, they may try to take advantage of your expertise too. Don't let them.

Keys to Success

Association management provides a great variety of duties and an opportunity to interact with interesting people. You will also get opportunities to learn about an array of topics at meetings and conventions. This is a great opportunity for those with philanthropic tendencies. To continually "wow" your association clients with top-notch management services that include Web site design and management as well as e-messaging campaigns to solicit members or donations, partner with some excellent Web designers who know how to stretch small dollars into huge returns on an attractive and fully functional Web site. Helping your clients to retain longtime members while adding new ones is your biggest challenge.

Auctioneer

Start-up cost:	$500–$1,000
Potential earnings:	$25,000–$150,000
Typical fees:	Flat fee of $150–$300, plus 3–5 percent of sales

Advertising:	Advertising in specialty publications (art/antiques, cars, farm equipment/livestock), business cards at each event, networking, your own Web site with links to auction houses
Qualifications:	A good, strong voice and the ability to stay on top of rapid-fire bidding
Equipment needed:	A gavel and a megaphone
Staff required:	One person
Hidden costs:	Travel expenses (be sure to build those into your upfront fee)

What You Do

Going once, going twice . . . SOLD to the buyers in your audience when you are an auctioneer! You will likely learn the business from another experienced auctioneer, who will teach you the ins and outs of facilitating deals and bargains with large groups of people. Whether you choose to specialize in auto, farm equipment, livestock, or fine arts and antiques, you will always be in the center of all the action when it comes to auctioning off items of interest to others. You will have to speak quickly and stay on top of the highest bidders at all times, so you'll need to have an extra-sharp mind with a good memory. Conflict-resolution skills may be necessary at times, especially when there is disagreement over who bid what and when. Hire a decent backup person to act as a witness and to help keep track of where the bids stand at each moment of the bidding process. Remember—you can auction everything from bric-a-brac to your home online!

What You Need

You really don't need much more than dependable transportation, a gavel ($10–$15), and a good megaphone ($150 maximum). Sometimes you'll be auctioning in places where microphones will be provided, but you can never be sure so you should always bring a megaphone with you.

Keys to Success

Once you become a visible fixture at local auctions, you will find that the business comes to you more easily. In the beginning, you might partner with a more experienced auctioneer or even one who is retiring, so that you can serve as stand-in when he or she cannot personally attend auctions. Soon you'll start building a name for yourself—riding the coattails of the pro you're replacing. That is a bargain at any price!

☞ Auditor

Start-up cost:	$5,000–$8,000
Potential earnings:	$50,000–$75,000
Typical fees:	Percentage of the savings you find for clients: often 50 percent for past savings and about 10 percent for two or more years into the future
Advertising:	Business and trade publications, direct mail, membership in business groups, networking, your own Web site with free, money-saving tips for businesses
Qualifications:	Accounting degree and certification, knowledge of area of specialty (utility bills, telephone options), excellent math skills, good detail orientation, selling skills
Equipment needed:	Cell phone (with or without hands-free accessories), office furniture, computer, suite software, printer, calculator, business cards, letterhead, envelopes, marketing materials
Staff required:	No
Hidden costs:	Ongoing marketing time and materials, continuing education

What You Do

As bills become more complicated, the opportunity for finding errors and over-charges in them increases. For most businesses, though, the tedious, detail-oriented work necessary to check each bill and interpret all the data is just too time-consuming. An auditing specialist can work through all the paper records, uncover overcharges, collect a percentage of the money saved, and make an excellent living. To be very successful, you will need the ability to consider what lies behind the rows of figures on a utility bill. Something as basic as a misplaced decimal point can have a huge effect, but it's harder to spot incorrect rate assignments, double billing for small segments of the service, or opportunities to use a different rate structure.

What You Need

You'll need a good place to work. This is a lot of detailed reading, calculating, and thinking, so your equipment needs to fit you comfortably (around $3,000 to start).

Keys to Success

If you focus on utility bills, look for organizations that consume large quantities of electricity, such as businesses that are open all night. Government organizations, churches, and other institutions with big buildings and inadequate staffing are excellent prospects also. Some auditing services focus on insurance costs or telephone charges. In spite of the clear benefits you will offer, however, marketing is a challenge. People aren't used to the idea of auditing specialists, and they probably have no idea how much money they are pouring down the drain each month in their businesses. In other words, they undoubtedly need your service, but they don't realize it. You will succeed when you find a way to help them understand the benefit you offer.

EXPERT ADVICE

What sets your business apart from others like it?

"I don't just punch numbers into a computer . . . I delve deeper to find out more about my customers and how I can help them on a long-term basis," says Dianna Stahl, President & CEO of E.R.S., Inc., in Akron, Ohio.

Things you couldn't do without

Stahl says she absolutely couldn't do without a computer and a phone.

Marketing tips

"Find a good mentor in whatever area you're weak in. I was weak in sales, so I found myself a good sales mentor and it helped immeasurably."

If you had to do it all over again . . .

"Know the people you're going to go into business with well before you do it. I was starting my business based on someone else's promises, and they didn't come through. Fortunately, it worked out."

Automotive Detailing

Start-up cost:	$5,000–$10,000
Potential earnings:	$30,000–$60,000
Typical fees:	$100–$500 per job
Advertising:	Newspapers, automotive publications, body shops, networking with dealers, regional coupon books (offer 10 percent off or one free service after five visits, and so on)
Qualifications:	A flair for the artistic
Equipment needed:	Cleaning equipment such as polish, rags, brushes, toothbrushes, cotton swabs; equipment such as airbrush, paint, sealer

Staff required: No

Hidden costs: Larger building as business grows

What You Do

Automotive detailing can be done anywhere and at your convenience. A relatively low initial investment will start you on your way. Although the number of auto detailers has grown significantly, you can remain competitive by creating a smart marketing plan, providing superior service, offering lower prices, and exhibiting sound management skills. Continually look for ways to provide services that your competition has overlooked.

What You Need

Aside from the cost of basic cleaning equipment, an airbrush and related art supplies will start at $2,500. It may be necessary to consider the location of your business. You may need to buy a small garage or shed in which to work.

Keys to Success

If you have dreamed of working at your own pace and during the hours you choose, automotive detailing can be a rewarding occupation. Individuals with artistic flair and an appreciation for well-kept automobiles are always in demand as many automobile dealers continue to farm out their detail work. Creativity is the key to keeping the competition at bay. Consider a mobile detail shop as your business van to allow on-site work, saving you and your customers valuable time. Your work is different everyday, so what's not to like?

Automotive Loan Broker

Start-up cost: $3,000–$10,000

Potential earnings: $50,000–$70,000

Typical fees: Percentage of loan amount from lender or borrower

Advertising: Classified ads in local and national newspapers and magazines, banner ads on sites like Cars.com, and a Web site of your own where people could prequalify for loans online (pending your review and approval)

Qualifications: Finance background would be helpful

Equipment needed:	Cell phone (with or without hands-free accessories), office furniture, computer with Internet access and Web site hosting capabilities, suite software, printer, fax, business cards, letterhead, envelopes
Staff required:	No
Hidden costs:	Utility bills

What You Do

A loan broker brings together the people who need money with the institutions that are in the business of lending it. As an automotive loan broker you will be specializing in a type of loan that almost every household in the country needs. There are roughly 1.8 vehicles per household in the United States, and most of the new vehicles sold are purchased through loans. That's a huge potential market. How can you become a part of this picture? You have a list of lenders, a long list. You have obtained their trust with a well-organized business plan. You advertise for borrowers in local automotive newspapers and Web sites like Cars.com. It is also possible that local auto dealerships might be good referral sources for you, so it would be worth some buddy-up time with them. The best part is, you don't have to restrict yourself to your own geographical area; much of this business can be done via Internet (through your Web site) and by phone. It is important to have a written agreement before you begin the loan search process, as most of your clients will use your service instead of a bank because they've had trouble securing credit in a more traditional way.

What You Need

The borrowers will visit the lender's office, not yours. Your initial start-up costs are your Web site, some advertising, and the equipment to support your paperwork and communications; all of these should be under $10,000. The Web site is crucial and should include a secure server, since your customers will be sending confidential information via the Internet through your site. Still, you should be able to generate significant business if you can promise decent terms. If you have true marketing savvy, you could earn as much as $70,000 from all of your efforts. In short, the potential for success in this business is high. All you need is the ability to produce. The more automated you make your business, the higher your profit will ultimately be.

Keys to Success

Clarity on goals and expectations is vital to the professional, ethical conduct of a loan brokering business. You make it clear to the potential borrower what expenses are to be reimbursed, and you take a fee only as a commission on a completed loan. Skill at bringing the two sides of the automotive transaction together can enable you to earn a very high income once you are established. Persistence pays off here, as it so often does in the world of small business.

Automotive Maintenance

Start-up cost:	$2,000–$5,000
Potential earnings:	$25,000–$50,000
Typical fees:	$25 and up per hour you spend on a job, plus part costs
Advertising:	Newspaper, radio, billboards, neighborhood flyers, direct mail, location, electronic mailing lists for car enthusiasts, a Web site with car care tips or photos of your best work
Qualifications:	Certified Automobile Mechanic, knowledge of environmental and governmental regulations
Equipment needed:	Automotive repair tools, inventory of wipers, motor oil, garage space (rented or owned), a computer for researching parts availability as well as for doing some self-promotion
Staff required:	No
Hidden costs:	Inventory, insurance, ongoing advertising

What You Do

Americans value our autos very highly, and we want excellent care for them. An auto maintenance service can be a wonderful way to reach this large group of customers, most of whom are keeping their cars years longer than they did in the past. You can focus your business just on maintenance and leave the complicated computer diagnosis and repairs and the big parts inventory to the dealers and garages. You'll have a limited, repeated set of procedures to follow, and you can build a loyal clientele if you keep people's cars running well and do it in a way that is convenient for their drivers.

What You Need

Costs will be fairly high to equip your business, unless you can buy a set of tools from another business for a reasonable sum. It will take some expensive marketing to launch your enterprise, and you will need to keep a certain level of advertising going throughout each year. If you are good, word of mouth could get you at least $25,000 the first year.

Keys to Success

So, what makes you think you can compete with Minit-Lube? The answer, of course, is personal service. You're not just a well-trained teenager in a clean uniform, you're an experienced, well-organized, customer-oriented maintenance person. You're the answer to the dreams of the little old lady who relies on her car for safe travel; of the incredibly busy executive who demands rapid, accurate service; and of the car nuts who drop in and want to "talk cars" with someone else who cares about them as much as they do. As long as there are cars, there will always be work for people who know how to fix them.

Expert Advice

What sets your business apart from others like it?

Paul Taylor, owner of a Midas Muffler franchise in Lawrence, New York, says his business is set apart because it's run by him. "I believe in the highest standards of equipment and service, and my customers know that about me."

Things you couldn't do without

"It really depends on the types of services you're providing. If it's just a muffler shop, you'll only need an air compressor, cutting torches, a MIG welder, and lifts; you'll need more equipment if you start adding brake services and other automotive repair services." Taylor says he couldn't do without multiline phones, an answering machine, fax, and printer in his office.

Marketing tips

"As an independent, you'll need to do more guerrilla-type marketing, going after wholesale work within a trade as a subcontractor for body shops or transmission services. If you're in a franchise operation, you should be getting all the marketing and technical support they can offer; after all, that's really the only reason for buying into a franchise."

If you had to do it all over again . . .

"I think I've done all the right things."

Automotive Paint Touch-Up Professional

Start-up cost:	$500–$1,000
Potential earnings:	$15,000–$25,000
Typical fees:	$30–$50 per job
Advertising:	Memberships to and active participation in car enthusiast events, direct mail, flyers, networking with dealers and auto repair shops, radio spots, classified ads in auto sales section of newspaper
Qualifications:	Some experience with auto paint work, sales skills, knowledge of environmental regulations

Equipment needed:	Inventory of popular paint colors, sander, brush
Staff required:	No
Hidden costs:	Inventory and disposal of used chemicals

What You Do

It's not the big things that drive us crazy; sometimes, it's the dings in our car doors and the chips off the hood. For an entirely new paint job or the replacement of a crumpled fender, plenty of sources are available in most communities. But how can people keep those little scratches and chips from slowly ruining the appearance and resale value of their cars? That's where your service comes in. You can fix the small stuff, which is important nowadays just to keep a car's body warranty in effect. Your business meets the need for a hassle-free, inexpensive way to maintain the smooth surface that your customers' vehicles had when new.

What You Need

Costs are low (about $500 for materials). Your skill in doing neat-looking paint touch-ups is your main product. On a part-time basis alone you could earn in excess of $15,000.

Keys to Success

Can you find a way to market to and serve a number of people in one place, perhaps even offering group discounts? Would it work to fix the scratches in every car in the parking lot of a huge company? Can you be an add-in to the work of a local detailer, car wash, or used car lot? You decide and market yourself accordingly.

Band Manager

Start-up cost:	$500–$1,000
Potential earnings:	$15,000–$25,000
Typical fees:	10 to 25 percent of a gig
Advertising:	Industry trade publications, local paper, direct mail, nightclubs, bulletin boards, musicians' associations, electronic mailing lists, and banner ads on Web sites for musicians; later, you might consider having a Web site of your own with testimonials from other bands you manage
Qualifications:	An ear for what will sell, management skills
Equipment needed:	Cell phone (with or without hands-free accessories), computer, laser printer, phone, letterhead, business cards

The 200 Best Home Businesses

Staff required: No

Hidden costs: Band could fire you without notice; it might be a good idea to represent several bands at once

What You Do

You're into the club scene. You know instinctively what's hot and what's not. You see a few up-and-coming bands who need representation (because, truthfully, most musicians lack business skills). If you have the ability to convince musicians that you can really sell them and make their jobs easier by handling all of the business details they'd probably rather not think of anyway, you could make a decent living. You'll need to be well connected on the club scene. If you are clued in on where to plug your band(s), you could successfully book them for regular gigs and earn a steady flow of income for yourself in the meantime. Of course, you need to really believe in your band, because if you don't, you won't be able to develop and promote them properly and it will show in your presentation. Good negotiation skills are a must.

What You Need

You'll need some initial capital ($500–$1,000) to help get the band off the ground and lay the ground for some publicity. The ability to negotiate good contracts is important not only to the band, but also to you since you get roughly 10 to 25 percent of what they make. With percentages like that, you could realistically make $15,000–$25,000 (depending on how many bands you represent).

Keys to Success

Expect to spend long hours on the phone trying to get bookings. You'll probably still have a day job in the beginning, so expect your evenings and weekends to be tied up and your cell phone to always be on. Start out at small clubs and work your way to bigger ones as your band(s) get more experience and confidence.

Bankruptcy Services

Start-up cost: $1,000–$10,000

Potential earnings: $25,000–$40,000

Typical fees: $350 per client; sometimes an additional percentage (5 to 10 percent) from the creditors

Advertising: Local newspaper ads, seminars, public service speaking engagements, a Web site that offers alternatives to bankruptcy filing and/or credit-restoration tips

Qualifications: Financial planning expertise, good people skills

Equipment needed:	Office furniture suitable for client conferences, business cards, computer with high-speed Internet access, letterhead, envelopes, marketing materials
Staff required:	No
Hidden costs:	Errors and omissions insurance

What You Do

Overextending is one thing; being completely out of financial control is another. Your clients are the people who realize that they can't manage the debt they've accumulated, and they may be so overwhelmed they can't manage the bankruptcy process either. You assist them in developing a clear picture of their financial situation, filing for bankruptcy, and planning for the consequences. In today's world of easy credit, many people find themselves in bankruptcy without quite realizing what hit them. They're distressed, humiliated, and probably very confused as well. Your assistance with the painful process of sorting out the facts from the feelings is a very significant benefit.

What You Need

Costs can be low (under $3,000), depending largely upon how extensive you choose to make your Web site. If you do it yourself and keep it simple, you can stay closer to a $1,000 startup. But if you choose a more interactive experience for your customers, complete with online evaluation of their situation, you could be looking at a much higher start-up cost of $10,000 or more.

Keys to Success

You are meeting your clients at a real low point in their lives, but you are the first step on their way back up. So the emotional temperature of your workday is going to be fluctuating wildly. Keeping a good psychological balance will be as important as getting the paperwork filled out correctly. Some of your clients will just have been irresponsible, but others will have been dealt an impossible hand by fate. Historically, the bankruptcy process has been designed to help these people by wiping the slate more or less clean. People facing bankruptcy are not generally easy to work with, so your skill in dealing with the human side of your business—which may include some raw emotions—will be essential.

Bartending Service

Start-up cost:	Under $1,000
Potential earnings:	$10,000–$20,000

Typical fees:	$15–$30 per hour or a flat per-event rate
Advertising:	Classified ads, bulletin boards, community newspapers
Qualifications:	Legal drinking age; ability to mix drinks without looking them up; some states require certification and familiarity with legal and liability issues
Equipment needed:	None, but a cell phone might be handy
Staff required:	No
Hidden costs:	None apparent, but watch your mileage

What You Do

Being a traveling bartender service for private parties is an exciting way to meet people and make money at the same time. You'll mix libations for everyone from wealthy executives to people at a family celebration, and the time will always pass quickly. You'll need to make sure that if you are expected to bring the beverages, you secure funds from your customer ahead of time. Be sure to add in the cost of delivering the goods as well. The best way to get started is to produce professional-looking business cards and leave them prominently displayed at a few of your first jobs. In fact, you may want to do your first five jobs for free if you feel you'll get a lot of attention. That may be a great way to start the highballs rolling!

What You Need

With virtually nothing to lose but your time, you could do far worse than start a bartending service. Invest in a few good mixology handbooks and you'll be off to a great start! You also may want to visit the more progressive bars in your area to see if the bartenders know of any interesting new drinks. The more you can offer your clients, the happier they will be.

Keys to Success

You'll really absorb the energy and variety of bartending work, but it can be tiring to stand on your feet in one place for too long. Remember to bring a bar stool for yourself and invest in a good pair of shoes with soothing inserts!

⬒ Bartering Service

Start-up cost:	$500–$2,000
Potential earnings:	$15,000 and up
Typical fees:	$15 or more per transaction

Advertising:	Community newspaper classifieds, bulletin boards, flyers, networking, participation in community activities related to recycling, cooperative grocery stores, Web site detailing your services
Qualifications:	Friendliness, attention to detail
Equipment needed:	A fast computer and high-speed Internet access
Staff required:	No
Hidden costs:	Phone bill may be higher than expected

What You Do

You know everyone. You never waste a penny. You love to solve problems and to help other people solve theirs. That's why you will derive great satisfaction from your barter system business. It's really just putting two and two together: what someone has with what someone else needs, and vice versa. Making it all work as a profitable business will be a bit more challenging than just this (which you have probably been doing on an amateur basis most of your life). Many barter systems are warehouse operations, with individuals buying bulk odd lots and then trying to trade them. You will need to become known, to gather the data, the offerings, and the needs, and to work continually at the matches. Creating some kind of valuation system for disparate objects and services may pose difficulties also: how does a car wash match up with a soccer ball? Trading small ski boots for larger ones is easier. Your best bet is to suggest cost or product categories (i.e., $10–$25 or "Sporting Goods") to keep people from trying to barter for more than they are offering. Your customers will be much happier when they are exchanging things like leaf removal service for snow-plowing, or art supplies for computer paper.

What You Need

Costs will be minimal (only about $500 to start). You'll need some way for your clientele to reach you, and some way to track what is bartered. Your resourcefulness is really what you're selling in this business. A part-time business should net you around $15,000.

Keys to Success

Barter systems appeal to people who try to live inexpensively and not wastefully: the cooperative market types, people in academic communities, and creative thinkers who are trying to step off the whirl of consumerism that keeps many of us in debt. You'll develop repeat customers if you can help people obtain their wants and get rid of their don't-wants at the same time without paying large sums of money—just a small fee to you for the privilege. This business is a classic example of making something out of nothing. Virtually no investment, no training required, nothing but hard work on your part.

☞ Bed & Breakfast

Start-up cost:	$60,000 (assuming you already own the building)
Potential earnings:	$35,000–$175,000
Typical fees:	$125+ per room, per night (depending on season)
Advertising:	Yellow Pages, B&B directories (both online and print), direct mail to travel agencies, Web site with reservation capability or booking calendar
Qualifications:	Permits for serving food to guests, may need zoning permit, knowledge of regulations
Equipment needed:	Beds and linens, towels, dining tables/chairs with enough seating for all guests, plates and drinking glasses, kitchen equipment, washer/dryer, large freezer, stationery/brochures
Staff required:	Yes (but it could be composed of family members)
Hidden costs:	Be sure your prices cover everything from electricity to food, as your utility bills and food costs will be significantly higher than usual

What You Do

Large verandas for after-dinner strolls . . . billowy white curtains blowing in the breeze . . . quiet meals by firelight. The sheer romance of a B&B can be intoxicating enough to entice you into starting one of your own. If marketing trends are on target, more and more folks are looking for unusual escapes from the stress of their everyday lives. And.what better place to recuperate than a peaceful, romantic inn? You'll need anywhere from two to twelve extra rooms for guest accommodations, in addition to adequate kitchen and dining space. You will need to be meticulous in your cleaning and make sure that all prepared foods follow strict regulations. Also, be sure to educate yourself on all of the tourist attractions in your immediate area. You'll be surprised how often customers will count on your local expertise in devising their travel plans.

What You Need

You'll need at least $100,000–$400,000 if you need to purchase a suitable home; you may also look into buying an existing B&B and simply taking over the business (turnover is relatively high, as some owners burn out after a period of ten years or so). If you already have a large enough home, put aside extra cash ($5,000–$10,000) for repairs and updates, in addition to another $10,000 to cover your initial operating costs. You'll spend between $1,500–$5,000 on your first six months of advertising as well. But considering that you'll charge clients $125 and up per night, you should be able to develop a steady cash flow within the first five years of your business plan's projections.

Keys to Success

You could easily be drawn in to the seemingly idyllic country inn lifestyle. But before you launder the sheets, put mints on the pillows, and open your doors to guests, give a lot of thought to the hard work ahead; most B&B owners will tell you that there are long hours of intense work (cooking, cleaning, and assisting guests in all of their needs). If you don't mind putting in a sixty-plus-hour work-week without the promise of grand riches, a bed and breakfast inn can be a great match. You'll certainly meet lots of interesting people!

Bicycle Rental

Start-up cost:	$7,500–$12,000
Potential earnings:	$50,000–$80,000
Typical fees:	$12–$15 per half-hour rental
Advertising:	Flyers/brochures (give some to the chamber of commerce or travel agencies), Yellow Pages, banner ads on travel or local chamber of commerce Web sites
Qualifications:	Knowledge of bicycle maintenance
Equipment needed:	Fleet of bicycles and repair kits; may need storage space
Staff required:	No
Hidden costs:	Liability/theft insurance

What You Do

Remember the days of the bicycle built for two, when tourists rented bikes to explore island areas where cars either didn't exist or were blessedly limited? Those days are still here—but the majority of bicycle rental businesses are now clustered around crowded tourist spots such as Michigan's Mackinac Island or Florida's sandy beaches. Many bicycle rental shops are now featuring Rollerblade rentals as well, especially in places like California. Regardless of what you decide to offer, you'll be amazed at how much money can be made in this relatively easy business. Each day you'll take a fee for short-term rentals, offering the possibility of instant repeat business or a large number of daily rentals. And since most bicycle rentals are cash transactions, you'll have instant money. What could be easier than that?

What You Need

Your main costs stem from the fact that you must buy a good fleet of bicycles, typically twenty to twenty-five of them at a cost of $300 or so each. If necessary, you can also rent garage space for $100–$300 per month. If you invest in only used bicycles, your maintenance costs could potentially be high. Considering that you'll be earning $12–$15 per half-hour rentals, you could make a sizable amount of money very quickly in this business if you're in a tourist area (especially one that doesn't allow many cars). Don't forget to spend some money on advertising; for instance, a few strategically placed banner ads on travel or chamber of commerce Web sites can bring significantly more tourist business than mere reliance on word of mouth.

Keys to Success

Do your homework and choose the right location for this business. Rental space should be included in your start-up costs. Obviously, it will only be seasonal in northern climates. Is that all you want? Or would you rather make money from this relatively simple, straightforward business all year long? You decide. Either way, you're bound to make a decent piece of change.

Boat Maintenance/Cleaning Service

Start-up cost:	$2,000–$10,000
Potential earnings:	$30,000–$60,000
Typical fees:	$75 per hour
Advertising:	Marinas, boat retailers, Yellow Pages, brochures
Qualifications:	Know the mechanics of a boat and the types of boats
Equipment needed:	Cell phone, tools, cleaning supplies, dock, storage space
Staff required:	No
Hidden costs:	Repairs to equipment (you will need to maintain your trailer on at least an annual basis), insurance

What You Do

Boat owners are nuts about their boats, and while they enjoy being out on the open seas, they often hate keeping up with the maintenance end. After all, boating is about getting away from it all, right? Usually, your clients have a lot of disposable income, since they've invested a great deal of cash in the boat itself; that's how you can be sure of your own earning potential. On a more practical note, this business is for you if you don't mind a little grease under your nails and working out in the hot sun occasionally. Know your boat types (fiberglass, wood, steel, aluminum) and what type of chemicals you can use on each without causing any damage. Certification as a boat mechanic will be helpful but not required. Advertise where people buy dock space and at boat retailers. Try to get the businesses (such as restaurants) along the shore to carry your brochure.

What You Need

If you are a good mechanic to begin with and have your own tools, your start-up costs could be minimal (about $500). You'll need storage space, possibly a dock, and all types of cleaners, paint, and detergents. Your basic fee to do a tune-up would likely be $50 per hour; add another $25 per hour to clean. Your salary will be in the $30,000–$60,000 range.

Keys to Success

This is a big undertaking, as boat owners usually pamper their boats. You have to be truly committed. If you like working with your hands and tinkering with engines, this would be a great opportunity for you. The payoff in the end could be great, too, as there are hundreds of thousands of registered boaters today. If you space your jobs out well, this could be a full-time job, and you could add staff before you know it.

≡ Book Indexer

Start-up cost:	$1,000–$2,500
Potential earnings:	$15,000–$30,000
Typical fees:	$2.50–$4.00 per printed book page
Advertising:	Direct mail to book publishers, Yellow Pages, industry newsletters, Web site with your credentials and rates (plus some testimonials)
Qualifications:	A strong eye for detail and subject matter; impeccable organizational skills
Equipment needed:	Computer with alphabetical sorting capability, indexing software, printer
Staff required:	No
Handicapped opportunity:	Yes
Hidden Costs:	Your time since you'll be getting paid by the page, not by the hour and indexes are complex and time-consuming to create

What You Do

When you're reading a book and you want to find information on a specific topic, you look in the index first. But it probably didn't occur to you that putting together an index is a job dependent upon painstaking accuracy and attention to detail. It's an area of specialization that sets professional indexers apart from other editorial types. These folks are typically not writers (although they can be), and they are not really editors, either. Their expertise is sought after the book is written and edited, but prior to publication. They provide readers with a service that enables them to locate topics of interest, saving them time in combing through the entire book. Obviously indexers work with nonfiction books, but the subject matter can be extremely varied and could include everything from automotive manuals to business or self-help guides. A good place to start if you feel that your organizational skills are up to this kind of work is the American Society of Indexers (*www.asindexing.org*), which has local chapters throughout the United States. Joining organizations such as this prestigious association could instantly raise your credibility level.

What You Need

Start-up costs are almost negligible for indexing; all you really need to purchase upfront is your indexing software if you already own a computer. A variety of good indexing programs are available for instant download on the Web. Begin with memberships in key organizations, then submit a letter of interest or resume to book publishers both locally and nationally. Set aside at least $1,000–$2,500 for working capital; also, you may want to furnish your office with a comfortable chair (a must). Charge anywhere from $2.50–$4.00 per printed book page; for example, a 200-page book will net you $500 minimum for your indexing work. Invest the time and energy to keep your Web site updated with an "index" of your latest projects.

Keys to Success

Low initial investment makes this a win-win if you don't mind detail-oriented work. The hours may be long, the turnaround time may be quicker than you had hoped, but the ability to generate income is there for those with talent.

Book Packager

Start-up cost:	$1,000–$5,000
Potential earnings:	$45,000–$80,000
Typical fees:	Sometimes a percentage of total production costs; often, a flat consultant's rate

Advertising:	Writers' and publishers' directories, industry trade magazines, direct mail, Web site with online portfolio of books you've helped produce
Qualifications:	Editorial background, top-notch organizational skills, broad understanding of publishing process
Equipment needed:	Computer with printer and Internet access, fax, desktop publishing software, cell phone
Staff required:	No
Hidden costs:	Insurance, cost of generating business (it can take a lot of networking and paid listing on Web sites to get work)

What You Do

Book packagers are often hired by publishers whose staffs are too limited to work on a multitude of projects simultaneously; in other words, these publishers are maxed out on projects and need outside help in handling additional ones. Some book packagers handle as much as 75 percent of a publishing house's projects, allowing the in-house staff to concentrate on future projects and expansion. You would do well as a book packager if you have an editorial background, a knack for organizing and pulling together all the details of a book project, and the foresight to set realistic goals about accomplishing publication. You will likely handle everything from hiring writers and photographers to production and sales/marketing management. You would do well to pick an area of expertise, such as high-quality illustrated books. Many publishers don't have that kind of expertise in-house and will gladly pay you for yours.

What You Need

Expect to spend between $1,000–$5,000 on your start-up, which will cover your initial advertising in addition to your complete computer setup (with printer, Internet access, fax, and desktop publishing software). If you can, develop your own simple, straightforward Web site, complete with samples of some of your work and testimonials from publishers you've worked with before. You'll need to work hard to make $45,000–$75,000 or more in this field, but it isn't uncommon (especially for those in close proximity to the publishing capitals of New York, Chicago, and San Francisco).

Keys to Success

Things could easily get out of hand when you are pulling together many different creative forces for a special project. Try to work out your worst-case scenarios early enough to form a game plan around them, and set deadlines that are far ahead of when you actually need a project to be completed. You'll see why after only one project.

What sets your business apart from others like it?

Andy Mayer, President and co-owner (with Jim Becker) of Becker & Mayer Ltd. in Seattle, Washington, says the ability to produce very complicated, production-intensive books is what sets his business apart. "My partner and I both have backgrounds in toy invention and design, and we can produce really interesting books as a result."

Things you couldn't do without

"Our staff! We couldn't do anything without them . . . so many good ideas come from them. From an equipment standpoint, we couldn't do without a phone, a computer, and a color printer to produce mock-ups for publishers."

Marketing tips

"Bring a lot of who you are to your company. Find out what your passions are and try to put that into the things you produce. Also, don't listen to people who try to tell you there's only one way to do something. Freely break the rules and see what happens."

If you had to do it all over again . . .

"I would have focused the business on book packaging much earlier . . . we tried to do both book packaging and toy invention, and that didn't work as well."

Bookkeeper

Start-up cost:	$2,000–$9,000
Potential earnings:	$20,000–$50,000
Typical fees:	$25–$35 per hour; more for financial statements and other tasks; flat monthly fees rather than hourly for some clients
Advertising:	Ads in Yellow Pages and trade publications, networking with CPAs, referrals, Web site with client testimonials and perhaps some simple record-keeping tips
Qualifications:	Knowledge of basic bookkeeping principles, some legal and tax knowledge, ability to use a computer, accounting/spreadsheet software, good eye for detail, honesty, good communications skills
Equipment needed:	Computer with Internet access, basic office equipment, a financial calculator and accounting software

Staff required: No

Hidden costs: Possibly association dues

What You Do

Small business owners, in particular, use bookkeeping services to keep up with the ever-changing tax laws and the constant flow of bookkeeping details for which they don't have time. Clients need help with such tasks as making deposits; reconciling bank statements; preparing financial reports; and handling payroll, billing, and accounts payable and receivable, to name a few. What's the difference between bookkeeping and accounting? Bookkeepers are the record keepers; an accountant's job is to analyze and audit the records. If you have a clear, logical mind and common sense, this may be a great business for you. It is recession-proof, essential work that can be challenging and fun.

What You Need

The required computer and office equipment can be acquired for as little as $2,000. Add another $500 or so for your first six months of advertising or the design and hosting of your own Web site, and you'll be all set. You might consider joining business owners' associations or your local Chamber of Commerce to generate business. Charges for your services will vary according to the extent of the project, but the average fees are $25–$35 per hour.

Keys to Success

This work gives you a great opportunity to learn more about the business world and about specific fields of business. The work requires close attention to each detail and necessitates your staying current about tax-law changes relating to payroll and record keeping. Mistakes may cause problems for your client with the government. Clients may also blame you for mistakes that they made. If you like numbers and enjoy working independently to solve problems, bookkeeping may be a great career for you.

⬒ Bridal Consultant

Start-up cost: $1,000–$3,500

Potential earnings: $25,000–$60,000 (depending on volume and location)

Typical fees: $35–$45 per hour (more in larger metropolitan areas)

Advertising: Bridal magazines (many areas have their own local versions), bridal salons, newspapers, Web site with some general wedding planning checklists or tips

Qualifications:	An eye for detail and a cool head
Equipment needed:	Cell phone, computer
Staff required:	Sometimes
Hidden costs:	Keep accurate records of the time you spend with each client, or you could short-change yourself.

What You Do

Wedding planning can easily turn any reasonable family into a temporary war zone—and that's where bridal consultants come into the picture. With most families spending anywhere from $10,000–$15,000 and up on the wedding extravaganza itself, what's a few extra dollars to take the headache out of the blessed event's planning? Your rates would range from $50 per hour to a flat fee of $1,000 or more for the entire wedding, so it is easy to see how you could earn a sizeable amount of money in a short period of time. But don't think you won't work hard for it. As a bridal consultant, you will handle every minute detail, from the number of guests to invite to what kind of champagne to buy. You are essentially in the hotbed of the action, with total responsibility for every aspect of the wedding.

What You Need

You will need to develop a strong word-of-mouth network. Try forging reciprocal referral arrangements with florists, bridal shops, and hair salons to build a good reputation. Also, since this is a people- and image-oriented business, you will need to make sure you look like you're worth it. Dress professionally and carry yourself with poise and an air of diplomacy. The bulk of your start-up costs will be in producing business cards and brochures in addition to placing newspaper and bridal magazine ads (count on forking over at least $1,000 for those items). You should also consider building a Web site that offers some general tips, preparation checklists, and an online photo gallery of some of your best-produced weddings. In this business, a picture is definitely worth a thousand words! Once you build a name for yourself, you may need additional staff to help you manage several weddings at once. You may also seek out partnerships with related services so that all of the responsibility doesn't fall on you. For instance, what if you become sick the weekend of the "big day"? Your job is to be prepared for everything—and to assure your client that all will be fine no matter what.

Keys to Success

The flash and excitement of impending nuptials can be intoxicating, as can the power involved in directing wedding parties to perform their best. Be careful not to offend people or step on their toes. Listen to what your customers tell you they want, and have the good sense to make them think all of the good ideas were theirs. While such ego-suppression is hard to accomplish in a high-profile job like this one, remember that the customer is always king (or queen).

☰ Bridal Show Promoter

Start-up cost: $5,000–$15,000

Potential earnings: $20,000–$40,000

Typical fees: $125 per booth rental space

Advertising: Flyers, radio and newspaper ads, bridal shops, direct mail, billboards, Web site (on which you can sell banner ads as well as offer some useful wedding planning tips or articles), videotape of previous shows to encourage participants and sponsors

Qualifications: Exceptional organizational skills

Equipment needed: Cell phone, computer with mailing list program, and desktop publishing software (to help create a low-cost, yet tastefully designed event program)

Staff required: Not initially

Hidden costs: Expensive radio ads; try to secure sponsors early in the game or arrange to split costs with them

What You Do

Bridal shows are popular in every town; there are always women who seek the best in wedding preparations. You should have no trouble securing an audience if you book in the right places (such as shopping malls, banquet halls, and hotels). Your biggest challenge will be to gain the attention, support, and dollars from participating vendors, who could be made up of businesses like caterers, florists, musicians, and cake decorators. You must be highly organized, however, to pull this one off convincingly. Lose sight of details and you'll instantly lose credibility with your audience as well as your vendors. The best advice is to secure your financial support up front to avoid any out-of-pocket expenses; in the event of a no-show vendor, you'll still have your cash.

What You Need

The $5,000–$10,000 you'll need to get this business off the ground properly will mainly cover your advertising and promotional costs. Remember that you'll need to have professional-looking promotional materials (brochures, videos, and a great Web site) to lure vendors in the first place, and then the flyers and billboards to attract your audience. Do it all correctly and you'll pull in between $20,000–$40,000 yourself, depending on how many shows you run per year.

Keys to Success

If you can't get at least fifty vendors for your first show, maybe you ought to rethink your marketing strategy. Try a novel approach, or get a well-known spokesperson or local celebrity to appear. Collect testimonials and put them on your Web site. Offer lots of great contests and prizes. Do everything humanly possible to attract attention.

Building Maintenance Service

Start-up cost:	$20,000–$40,000
Potential earnings:	$45,000–$75,000
Typical fees:	Monthly contract of $150–$350 per client/building per month
Advertising:	Yellow Pages, direct mail to building owners and rental property managers, networking, cold calls
Qualifications:	Handyman experience, preferably with some background in electrical work and building systems
Equipment needed:	Cell phone, van equipped with tools, chemicals/solvents, ladders and small power equipment
Staff required:	No
Hidden costs:	Insurance

What You Do

Nearly all of the apartment complexes, office buildings, and universities in your community need to be maintained by someone. And if you have a technical, hands-on background in building maintenance (or even more generally, as a Mr. or Mrs. Fix-It) you can parlay that talent into a building maintenance service quite nicely and logically. You'll need to position yourself in this competitive business as a small-but-mighty industry leader with stability and a commitment to keeping everything running smoothly. Of course, you can't promise that every single light switch will always work perfectly, but you can offer a pager accessibility and twenty-four-hour service so that your clients can rest comfortably knowing that you're in charge of those three-o'clock-in-the-morning emergencies. And isn't that the time most things go wrong?

What You Need

Your costs to launch this business will be moderate ($20,000–$40,000) due to the fact that you'll need a good van filled with everything from wrenches and sockets to small pneumatic drills and large ladders. If you're a hard worker, as most maintenance folks are, you could make $45,000–$75,000 (depending on how many clients you serve). Of course, the more you make, the more likely you'll need additional staff, since one person can't simultaneously fix all the light switches and circuits in a dozen buildings.

Keys to Success

Be prepared to spend long hours doing the kind of work that tinkerers like to do most of all: figuring out what went wrong with that blower or electrical system and being the hero when the problem is solved. It's not a bad way to end each day, even if it is long.

Business Broker

Start-up cost:	$2,500–$7,000
Potential earnings:	$100,000 (based on one sale a month for 10 months of the year)
Typical fees:	Standard 10 to 12 percent of the selling price of the business
Advertising:	Direct mail, telemarketing, networking, ads in Yellow Pages and business publications, banner ads on entrepreneurial Web sites with a link to your own informative Web site
Qualifications:	A real estate broker's license in some states, ability to understand financial reports, solid business background, considerable legal knowledge, good sales and communication skills
Equipment needed:	Cell phone, computer with Internet access, office equipment, business cards
Staff required:	No
Hidden costs:	Travel, phone costs of arranging long, drawn-out deals, liability insurance

What You Do

Business brokers match clients who are interested in selling their businesses with others who want to buy. Many such businesses are home-based. This field is growing. Many people think it's less risky to buy an existing business than to start a new one. Nearly all brokers represent the client who is selling a business, but a few choose to represent the buyer. Specializing in a particular size or type of business, or in a particular geographic area, brings success to many home-based brokers. Excellent communication skills are vital, particularly the ability to express empathy and to listen carefully. Strong sales skills, coupled with the essential legal knowledge and business background, will help you establish what could be a most lucrative business.

What You Need

A computer, printer, and software (some specialized) will cost an average of $3,500. Add to this at least $700 for office furniture, phone, letterhead, and supplies. Your earnings will hinge on whether you're able to strike a deal; if so, take a 10 to 12 percent cut on the selling price.

Keys to Success

Network, network, network! Talk to people who own businesses, figure out what associations they belong to, and join them. Get referrals from lawyers, accountants, and bankers. Take some adult education courses, if necessary, to help you learn more about the unfamiliar aspects of your new business. Getting businesses to sell is hard work, but remember that it helps to specialize. It's fun to act as matchmaker and satisfying to help your clients succeed. Your expenses and start-up costs are low, and the opportunity to make a great living is excellent. Nothing succeeds like success, so once you make a great match, you'll have a basis on which to build future business.

Business Form Production and Sales

Start-up cost:	$20,000–$40,000
Potential earnings:	$35,000–$60,000
Typical fees:	$25–$30 per form; more if it's a complex custom design versus a predesigned template
Advertising:	Yellow Pages, classified ads, direct mail, Web site with e-commerce capability (for easy online purchasing and downloading of forms)
Qualifications:	Basic editing and desktop publishing/design skills, knowledge of e-commerce, sales experience
Equipment needed:	Computer, Adobe Acrobat software (for .pdf creation), printing equipment (if not using a subcontractor), extensive online or color catalog of your goods, inventory of a wide variety of forms
Staff required:	No

Hidden costs: Costs of cold calls—use the Internet to your highest benefit by advertising your Web site in as many places as possible

What You Do

This type of business is so standardized and easy for people to learn that it is among the top franchise businesses on the market today. All you need to do is find out what potential customers are using for business forms (such as inventory records, receipts, invoices, and other important documents). Then you sell them on your customized service, quick turnaround, and easy terms. Remember, though, that you will be competing heavily against some fairly large organizations (such as Office Depot and Office Max) as well as other independents like yourself; you will need super sales skills to stay on top of it all and make your regular goals. In the old days, cold-calling was the primary way of finding new business, but now you can place banner ads on entrepreneurial Web sites and you're one click away from finding new customers on a regular basis. The income potential is great for those who sell online and who can stomach the competition. If you capitalize on your strong points, you should be able to come up with forms that make every customer happy (and, ultimately, result in your own profitability). You can either design your own forms, or purchase them from paper suppliers and related sources found on the Internet.

What You Need

You'll need between $20,000–$40,000, particularly if you buy into a franchise operation, but can get away with $5,000–$10,000 if you do the whole thing on your Web site. This investment will usually cover your catalogs, inventory, and training materials, and may also cover printing equipment (typically including specialized software). You may also partner with a supplier who helps you develop your own Web page that links to their site, and from which your customers can purchase and download forms. You'll charge $25–$30 per type of form; more if it's a complex custom design your customer wants you to create from scratch. In the end, you'll wind up making between $35,000–$65,000 per year if you're working full-time and full-throttle. Expect to make anywhere from $20,000–$40,000 per year, but more like $35,000–$60,000 as a Web-based business.

Keys to Success

There is probably no more straightforward, easy business to learn than this. But do recognize that you're going to need to be well connected to get regular, dependable business. Network with anyone who's anyone, and make the daily fifty or so phone calls it may take to get one fresh, new lead. After all, you're competing against major office store chains, and you need to tell people that what sets your business apart is the customized service. On the Web, offer special deals (such as 10 percent off) to customers who purchase three or more forms at one time.

Business Networking Service

Start-up cost:	$5,000–$10,000
Potential earnings:	$20,000–$80,000
Typical fees:	$200–$300 per year per member
Advertising:	Business publications, newspapers, Yellow Pages, direct mail, networking, subscriber-only Web site
Qualifications:	The ability to organize and lead groups, some business experience would be helpful as well
Equipment needed:	Computer with Internet access; cell phone
Staff required:	No
Hidden costs:	Phone calls

What You Do

There are at least 5,000 new businesses launched every day of the week, and all of them need to connect with other businesses to exchange leads and helpful ideas. Your business brings these entrepreneurial minds to the table, encouraging interaction and support. That's what your members essentially get from joining a business networking service. What you get from this service is a steady income and the rewards of facilitating the success of others. You'll round up as many new business owners as you can, invite them to an introductory session, and hook them up with seasoned professionals. Then, secure a financial commitment of anywhere from $200 to $300 per year from each member, and you have a business networking service. What sets you apart from other associations (such as the Chamber of Commerce, for example) is that you provide expert ability to mix exactly the right combination of professionals, allowing only one company to join in a given category so that there is not direct competition. You can also provide monthly speakers to inspire and motivate the entire group to continued success.

What You Need

You'll need to advertise your service extensively at first; set aside at least $1,500 for this necessity until your own networking members bring you additional business. You will also need to rent a meeting place one a month. Check hotels, churches, and universities for the best rates, and negotiate special rates based on frequency.

Keys to Success

If bringing people and businesses together to work for the group's common good pleases you, you will be pleasing others and making a great deal of money doing it.

However, be sure not to invite any unethical businesses into the group; check each out with the Better Business Bureau before accepting their application. It will go miles toward preserving your credibility.

☞ Business Plan Writer

Start-up cost:	$5,000–$10,000
Potential earnings:	$30,000–$100,000
Typical fees:	$3,000–$6,000 per plan (about two weeks of work); $45 per hour
Advertising:	Teaching courses on business development; networking, including with bankers and at entrepreneurship centers; business associations; advertising in local business newsletters and with banner ads on entrepreneurial Web sites; your own Web site with general business-planning tips and testimonials from your best clients
Qualifications:	Understanding of financial statements, savvy business sense, excellent oral and written communication skills, ability to get people to work together, experience writing business plans
Equipment needed:	Computer with Internet access, fax, laser printer, suite software, business-planning software, office furniture, business cards, letterhead, envelopes, brochures
Staff required:	No
Hidden costs:	Association dues, business periodical and newspaper subscriptions, insurance

What You Do

Businesses are being created all over the country at a phenomenal rate. There are two main reasons for these new enterprises to want a formal business plan. First, the plan structures the efforts of everyone involved, outlining what needs to be done and describing the means by which those goals will be achieved. It highlights the feasibility of the products or services that the enterprise will be marketing. Most importantly, it estimates expenses and revenues, along with projections. If the revenues won't cover the expenses, it doesn't matter what wonderful things could happen down the road. The cash-starved business won't be able to get there to achieve them.

The second main reason to have a business plan is to obtain financing. A business plan is essential for obtaining bank loans and most other types of outside financing. You can take your good sense of business and finance, your high-level business writing skills, and your ability to communicate with fledgling entrepreneurs and earn a hefty annual income writing business plans.

What You Need

The equipment and materials to present a professional image are fairly costly (in the neighborhood of $3,000–$10,000). You'll need to be able to produce a very polished printout of the final plan, most likely using one of the better-quality business plan software packages available (about $150–$300). But you can charge $3,000 and up for each package, with hourly fees of $45 or more depending on your location. You may also opt to automate your services via your Web site, where customers can fill out a detailed information form, enter their payment details through a secure server, and receive their finished proposal in a week to 10 days. For this type of service, you can charge $500–$800 for each proposal you create.

Keys to Success

If you have developed the wide range of skills necessary to do this work, you undoubtedly are the kind of person who loves this job and can tolerate the tedious parts. What can be more rewarding than helping a new enterprise take wing and fly? You will really be a combination counselor and consultant for the entrepreneurs. It is very difficult to write an effective business plan, but that is the very reason your market exists. Each situation is different, which means that there are opportunities for continuous learning on your part. Once you complete a plan, you will need to have another client waiting, so your marketing must be ongoing. Who sees your clients right before you do? Perhaps you might network with business incubators, career counselors and your local university to develop a strong referral base. On another note, it's a good practice to ask for a 50 percent deposit up front. While most businesses fail due to poor marketing and undercapitalization, some business start-ups are shady.

Cake Decorator

Start-up cost:	$100–$200
Potential earnings:	$5,000–$25,000
Typical fees:	$10–$1,000 per cake
Advertising:	Newspaper ads, neighborhood bulletins, brochures

Qualifications:	Cake baking and decorating knowledge; knowledge of health regulations; possible food preparation permits; patience and good marketing skills
Equipment needed:	Baking pans and utensils, decorating supplies, ingredients, oven
Staff required:	None
Hidden costs:	Possibly a second oven or other facilities as business grows; need vehicle if you deliver

What You Do

People love home-baked goodies. All it takes to satisfy that need is an oven, some recipes, and a way to let people know that you're in business. Birthday cakes for children are especially popular; a home baker can customize and personalize them in countless ways to please the customer. Creating and selling wedding cakes can be very lucrative but require more time and equipment than cakes for other occasions. Nowadays people want to choose from more than chocolate, vanilla, or yellow cakes—the sky's the limit!

What You Need

The start-up cost for a cake-baking business is minimal. Some great recipes, baking pans, decorating supplies, utensils, and an oven are all that you need. You'll also need to be aware of food preparation codes, and you may need to pay for inspection and permits. If you can't easily learn to decorate cakes from a book or by trial-and-error, you may want to invest in an inexpensive cake decorating course. If you plan to deliver the cakes, you will need an appropriate vehicle.

Keys to Success

The potential market is huge, especially since most working women and men don't have time to bake, but still want homemade cakes. There are so many special occasions to celebrate, and most of them feature great cakes: graduations, birthdays, anniversaries, retirement parties, baby and wedding showers, weddings . . . the list is endless! A cake that can be made for as little as 60 cents can sell for as much as $9—a nice profit for your efforts! On the downside, it may take some practice to make beautiful cakes.

Calligrapher

Start-up cost:	$150–$500
Potential earnings:	$10,000–$15,000

Typical fees:	$50–$75 per invitation, other items on a per-job basis
Advertising:	Classified ads, bridal magazines, bulletin boards
Qualifications:	A steady hand and a love for lettering
Equipment needed:	Calligraphy pens and ink, parchment or specialty paper
Staff required:	No
Hidden costs:	Advertising

What You Do

The fine art of calligraphy began in medieval times, when monks joyously and laboriously produced biblical text using intricate, artistic lettering. This regal writing appears today in items such as wedding invitations, birth notices, and certificates of merit. You could also produce suitable-for-framing family trees. (The customer would, of course, need to supply the data.) Without a huge initial investment, you can offer your services to schools for diplomas, brides-to-be for addressing invitations, athletic teams, and even corporations that have recognition programs. The market is large, diverse, and challenging because there are many paper companies that offer programs for producing certificates having the same look as a hand-produced one. But for many folks, nothing can beat the beauty and craftsmanship of a handwritten calligraphy invitation.

What You Need

Calligraphy pens and paper are all you need to start this business, although you will have to work hard to get the word out. Perhaps you could mail invitations to those who might need your service, inviting them in for a free consultation. Networking with bridal salons may also help build business. Charge at least $50 per hour for your service, since it is specialized and can be time-consuming.

Keys to Success

The creative nature of this age-old art form is in demand by those who still place value on the handmade; but, with the ability to quickly generate calligraphic style on a computer, you may find the market challenging, at best. Being a professional calligrapher isn't necessarily going to make you rich, but it's not a bad way to earn some extra pocket money, either.

⬚ Career Counselor

Start-up cost:	$10,000–$15,000
Potential earnings:	$30,000–$65,000

Typical fees:	$350 and up for an hour-long session, unlimited e-mails, and production of a professional resume
Advertising:	Yellow Pages, classified ads, job fairs, human resource newsletters, Web site with career tips and/or job listings
Qualifications:	Many states require certification
Equipment needed:	Computer, assessment software programs, TV and VCR or DVD for educational videos
Staff required:	No
Hidden costs:	Any type of counselor must keep an eye on the clock if he or she is billing by the hour. Remember that time is money; clients often need to be told when their time is up

What You Do

There are literally thousands of careers out there. With so many choices, a career counselor is in high demand to provide personal guidance. You can assist first with personality assessment, then with matching your client's goals and interests to a potential career. Next, map out a success plan for achieving that new job or business. (Yes, many people do discover through career counseling that they would really rather work for themselves.) You can use formatted questionnaires or conduct personal interviews (or a combination of both) to arrive at some career-forming conclusions. But your counseling efforts don't have to stop there; you can also offer resume services, viewing of motivational videos, cassette tape rental, and a library of resource books. The best part is, your business is recession-proof and corporations often contract with career counselors during periods of downsizing. The difficult part is reaching those who may need your services but who are currently unaware that these services even exist.

What You Need

Your start-up cost primarily reflects your office furniture and assorted resource/testing materials ($10,000–$15,000 is about right if you don't already have a computer). But the going rate for career counseling services is $350 and up (in medium to large metropolitan areas; in smaller, rural areas, rates can be as low as $45 per hour but this typically does not include resume services). With at least one good corporate client and a few stragglers, you should be well on your way in your own career path!

Keys to Success

You will be working with many different types of people, but they do have one thing in common: they are not sure of which direction to take their careers. This can be frustrating to them, and no doubt that will translate into work for you, which is part information-giving, part hand-holding. If you're well-adjusted enough yourself to help others deal with a career catharsis, you'll probably benefit professionally and personally from this type of service. You can even offer your counseling services via the Internet or phone.

⤢ Carpet/Upholstery Cleaning

Start-up cost:	$1,000–$3,000 if leasing equipment initially; $4,000–$10,000 if buying equipment
Potential earnings:	$35,000–$50,000
Typical fees:	20 cents per square foot first room; $40 each additional room
Advertising:	Direct mail, Yellow Pages, newspaper ads, coupon books
Qualifications:	Physically able to do manual labor, some prior experience
Equipment needed:	Cleaning machine, large quantity of chemical cleaners, some mode of transporting materials
Staff required:	No
Hidden costs:	Fuel for vehicle

What You Do

If "Out, damned spot!" is your battle cry, getting others to enlist your services in the carpet/upholstery cleaning business shouldn't be too hard. After all, we've all spilled food or drink on at least one piece of furniture in our homes—and we've all thought of paying a professional every once in a while to freshen up the house with a good carpet cleaning. That is why this is such a recession-proof business; the need for clean places to live never goes out of favor with consumers. You could offer your cleaning services to everyone from homeowners to managers of apartment complexes and even corporations. The best way to get your name out there is through excellent, timely service and its resultant good word of mouth. You'll sweep the surface dirt from furniture and floors, perform an overall general cleaning, and use industrial-strength spot removers on tough stain areas. Since each room takes approximately an hour to service (if there are few stains requiring more attention), there is the potential for making lots of money once you learn to work quickly and efficiently while maintaining high-quality standards. One final note: buying cleaning fluids will be slightly more expensive if environmentally safe products are chosen. Many people prefer "green" cleaning products, especially for health reasons, and customers will feel safer and more satisfied when they know there are no toxic residues in their house.

What You Need

Deciding whether to buy or lease equipment at first will depend upon how much capital is available to invest. A carpet cleaning machine will cost from $600–$3,500, while leasing will run about $300–$400 per month. Rotary shampooers and steam extractors are the two current types available. While each has its advantages and disadvantages, rotary shampooers are the preferred method because they clean more deeply. A good, strong vacuum cleaner is the next most vital tool, and buying a sturdy canister model with a variety of attachments will cost $400–$600. The leasing option will be anywhere from $100–$200 per month. Access to a reliable vehicle large enough to tote around all equipment and supplies (and gasoline to run it) is another expense involved in this business, but really won't amount to much if you already have a station wagon/truck/van. Include advertising in your budget, which could run anywhere from $600–$3,000 for half a year. Coupon books seem to be fruitful ground for carpet cleaning businesses as a starting point for bringing in new customers. For carpets, fees are often 20 cents per square foot plus an additional $40 or more per each extra room depending on size. Upholstery cleaning is usually done per piece, with fees ranging from $50–$150.

Keys to Success

Working for another local company first may give you a good idea of what's needed to get started and how to proceed from there. As in most trades, experience is essential to success. Knowing which contracts to take and which are just impossible, what are appropriate fees for your area, how billing works, and other aspects of the business will make your start-up smoother. Sales skills are a plus since most people don't realize that they might need your service, or know how often they need it. Calling former customers to find out if the work was performed satisfactorily and offering to repeat it will keep you busy.

⬏ Catalog Retailer

Start-up cost:	$15,000–$60,000 (depending on whether you're marketing your own or someone else's products)
Potential earnings:	$25,000–$50,000+
Typical fees:	Products can sell from $5–$500 or more; you'll charge one-third more than the retail price
Advertising:	Direct mail, advertising co-ops with other catalog retailers in national publications, banner ads with links to your own catalog Web site
Qualifications:	Sales/marketing background

Equipment needed: Postage meter, computer with Internet access, printer, fax, phone with 800 number for ease of ordering, credit card processing equipment (for print catalogs); Computer with DSL line, Web site, and online ordering/e-commerce capability (for online catalogs)

Staff required: Not initially

Hidden costs: Insurance, purchase or lease of specialized mailing lists

What You Do

Catalogs have been around as long as there have been products to sell. But what seems to work best in the catalog/mail order business is to use niche marketing; that is, pick an area of specialization and only offer products related to that area. For instance, you might sell only products for golf lovers or only baby items. Choose an area that is specific enough to catch instant attention, yet broad enough to include a wide variety of products. You'll build your customer base from lists you either rent or purchase; if you specialize, this will be an easy process for you (and will cost less in the long run). Your days will be spent taking and filling orders in the most efficient way possible (hint: online ordering with drop shipping would be ideal); you'll also be handling customer service and possibly returns. That is why, in addition to a terrific marketing background, you'll also need some accounting skills. It all gets to be quite complicated when you're dealing with hundreds of orders, which you'll need to break even. Make sure you have adequate storage space for all of the goods; you may run out of space quickly in your basement.

What You Need

Your earnings potential is unpredictable because you're dealing with various products at different prices and hoping they will all sell within a short period of time. Because you'll need to send out a thousand or so catalogs to make your sales efforts pay off, and because you'll need everything from a postage meter to credit card processing equipment and a computer system to maintain and run your business, expect to spend $15,000–$60,000. It'll be closer to the high end if you're actually selling your own product line; obviously, it's a little cheaper to work out agreements with other manufacturers and get a percentage of their take (usually 15 to 20 percent). Don't forget printing costs, either, which could run as high as $10,000–$15,000 per issue. If you choose to do an online-only version of your catalog, you will save on printing costs but will still need to pay design, updating, e-commerce and hosting fees associated with your site. You could potentially earn $25,000–$50,000 or more, depending on the market for your product line and how much of a price variance you offer.

Keys to Success

On the positive side, you'll be able to work in your pajamas if you want to, since you'll be in your office most of the day. The downside is, if you're having a bad day, orders won't get filled and you'll wind up losing money. Be sure that you're selling quality products—ask for samples.

Caterer

Start-up cost:	$15,000–$23,000
Potential earnings:	$30,000–$80,000
Typical fees:	$800–$15,000 per event
Advertising:	Brochures, press kits, direct mail, networking
Qualifications:	Cooking and menu planning experience, knowledge of health, safety, zoning, product liability, and other laws and regulations; good people skills; good recordkeeping skills
Equipment needed:	Cooking equipment and supplies; a commercial kitchen (which may be rented or shared) and appropriate permits
Staff required:	Not initially; may be needed to grow
Hidden costs:	Travel costs associated with delivering food

What You Do

If you have the right mixture of cooking know-how, business acumen, and good communication skills, catering can be a profitable and enjoyable enterprise. Although a commercial kitchen may be required after your service starts to grow, most catering services begin at home and then move to shared facilities in order to keep capital costs low. One fast-growing segment of this business is food delivery—especially lunches—to offices and corporations. Catering opportunities abound in preparing private banquets at hotels; furnishing meals to airlines; cooking for parties, fundraisers, and other events; or serving as an executive chef in a company dining room. Specializing in a particular item, such as gourmet wedding cakes or chocolate chip cookies, is another option. Caterers must observe health, safety, zoning, product liability, and other laws and regulations. Detailed recordkeeping is also needed.

What You Need

Access to a commercial kitchen can range from about $8,000–$12,000; appropriate equipment (pots, pans, etc.) will be $500–$1,000. In addition, allow

$3,000–$10,000 for legal and insurance fees, a license, and advertising. You will also need a delivery vehicle.

Keys to Success

Successful catering requires a lot of hard work and careful planning. You have to devote time to meeting with—and cooking for—potential clients even though you may not be chosen to cater their event in the end. Social catering involves weekend and evening work, and is also often seasonal in nature. Keep in mind that you also will be responsible for serving and cleanup, as well as menu planning and cooking, unless you hire others to do these tasks. On the other hand, cooking is fun! It's a creative process, one that nourishes the cook as well as those who eat the food. You can control how much or how little you work. And you'll always be welcome in everyone's kitchen!

Childbirth Instructor

Start-up cost:	$500–$1,000
Potential earnings:	$15,000–$35,000
Typical fees:	$175 per couple for three to four classes
Advertising:	Bulletin boards, parents' newsletters, OB/GYN offices
Qualifications:	A nursing degree would be helpful and respected by those needing your service, but you will likely need state certification as a licensed childbirth instructor
Equipment needed:	No
Staff required:	No
Hidden costs:	Liability insurance and educational materials such as models, books, and videos

What You Do

Giving birth is a very natural experience that doesn't come naturally—that's why we need childbirth instructors to show us the way. Childbirth instructors are experts in labor stress and pain management. First-time parents are especially uneasy (even frightened) about the pending event, and their fears are best calmed with detailed and expert information from a reliable source. If you've been in a delivery room, and have a nursing degree or related training, you would be a terrific candidate for this type of work. A childbirth instructor is essentially a teacher, so you must develop (and stick to) a teaching plan much the same as any other teacher. Most childbirth classes meet once a week for four to six weeks, so space your lessons out accordingly. Begin with the basics and end with a strong visual, such as a childbirth film. Be sure to answer all questions, even the most common ones, courteously and compassionately. After all, many of your customers haven't a clue what they're in for, and it's your job to make their fears subside for a calm, secure birthing experience.

What You Need
You can contract with hospitals. If you decide not to, spend some advertising dollars to get your name out there since you will be competing against them. In addition to advertising in parents' newsletters, you might also want to consider advertising at a children's consignment store, which often have bulletin boards for child-related services. You could offer to provide some referrals for them in return. You should also get to know a few obstetricians and midwives, who will comprise your strongest source of word-of-mouth business. You might also want to have a Web site or do some advertising on pregnancy Web sites, since there are so many of them. Include testimonials that speak to how you helped calm the fears of parents-to-be.

Keys to Success
The birth experience is a joyous occasion, and you will likely enjoy telling and retelling the story of this miracle of life.

⇐ Child-Care Referral Service

Start-up cost:	$500–$3,500
Potential earnings:	$20,000–$65,000
Typical fees:	Free browsing through your Web site; membership fee of $150 per year for parents to use your search services and interview and/or book childcare providers through your Web site
Advertising:	Classified ads, display ads in local newspapers or regional parenting magazines
Qualifications:	You may need to be bonded or licensed in your state
Equipment needed:	Pager or cell phone, computer with database program, high-speed Internet access
Staff required:	No
Hidden costs:	None

What You Do

This is a perfect job for those who like to work alone and as a valued resource person. As a child-care referral agent, you will develop a database of names and phone numbers of reputable child-care professionals in your area at a cost of about $150 per member. Be sure that the database does its own background checks on the child-care professionals, or you will need to do background checks for each prospective hire. You would most likely get your start by placing a classified ad in your local newspaper, then talking with parents/prospective clients to discuss their needs. For instance, some single parents or career couples are in need of a caregiver to watch their kids all week long, while others just need part-time care for their children. Some will want to interview each potential caregiver on your list, while others will want you to do the legwork.

What You Need

First of all, you'll need the ability to multitask and pay attention to details. But with a minimal start-up cost of $500 for your advertising and Internet expenses, you could begin to pull in a profit with this business almost immediately. You will need to build a vast network of reputable child-care professionals, which you can easily accomplish by posting flyers in public places (such as Laundromats and grocery stores) and combing the ads in your local newspaper to find babysitters who are offering their services. If you have a little bit of extra money to play with at the beginning, you should also invest in professional-looking stationery and business cards to convey the best possible image to your babysitters as well as to parents. You might need to charge each prospective caregiver an annual membership fee of $150 and use some of those funds to conduct online background checks.

Keys to Success

What's not to like about setting your own hours and having essentially complete control over a low-overhead business? While this business might not work well if you live in rural area, it could really provide some decent cash if you live in a city or suburbia.

Collectibles Broker

Start-up cost:	$5,000–$15,000
Potential earnings:	$500–$20,000
Typical fees:	Varies from one collectible to another
Advertising:	Online auctions, flea markets, swap meets, antique fairs, flyers, brochures

Qualifications:	Knowing how to spot money from junk
Equipment needed:	Computer, digital camera
Staff required:	No
Hidden costs:	Listing fees at auction sites such as eBay, table/space rental fees for flea markets, travel and setup time

What You Do

Everything old is new again! Remember the Morton Salt Girl or the Brady Bunch lunch boxes with radios in them? In mint condition, they are in popular demand right now and bringing in top dollars ($100 or more each). And so is anything retro: salt/pepper sets, board games, clothing, limited edition plates, Presidential items, cereal boxes, you name it. But that doesn't relieve you of the responsibility to heavily market your service. You can specialize in one era, such as the '50s, and carry everything from that time period. Or, you can specialize in one item, such as toasters through the twentieth century. Try to hit as many antique fairs, swap meets, and dealer conventions as possible. But the online auctions are where you'll probably spend the least, but earn the most.

What You Need

First off, you should have twenty to thirty collectibles to start. You will need equipment to show off your stuff, so that will be the biggest expense (about $1,500 for a computer and digital camera). The next biggest will be your advertising and marketing. When you go to shows, plan on paying $15–$100+ to rent a table or space to showcase your merchandise. Earning potential will be initially slow—$500–$20,000—until you're-established.

Keys to Success

People are crazy for the past. Collecting has become a $6-billion a year business, so if you have a collection you're willing to part with, you could make some serious money. Collecting interests tend to run in twenty-year cycles, so this is a long-term possibility if you have an eye for what is collectible and what will sell. The danger is getting so caught up in acquiring certain pieces that you aren't willing to part with them yourself. Beware—collecting is intoxicating to those who enjoy it!

Collection Agency

Start-up cost:	$3,000–$10,500
Potential earnings:	$30,000–$60,000

Typical fees:	25 percent commission
Advertising:	Phone solicitation, networking, writing articles for local publications, public speaking, Web site with client testimonials
Qualifications:	Good communication skills; patience; high self-esteem; budgeting skills; clear understanding of the Federal Fair Debt Collection Practices Act and any relevant state laws; understanding of health insurance policies and billing practices if working with the medical field; state, city, and/or county licenses are typically required
Equipment needed:	Computer, printer, fax, wordprocessing and spreadsheet software, specialized collection software, and phone with optional headset
Staff required:	No
Hidden costs:	Association dues for networking purposes; possibly licensing fees

What You Do

Are you an addict of *Unsolved Mysteries?* Collectors are often put to the test as they track down elusive debtors. State laws typically require people who do collections to be bonded and licensed. Generally, it is not difficult to obtain the proper license provided your state does not prohibit home-based agencies. Using special collections software and a PC reduces the time and labor for handling mail and accounting, making the collection service more efficient. Additionally, services provided by Internet search engines cut the cost of tracking debtors considerably.

What You Need

It is essential that you take advantage of the many high-tech devices that will make the collection process easier. A computer is essential, as is customized collection software. Costs ranging from $2,000–$7,000 for these basics are average. Don't forget to shop around for the best rates on Internet Service Provider packages, which can run anywhere from $9.99 to $79.99 per month.

Keys to Success

The collection process is often frustrating. Keeping your self-esteem intact in the face of rejection is necessary. Although confronting people about their unpaid bills can be emotionally draining, the work never ceases to be challenging and rewarding. In some cases, you are able to solve debtors' financial problems and keep them from bankruptcy. When all parties agree on a suitable payment plan, everyone wins.

What sets your business apart from others like it?

"There are a lot of good agencies, and we all basically do the same things," says Deloris C. Lewis, President of Debt Credit Services & Associates in Akron, Ohio. "I cater to the needs of my clients and go out of my way to help them. I try to be fair to both the creditors and the debtors."

Things you couldn't do without

Lewis says she couldn't do without an excellent, well-trained staff, speed dialers, computers, integrated skip tracing and bookkeeping software, a phone system, and mailing equipment.

Marketing tips

"Go after the large-dollar, small-account commercial business that's out there. Stay away from health care; if you're new, it will be too demanding and intense for you. Use networking and advertising to bring in new business, but depend heavily on referrals."

If you had to do it all over again . . .

"I'd have started with more capital . . . that means developing a sound business plan, which I didn't do in the beginning and which has held me back. I winged it—and now I'd be more organized so that I could get better funding."

College Application Consultant

Start-up cost:	$500–$1,000
Potential earnings:	$15,000–$30,000
Typical fees:	Extremely varied; some consultants charge as little as $150 or as high as $1,000 for this service
Advertising:	School and local papers, direct mail, Yellow Pages, banner ads on college-oriented online message boards, your own Web site with helpful information
Qualifications:	Familiarity with various colleges and programs
Equipment needed:	Computer, variety of available databases, reference materials
Staff required:	No
Hidden costs:	Long distance phone calls and Internet Service Provider fees

What You Do

Nowadays the hardest part of getting into a college is choosing the right one; it's a vital decision for a young person's future, one with far-reaching implications. Now more than ever, a bachelor's degree is almost a requirement to secure a decent, well-paying job. And although some high schools do have respectable advising departments, many do not invest the time and money into this important aspect of continuing education that they could and should. That's where you come in. As an independent college application consultant your services are in high demand in a low-competition field. What more could a business person ask for? If you are amenable to long hours of research and documentation, this business could provide you with just the intellectual challenge you need. Your main hurdles are problem-solving for high school seniors and their families and dealing with emotional/sentimental issues (primarily of the parents). You would conduct a skills/needs assessment, match them to an appropriate choice of universities, assist the customer in obtaining and filling in financial aid and application forms properly (and mailing them on time). You will also relay necessary facts about ACT/SATs, placement tests (such as math, English, and foreign languages), degrees, program requirements, extracurricular activities offered by schools that might be of interest to students, and so on.

What You Need

A computer is the largest expense at about $1,500, if you choose to buy one. It isn't a necessity but it will tremendously speed the search process. College catalogs available online show listings of courses and a description of each, as well as some information about application procedures, fees, deadlines, requirements and other general facts about the schools. Buying many of these print catalogs, as well as a few specialized publications that rate universities or give little-known information about them, will cost several hundred dollars. Placing only small ads will help keep advertising costs down to $100 or so, but the price of calls to colleges may add up quickly, so remember to monitor your phone time. Charges for these tasks could be determined a number of ways: per task, per package of tasks, hourly, or however else seems reasonable for the area and best covers the particular request.

Keys to Success

Good listening and problem-solving skills are your biggest assets in this business. Customers are trusting you with a very important part of their lives: their futures. High self-motivation and research skills will also help keep you enthused and knowledgeable about colleges and what's new on campuses. If you enjoy being the middleman, then college consulting is for you.

⫷ College Internship Placement Service

Start-up cost:	$1,500–$3,000
Potential earnings:	$20,000–$50,000
Typical fees:	$75–$175 (paid by student/parents); hiring companies may also pay from $75–$150 per listing if they want to post openings
Advertising:	College newspapers, campus bulletin boards, direct mail to parents, Web site with internship offerings and capability for students to apply via e-mail
Qualifications:	Background in placement services would be helpful
Equipment needed:	Computer with printer, Internet access, fax
Staff required:	No
Hidden costs:	Insurance, Internet Service Provider fees

What You Do

It used to be that companies offering internships contacted colleges to find students for summer or short-term work. But, in this era, such companies are relying increasingly upon services such as yours to bring them talent. It's challenging work to find a suitable internship for a student (and vice versa), but you'll have enough resources from which to choose at your local library. There are plenty of books that detail such opportunities, and there should be plenty of postings for internships through online services or the Internet. You'd have to work pretty hard to exhaust all of the possibilities. You'd be wise to market to the parents of students in addition to the students themselves, since parents are typically the ones with the foresight to see the importance of an internship. You can deliver your service in one of two ways: (1) as a consultant who finds and recommends several internship possibilities for a student, or (2) as the liaison between hiring companies and students, even going so far as to screen applicants and finalize the deal just as a professional recruiter would do. You will obviously make more money with the second option.

What You Need

You'll need to have at least $1,500 for your computer system and another $1,000 or so for advertising in your first six months. If you choose to do internship placement for hiring companies, you will need to network with several such companies in order to get their business. Contact management software would be a good investment for this type of business.

Keys to Success

Your work will be different every day, and the challenges will present themselves on a regular basis, too. Sometimes you'll work with folks you simply can't seem to please, or who don't come across as highly motivated. Remember that part of your job is to sell students on the importance of choosing the best internships.

Color Consultant

Start-up cost:	$2,000–$4,000
Potential earnings:	$30,000–$50,000
Typical fees:	$35–$75 per hour
Advertising:	Local newspapers, business publications, direct mail, Web site with latest color trends and client testimonials
Qualifications:	Possibly training through cosmetic firm, paint company, or similar business; certification
Equipment needed:	Computer, color swatches, color charts, cell phone
Staff required:	No
Hidden costs:	Travel expenses

What You Do

Have you ever wondered exactly how the major automobile manufacturers and appliance makers decide which colors to use on their products? Or where the world of fashion comes up with the latest hues? They use color consultants—experts who know the entire spectrum of the rainbow, including minute variations and redefining nuances that are invisible to the untrained eye. It is essential that a color consultant have a strong understanding of how color affects people in addition to the natural ability to distinguish slight color variations. The former is a learned skill, while the latter is a natural talent that must be present if you are to be successful in the field. Once established in this business, your days will consist of working with a wide range of clients, including individuals, cosmetic companies, corporations, appliance/furniture manufacturers, and so on. People will look to you for the trends of the future.

What You Need

Training with a company that teaches color and color dynamics is the biggest initial expense involved in becoming a consultant. Most often, the program is a week of intensive instruction on color theory and analysis, marketing techniques, and applications; expect to spend at least $1,200 on classes/certification (if available in your area). Other costs are directly related to visual materials to use in consultations and demonstrations, which can run anywhere from $25–$1,000. Consultations often last an hour, with the average fee being $50–$75, depending upon the industry and geographic area of the country. Once you are trained, you will work with corporate and individual clients to determine the best color combinations to use in everything from new product launches to color schemes on the walls.

Keys to Success

Working with people is always a challenge, but more so when it involves personal issues such as what's aesthetically pleasing and what's not (which can be quite subjective). Staying on top of the latest color trends can be an exciting challenge, so if you like the idea of making other people look good and making money while doing it, this could be the career for you.

Commercial Cleaning Service

Start-up cost:	$700–$5,500
Potential earnings:	$45,000–$75,000
Typical fees:	$25–$50 per hour or a monthly fee of $500–$2,500 (depending on size of facility)
Advertising:	Local business publications and newspapers, Yellow Pages, Web site
Qualifications:	License
Equipment needed:	Janitorial cleaning equipment and supplies
Staff required:	Most likely
Hidden costs:	Liability insurance, licensing/bonding fees, high turnover if you employ a staff

What You Do

There will always be a need for commercial cleaning services. Offices are only one piece of a prosperous pie: You can also count apartment buildings, retail shops, and even health clubs among your best customers. Starting small with a home-based cleaning business will keep your overhead low, allowing you to reach a break even point much more quickly. You can even branch out to several locations by offering some of your best employees their own territory. If you're willing to put in the time and energy necessary to continually win new clients (while keeping the old ones clean and happy), you can enjoy a very healthy income doing something that is relatively easy. Best of all, you can set your own hours.

What You Need

If you want to promote yourself as an environmentally friendly cleaning service, you will likely spend a little bit more for your cleaning solutions; however, you can easily recoup this in charging slightly higher fees for your services. Should you choose a more traditional route, you can get away with a cart of cleaning solutions, one industrial-size vacuum, and a supply of garbage bags (about $500 worth of supplies to start). Don't forget rubber gloves to protect your skin. If you decide to invest in heavy-duty cleaning supplies that include professional-quality vacuums and power cleaners, expect your start-up costs to be as high as $5,500.

Keys to Success

The hardest part of running a successful cleaning business is keeping it running. While that may sound like a riddle, it's no joke that the turnover in the cleaning business is quite high. So look for innovative ways to keep your employees happy and motivated. Run contests for those who bring in the most business or award time off for those who put in a high number of hours. Also, you should constantly strive to set yourself apart from competitors, especially larger chains with bigger advertising budgets than yours. What you offer is personalized service and attention to detail. With your company, customers are not just numbers on a spreadsheet.

EXPERT ADVICE

What sets your business apart from others like it?

Lillian Lincoln, President of Centennial One, Inc., in Landover, Maryland, says her company distinguishes itself from others by emphasis on quality. "We place a great deal of emphasis on giving our clients a comfort level that assures them that their building maintenance requirements will be adequately addressed."

Things you couldn't do without

Vacuums, buffers, scrubbing and shampooing machines. "No equipment is needed until some work has been secured. No lead time is needed unless the job requires specialized equipment, so purchase only the equipment needed for each job as they roll in."

Marketing tips

"Industry knowledge as well as business acumen are great assets. Too many people have the mistaken impression that this industry is a 'mop and bucket' business. Far from true! It requires knowledge of chemical and equipment usage, time management, human relations, and a number of other skills. For anyone going into this business for themselves, I advise them to work in the industry for a minimum of six months first."

If you had to do it all over again . . .

"I would spend more time working in the field to learn more about on-site operations. I made some mistakes early on because I was not as knowledgeable as I should have been about the basics of the business."

Commercial Photographer

Start-up cost:	$3,000–$5,000
Potential earnings:	$35,000 and up
Typical fees:	$35–$50 per hour
Advertising:	Classifieds, trade publications, business groups, direct mail, Web site with online portfolio
Qualifications:	Photographic skills, excellent time management skills, ability to market and sell your services
Equipment needed:	Excellent camera equipment including traditional and digital, cell phone, computer with Internet access and photo printer, fax, business cards, letterhead, envelopes
Staff required:	No
Hidden costs:	Equipment upgrades and repair, travel costs

What You Do

Commercial photography is an ideal business for the individual who can produce. If you can "see" the images needed by a business segment in your community, and produce them on time for a competitive cost, you can probably develop relationships with your customers that will bring you an ongoing stream of business. Photos always seem to be needed, but often at the last minute. You will need to produce under pressure and have a reputation for getting it right the first time. Commercial photography requires an interesting combination of technical, artistic, sales, and business skills. If you have this mix, or can develop it, you can go far.

What You Need

The photographic equipment you use is, of course, the vital component of this business. (A top-of-the-line digital camera will generally run $3,000.) Having an effective home office is also necessary for supporting the "business" side of your business: receiving assignments, preparing invoices, and so on. You could earn upward of $35,000 in the beginning, and the sky's the limit once you develop a healthy reputation.

Keys to Success

Most successful commercial photographers specialize. And some have gone beyond providing the photographic image alone to offering related services—preparation of brochures, scanning and retouching images, or working in close association with graphic artists and copywriters to provide a completed piece. If you become known for excellence in photography of construction projects, retail store installations, or company board retreats, you will have a leg up on the competition. This is another crowded field with plenty of room at the top.

EXPERT ADVICE

What sets your business apart from others like it?

Tom Uhlman, owner of Tom Uhlman Photography in Cincinnati, Ohio, says that he stands apart from other commercial photographers by offering sound editorial judgment in addition to providing quality photographic work. "I'm dependable at finding interesting situations, giving publications the kinds of unusual photos they want and need without having to wait for assignment." Uhlman's photos have been picked up by the Associated Press and have appeared in *Newsweek*, the *New York Daily News*, and *USA Today*.

Things you couldn't do without

Uhlman says he couldn't do without top-quality cameras with motor drives, flash equipment, better-than-average lenses, and dependable transportation. "I would also buy a police scanner, so you can shoot 'hard' news as it happens. It's the best way to break into newspapers, because they often don't have the staff or time to get these shots."

Marketing tips

"Look at the work of others and learn from it. But you'll probably learn the most from being out there and getting your own experience. Find photos that tell good news stories, and you should never have a problem selling."

If you had to do it all over again . . .

"I pretty much did everything in the right way and time. I learned early on that doing is what gets you there."

Commercial Plant Watering Service

Start-up cost: $800–$1,000
Potential earnings: $30,000–$60,000

Typical fees:	$25–$50 per day (per customer), some work on monthly retainers of $500 and up
Advertising:	Referrals, Yellow Pages, affiliations with nursery businesses
Qualifications:	Knowledge of plants' requirements
Equipment needed:	Vehicle, cell phone
Staff required:	No
Hidden costs:	Associated travel expenses, including mileage, gas, etc.

What You Do

Interior plantings are more common in some parts of the country than in others, but almost all large businesses maintain some kind of greenery to soften their offices. Once you show these organizations that you can care for their plants and keep them healthy and attractive, you will have the opportunity to develop an ongoing business that brings you a steady income stream.

What You Need

Costs are minimal. You will need a car or truck to drive from client to client and possibly business cards that you could leave near the plants to generate more business. Most larger plant maintenance services charge a flat monthly rate of $500 or more; if you're smaller, however, this will likely be a part-time job, earning you between $25–$50 per day (per customer).

Keys to Success

This is definitely a business for plant lovers. If you enjoy making things grow, you'll find plant watering to be a rewarding enterprise. However, there isn't much change from day to day, although you are in and out of different environments as you go from customer to customer. This is not a business for people who thrive on excitement and not exactly a get-rich-quick enterprise either.

Computer Consultant

Start-up cost:	$5,000–$13,000
Potential earnings:	$40,000–$100,000
Typical fees:	$75–$150 per hour
Advertising:	Referrals, direct mail, publications, networking
Qualifications:	Technical knowledge, specialty knowledge, people and time-management skills

Equipment needed: High-end computer, a sufficient supply of hardware and software, copier, fax, office furniture, business cards, letterhead, envelopes

Staff required: No, but must be able to subcontract outside of specialty

Hidden costs: Internet Service Provider fees, time and expense of staying current in fast-changing field

What You Do

It's getting very hard to operate any business without a computer system, so almost anyone is a potential client if you know how to match up a computer system with his or her needs. Computer consulting is a big field today and will continue to grow as long as there are computers and users who need help keeping them alive and well. Many computer consultants become as essential to their clients as the systems themselves, earning a steady income in the process. This field is for individuals with wide expertise in hardware and software. Even more important is an ability to see issues from the client's point of view. What are his or her real problems, and what creative solutions to those problems will be best served using computer technology? You will probably need to focus on one area of specialization, such as networking computers, or on one type of business, such as retail outlets or physicians' offices.

What You Need

Your own business must have a computer system, including software that is comparable to those of your clients. This will be your major expense, but if you have the expertise to operate this business, you probably have much of the equipment and software already. You'll also need a high-quality copier and a fax. The essential association dues and online services can also add surprisingly to your operating expenses. But if you charge the going rates of $75 and up per hour, you should be able to earn back your initial investment in as little as six months.

Keys to Success

Computer consulting is for big-picture people also skilled in keeping track of details. Each client and situation is different, making for a very stimulating work life. You will likely need to function outside of normal office hours, since that's when most major computer overhauls typically occur in an effort to minimize business interruption. As a result, you probably won't find competitors undercutting you with cookie-cutter services. But computer consulting is extremely demanding. You will often be working under a deadline or in a crisis situation. You must produce what you promise and be able to train your clients' employees to make the system work under real conditions. Bidding for jobs is challenging, especially at first; keeping track of billing is essential.

What sets your business apart from others like it?

Lee Hughes, Systems Engineer at Hughes Information Systems in Cloquet, Minnesota, says his business is successful because it streamlines and automates other businesses' operations. "We take an engineering approach to solving problems."

Things you couldn't do without

"A personal computer, printer, and phone."

Marketing tips

"It is virtually impossible to accurately estimate project costs. Try to build in a cushion when you provide an estimate."

If you had to do it all over again . . .

"I would educate myself much more in business management, sales/marketing, presentation, and negotiation skills."

Computer Maintenance Service

Start-up cost:	$5,000–$10,000
Potential earnings:	$50,000–$70,000
Typical fees:	$50 per hour on cleaning or repairs
Advertising:	Yellow Pages, flyers, business card, opportunities to teach classes, Web site with links to related resources
Qualifications:	Knowledge of computer hardware and interfaces, ability to deal with upset clients diplomatically and sympathetically
Equipment needed:	Computer with Internet access, printer, fax, tools, cleaning supplies, diagnostic software, spare parts, office furniture, business cards, reference books
Staff required:	No
Hidden costs:	Staying abreast of new technology

What You Do

Computers and dust don't mix. That seems like a simple idea, but many people have little understanding of that concept. They don't understand why computers tend to crash without regular maintenance, and they need much reassurance before they will trust you to remove a cover and begin cleaning the drives. Once you gain trust and develop your clientele, though, you'll be able to negotiate ongoing service contracts that will give you a steady flow of work, and income. Twice a year you can service each client on your list, cleaning the vital components of the machines that keep their businesses running. You may also develop connections to possible add-on services you could offer, such as training, software installation, file backups, and so on.

What You Need

The computer for your own office is the largest expense because the actual computer cleaning tools are quite simple and not very costly. Fees are usually in the $50 per hour range. Your biggest challenge is to make potential clients aware of the benefit of maintaining their systems. All too often they'll wait until something catastrophic happens before they call you. Consequently, a decent Web site, some advertising and maintenance reminder cards will cost you at least $1,000–$2,000 per year.

Keys to Success

If you have the ability to clean computers and peripheral equipment, you can provide a service needed by almost all businesses and many individuals as well. Satisfied customers will probably provide you with plenty of referrals, but you will occasionally be working with distraught clients. You might need to work at your customers' sites, so careful planning is necessary to make best use of travel time.

🖅 Computer Programmer/Database Consultant

Start-up cost:	$1,500–$5,000
Potential earnings:	$75,000–$150,000
Typical fees:	$125–$150 per hour or quoted on a project basis
Advertising:	Online advertising, direct mail, networking with business professionals who might need your services or who can refer others
Qualifications:	Programming experience or professional certification (Microsoft certified programmers tend to make more money based on name recognition)
Equipment needed:	At least one computer, database and programming software, printer, business card
Staff required:	No
Hidden costs:	None

What You Do

As a computer programmer/database consultant, you will work with clients to improve the efficiency of their businesses. Perhaps it's as straightforward as building a client database that enables your customer to analyze where its sales are coming from and how to maximize sales potential. Or maybe it's programming the back-end of a database-driven Web site that is user-friendly and highly functional, allowing the site owner to capture data about each visitor to their site for demographic and sales/promotional purposes. If you have a strong working knowledge of programs like LINUX, dBase+, and DreamWeaver, you will be able to find work as long as you market yourself in a visible manner. A strong Web site with links to your finished work will do, but then you need a powerful marketing piece to drive visitors to your site. You can accomplish this through a printed piece, such as a four-color postcard (which can be economically produced through sites like amazingmail.com and modernpostcards.com), or develop a slick, interactive e-marketing piece. For these marketing pieces, you'll need to purchase a good list of prospects, and be sure you comply with the CAN-SPAM Act by including an opt-out and your company's physical address.

What You Need

You may need one powerful computer or perhaps several if you have others working with you or if you need to view your work on different-sized screens. Your biggest start-up cost is likely to be software, which can run anywhere from $150–$1,500 depending on the level of sophistication or specialization. Plan on setting aside another $500–$2,500 for your initial phase of marketing and advertising materials. You'll need to spread the word before the referrals start rolling in.

Keys to Success

You would do well to join a professional association of computer programmers. Such an organization will likely offer terrific guidance on how to start your business, as well as provide you with great networking opportunities with others in your field. Often you can get your start taking on the overflow of other programmers. You might also find lots of work on Web sites such as SoloGig.com and Dice.com. The work is definitely out there for talented professionals like you.

⋲ Computer Trainer

Start-up cost:	$5,000–$16,000
Potential earnings:	$40,000–$100,000 (a computer trainer typically has several students at once, each paying $75 per hour)
Typical fees:	$75+ per hour

Advertising:	Speaking at business meetings, referrals from software companies, networking, direct mail to specific companies, computer and trade publications, Web site with general computing tips and your most recently updated class schedule
Qualifications:	Computer skills and/or certification by software company, writing and presentation skills, ability to handle group dynamics, background in teaching or instructional design
Equipment needed:	High-end computer, hardware and software, laser printer, office furniture, brochures and/or presentation folder, business cards, letterhead, envelopes
Staff required:	No
Hidden costs:	Certification training to teach specific programs

What You Do

As computers become even more important in the business world, so does computer training. New software is powerful, but added features mean that almost every employee needs training to use it productively. To be a successful computer trainer, you need a range of skills, beginning with expertise in each software package. Beyond the ability to use the software yourself, you need to understand how others use it. Computer trainers may work as tutors with one or two individuals at a time, but more often they teach classes to groups at a business location. Teaching and presentation skills are essential. Computer training can be a successful business for people who have computer skills, find teaching to be a creative enterprise, and like working with adults. You will need to focus on the areas in which you can keep updated: word processing, databases, or accounting programs, for example.

What You Need

Your computer, software, and laser printer will be the largest start-up expenses, totaling as much as $10,000–$15,000. You will also need to produce your own training materials, and these will change as new versions of the software packages are installed by your clients. Most training is conducted on clients' premises, so your own office equipment can be added later. Charge at least $75 per hour to cover your expenses and to make a tidy profit.

Keys to Success

If you are good at teaching, you can make a big difference in the work lives of the people you train. They must use computer equipment to complete their tasks, and knowing how the programs operate will greatly increase their efficiency. You will know that the services you provide are important to the employees you train and to the businesses that depend on them. You'll need to be good at defusing their computer anxiety, though. People who don't understand the intricacies of a program start pulling their hair out almost immediately. You will need to coax them gradually through each skill level until they gain confidence. Students who are new to an area often don't ask clear questions; anticipate that and listen carefully to give the right responses. Some adults find it very difficult to become students again. Also, there is a lot of competition in this field today. You will need to find a way to distinguish from all of the others what you can offer. Finally, preparing training materials can be time-consuming and labor-intensive if you're not used to step-by-step approaches.

Concert Promoter

Start-up cost:	$15,000–$25,000
Potential earnings:	$50,000–$100,000+
Typical fees:	25 to 30 percent of the concert gross
Advertising:	Promoters' magazine, industry trades, newspapers
Qualifications:	Should be well connected in the music industry
Equipment needed:	Basic office setup, cell phone
Staff required:	Yes
Hidden costs:	Insurance, travel/entertainment costs

What You Do

Rock, opera, classical, folk . . . there are as many different acts to promote as there are types of music. If you are a real go-getter and have had an extensive background in the music industry, you stand a chance of making it as a concert promoter. You'll need to be supremely well organized and detail-oriented, since your business hinges on every little detail. You will solicit agents by telling them that you will promote their clients aggressively if they bring them to your town. Network with local media to ensure good public relations, but don't promise agents the moon if you can't deliver. This business is full of hyped-up promoters who are really ripoff artists. You can't afford to be greedy until after you've established yourself; once you have a solid track record of successful promotions, you can go for the big bucks.

What You Need

Your start-up cost ($15,000–$25,000) will be wrapped up in getting your name out there and presenting a professional image. You have to be fairly well-known before people will let you promote their acts. Your fee will be 25 to 30 percent of the concert gross; if it's a big name, you could earn as much as $150,000 per show.

Keys to Success

There are long hours involved in this occupation—and a lot of socializing too. It's not necessarily a good deal for a person with a family, but it's workable if you have a strong support staff. Expect a lot of trial and error in the beginning; learn from each experience and improve yourself with time.

Consulting Engineer

Start-up cost:	$20,000–$50,000
Potential earnings:	$40,000–$85,000+
Typical fees:	Depends on length and extent of project; can be as little as $175 for a minor project and as high as several thousand for the larger ones
Advertising:	Trade journals, classified ads, federal publications, networking, banner ads on building- and construction-related Web sites that link to your own informative site (which may include case studies showing how you solved engineering problems)
Qualifications:	Degree and certification necessary (sometimes in each state you do business in)
Equipment needed:	Drafting equipment and reference materials, computer-aided design (CAD) software, perhaps surveying equipment
Staff required:	Not initially, although you may want to hire an administrative assistant early on
Hidden costs:	Liability insurance, mileage

What You Do

When a big project is launched at a corporation or even in a municipal environment, the expertise needed to actually create the "great idea" isn't necessarily in-house. You can really carve a nice niche for yourself as the "hired gun" who pulls together all the necessary finishing touches for construction, manufacturing, or technical situations. Consulting engineers offer their expertise or hands-on abilities to bring special projects to fruition. This could involve anything from creating CAD designs to developing a better means of production for wiring harnesses. If you don't mind the pressure of coming into a potentially volatile (and political) situation, and particularly if you are amenable to long hours for a short-term project, this could be a perfectly workable business for you.

What You Need

Your start-up costs will consist mainly of basic equipment. Expect to spend at least $20,000 (more if you're planning to have others working along with you). Invest in a professional-looking Web site, at the very least. But if you're good at what you do, you'll be able to earn a considerable amount of money within the first year or two—perhaps as much as $100,000 or more.

Keys to Success

The key to success as a consulting engineer depends heavily on your ability to establish yourself as an industry expert of some kind. The more well-known you are for solving manufacturability problems, for instance, the more calls you're going to get—and the richer you'll become.

Cooking Instructor

Start-up cost:	$1,000–$5,000
Potential earnings:	$10,000–$20,000
Typical fees:	$20–$45 per student per class
Advertising:	Newspaper ads, brochures, flyers, Web site with your latest class offerings and the ability to register for them online
Qualifications:	Cooking experience, teaching ability, some marketing skills; knowledge of state/federal regulations related to cooking in a home (if that's where you'll be teaching); possibly permits
Equipment needed:	Cooking equipment and supplies, a place to teach (if not teaching at home)
Staff required:	No
Hidden costs:	Possible need to rent a facility to teach the classes; must have adequate stove(s), generous counter space

What You Do

Gourmet cooking and dining have always been popular. There are many television shows featuring chefs and cooks whose creativity pleases the palate, and gourmet restaurants and cooking supply stores abound. If you have (or can learn) the basics of cooking and have an interest in teaching others to do the same, this might be the business for you. You might check out the possibility of teaching in a home economics room at your local high school. This business can also be conducted easily from your home.

What You Need

Start-up costs can be minimal if you already have the cookware and utensils needed. In addition, factor in the purchase of a professional stove, if you don't have one, and the cost to rent a facility for the classes, if you don't want to teach at home. Teaching at home is only recommended if you have a large kitchen. The costs of your raw materials will need to be factored into your class fees.

Keys to Success

A cooking class business can be very rewarding. Everyone loves to eat, and learning to produce delightful meals will please your students. Marketing is probably the big hurdle for this type of business. You will need to advertise. You might be able to find related businesses to sponsor you or to spread the word about your classes. For instance, you could build a relationship with the owner of an upscale kitchen products company or offer your classes as "continuing education" through a local college.

Corporate Art Consultant

Start-up cost:	$1,000–$5,000
Potential earnings:	$35,000–$100,000
Typical fees:	$50 per hour
Advertising:	Web site with your credentials and an online gallery sampling of your "art catalog," trade publications, business periodicals, service on local community boards or in charitable organizations, networking
Qualifications:	Degree in art or related field, extensive gallery or museum experience, interior design credentials
Equipment needed:	Business cards, letterhead, envelopes, cell phone, digital camera or scanner, laptop computer with Internet access
Staff required:	No
Hidden costs:	Membership dues, subscriptions to art periodicals, travel, Web site development and maintenance

What You Do

The corporate art consulting business is where connoisseurship and corporate image issues come together. It's a rare combination, and you'll need a strong eye for art and a reputation for awareness of business image requirements to create a successful enterprise. The art world often has trouble communicating with business people. Your ability to move in both worlds will be a major factor in your success.

To a large degree you will be selling yourself, and you will do this by listening well, understanding corporate culture, grasping the needs of your client, and presenting each organization with choices that will enhance their workplaces and their image. You will transform your own appreciation for art into a service that adds value to your clients' enterprises.

The ability to locate the perfect piece of art for the corporate environment is rare. You'll need to visit every art show or trade convention you can and collect catalogs from dealers worldwide. Then you'll negotiate fair prices, which includes using your expertise to help newly discovered artists price their work to sell.

What You Need

You'll be meeting people at your clients' premises, in galleries, and so on, rather than at your own office. As a result, your home office will only have to support your business needs, not to impress. In the beginning, particularly, you will need to build your reputation through use of impressive direct mail pieces, networking, and a high-quality Web site that showcases some of the work you have available. Take a laptop computer ($2,000–$3,000) with you for presentations and log in to your online catalog. Then you will be speaking the language of business while spreading the treasure of original art.

Keys to Success

Establishing yourself as a corporate art consultant will take time, determination, and persistence. Comb the local business pages for stories or announcements about new corporate office buildings, which will likely need some artwork to make their new offices truly outstanding workplaces. Where you live will control your avenues of approach. Operating independently, without an association to back you or sponsor you, will be possible only in one of the major U.S. cities. Elsewhere you'll need to be associated with a commercial interior design firm or an art gallery that can provide you with a steady stream of business referrals.

Counselor/Psychologist

Start-up cost:	$3,000–$5,000 (after college expenses)
Potential earnings:	$65,000–$150,000
Typical fees:	$60–$85 per hour
Advertising:	Newspapers, referrals from physicians, Yellow Pages
Qualifications:	Degree and certification
Equipment needed:	Phone, fax, and answering service to field calls when you are not available

Staff required: No (possibly an assistant for handling insurance claims)

Hidden costs: Keep scrupulous records of every meeting you have with a client—emergency meetings are frequent and could slip through the cracks when billing if you aren't careful

What You Do

Do you have a knack for getting to the heart of a problem? Are you on top of all the self-help ideologies out there—and their potential for both helping and worsening the problems of others? If so, you are well suited to the profession of counselor/ psychologist. You will not only listen to your clients' problems, but you'll also guide them to finding their own healthy solutions. You'll offer them resources to expand their own abilities in problem-solving and provide creative exercises to get the clients to relax and open up their lives to you. But your job doesn't stop there. You must also keep accurate records of your meetings, spending time reviewing these records before and after each meeting. Therefore you must love details and be able to budget your time appropriately in order to stay on top of your workload.

What You Need

Your initial costs are moderate and primarily cover advertising and promotion. You'll need business cards and stationery with which to invoice your clients. Add to that the cost of continuing your education via seminars and conferences (generally around $1,000 annually). Finally, you'll need someone who can process medical claims if you are not able. The insurance companies can be tricky to deal with if you're a novice at it. Your clients will be dependent upon you very heavily at first, then may possibly disappear altogether when they feel they are better.

Keys to Success

You may relish the opportunity to make sense out of someone else's life, but being a successful counselor or psychologist often means giving with a capital "G."

Courier Service

Start-up cost: $300–$500 ($15,000–$25,000 more if you purchase a dedicated delivery vehicle)

Potential earnings: $25,000–$65,000 (more in a major metropolitan area)

Typical fees: Depends on mileage, but you can set flat rates for specific types of courier service (such as international adoption paperwork for which couriers typically charge $150–$350 for taking papers to consulates for certification and redelivery to parents or adoption agencies)

Advertising:	Web site, business publications, adoption agencies,
Qualifications:	Administrative skills, attention to detail
Equipment needed:	Computer, dependable transportation to government offices and delivery services, cell phone with hands-free accessories (if mandated by your state), e-mail accessibility
Staff required:	No
Hidden costs:	Transportation fees should be built into your services—they may seem negligible but do quickly add up; you will also need good insurance (including liability)

What You Do

When important papers absolutely must be delivered to waiting hands, the answer isn't always overnight delivery. Often, a courier is needed to take contracts, storyboards, or other important business documents to another city or state—and a courier service can be ready to deliver at the drop of a hat. That is even faster than overnight, right? If you have a good working knowledge of the lay of the land, you can maximize the profits of your courier service by choosing the fastest, most economical routes to the delivery site, and even group a few deliveries together whenever possible. You will be entrusted with original documents, so take extra care not to lose or misplace them or you will be liable for their replacement. Deliver what your clients entrust to your service, and then go the extra mile to be sure they are notified of safe, efficient delivery. Communication is what it's all about.

What You Need

Dependable transportation is a must, so be sure you either have a vehicle in good working order or have constant access to fast, reliable public transportation. You will be able to respond much more quickly if you have your own car or van and a cell phone with hands-free accessories (if mandated by your state) or paging system. Being accessible and able to respond quickly is what will win you the big bucks.

Keys to Success

You are always dependent upon referrals and repeat business, so friendly and dependable service is a must. The customer is always right, and you should go out of your way to keep your customers happy, since they are the well of eternal hope for your business. Offer nice little extras that set you apart from the competition; for instance, you might offer coupons or gift certificates from businesses with which you align yourself (such as hair salons, copying services, or even local restaurants). Also, being a notary can make your courier business value-added service, since you could also offer traveling notary services to office workers that are in need of a notary but don't have time to leave the office during regular hours to find one. Think strategically and creatively and consider what you might want from your own local courier service. You'll soon see how far the little things will take you.

Credit Consultant

Start-up cost: $2,000–$3,000

Potential earnings: $25,000–$40,000

Typical fees: Percentage of debt from client and from creditor (usually 10 to 15 percent from each)

Advertising: Yellow Pages, seminars, speeches to community groups, classified ads, newspapers, radio spots, banner ads on financial Web sites, your own Web site with consumer credit tips and links to helpful online resources

Qualifications: A background in finance would be ideal

Equipment needed: Business cards, letterhead, envelopes, computer, printer, fax, spreadsheet software

Staff required: No; may need administrative support

Hidden costs: Insurance

What You Do

As a credit counselor you work with people who have overextended themselves financially. Your clients will come to you for help in dealing with an unmanageable credit burden. How big is this market? We've all heard the stories about the credit cards that pour into people's mailboxes, even cards with "Fido" printed on them in gold letters. Fido's credit rating has "already been preapproved." Credit card debt is at an historic high right now, and not everyone has budgeted for the payments. You will negotiate with the creditors to develop a manageable payment plan. Your client pays you a small percentage of what is owed, and the creditors also compensate you as the plan you work out most likely prevents the debt from being a complete loss.

What You Need

Your office can be quite minimal at first; you should be able to get away with spending $3,000–$5,000 maximum. Since your business depends on how many clients you can secure (i.e., how many stay with the program, so to speak), you should be able to make a decent living ($25,000–$40,000).

Keys to Success

You're providing a valuable service to desperate, guilty, and frustrated people. This situation can be rewarding or draining, depending on the individuals involved. For most debtors, dealing with the pain feels much better than watching it spiral out of control. You will probably have the opportunity to add some education and psychological support into your services. This will allow you to gain the satisfaction of knowing that you have helped to improve a person's or family's financial standing.

☞ Damage Restoration Service

Start-up cost:	$15,000–$20,000
Potential earnings:	$40,000–$65,000
Typical fees:	Varied according to damage; can be as little as $500 and as much as several thousand
Advertising:	Yellow Pages, coupon books, networking with Realtors and contractors, possibly a Web site with a photo gallery featuring "before" and "after" photos of your best restoration work
Qualifications:	Should have extensive knowledge about building structure and repair and codes and regulations regarding hazardous chemicals
Equipment needed:	A complete set of tools, painting/wallpapering equipment, varnishes and woodworking equipment, special solvents for cleaning up waste byproducts, computer and cell phone
Staff required:	No
Hidden costs:	Insurance

What You Do

When a hurricane or other natural disaster strikes, any kind of professional who can fix homes or offices is called in to assess the damage, create an estimate, and work with insurance companies to get the job done. A damage restoration service is just one of the many services that can help fix the havoc that nature wreaked on a property. But it doesn't need to be a major natural disaster for your services to be called upon; more often than not, a fire or severe storm warrants repair work. Both fire and flood can cause structural damage to a building, but they can also ruin floors and walls. As a damage repair service professional, you'll spend the majority of your time fixing walls, ceilings, and floors, so you'll need to be familiar with every kind of chemical that cleans, repairs, or restores such surfaces. If peeling paint and waterlogged walls are up your alley, you'll enjoy each of the projects that comes your way. One thing is certain: this kind of work is never without its challenges.

What You Need

The smartest thing you can do is lease your equipment (and possibly even your tools) until you're sure of enough business to cover expenses. Leasing can cost you between $150–$300 per month, as opposed to a large initial outlay of cash ($10,000 or more) for repair equipment. Your charges will depend on the extent of damage done to the building; some repair jobs bill at a mere $500, while others are $1,500–$80,000.

Keys to Success

This business can be quite lucrative if you're in a hurricane- or tornado-prone area, but sporadic in other areas of the country. You might consider adding on related services, such as wallpaper installation or faux finishes, to keep the money rolling in.

Dating Service

Start-up cost:	$15,000–$150,000 (depending on how high-tech you want to be)
Potential earnings:	$50,000–$1.5 million
Typical fees:	$150 per client (for a six-month subscription)
Advertising:	Yellow Pages, classified ads, 900 numbers, television ads, singles magazines, banner ads on singles sites
Qualifications:	None
Equipment needed:	Extensive phone system for 900 numbers, computer (with many using computer video programs to showcase their clients), Web site with candidate sign-up, screening, search and match capability
Staff required:	Yes
Hidden costs:	Computerized systems can run as high as $40,000

What You Do

"Matchmaker, matchmaker, make me a living." Today's dating scene is vastly different from the old days, when a village woman made matches based on how her knee was feeling that day. Tired of meeting people in bars and the regular "sweat shops," many young professionals simply want a confidential, efficient way to meet the man or woman of their dreams. The Web offers an even more accessible way for them to accomplish their goal of finding the perfect mate. Because your clients don't have the time to screen a hundred or so applicants, you can provide this service for them—and at a competitive rate. (Just because they don't have time certainly doesn't mean they don't have money.) You'll need to first decide what kind of dating service you'd most like to offer: a well-respected, high-profile Web-based agency; an impersonal (yet profitable) 900 number. Either type requires you to manage profiles of your clients, so you'll need to have them answer questionnaires detailing their hobbies, interests, and desires in a potential mate, which is easy if your service is Web-based. The next steps are to make this information readily available to your client base—and keep track of your successes!

What You Need

Your start-up costs can be quite high, based on the fact that most of your competitors (both large and small) are investing in Web-based technology that does it all in a few steps: first conducting the interview, then recording the interviewee and, finally, selecting a potential match from the data bank. All of this could run anywhere from $40,000–$150,000, so be sure to investigate those costs well enough to document them in your business plan, particularly if you are going to need investors.

Keys to Success

This is the love business, so what's not to love? For one thing, you'll be meeting quite an array of interesting people, and you'll be helping them to find long-lasting happiness. But what if it doesn't work out? Are you prepared to deal with broken hearts, all the while encouraging them to stay in the game? If the answer is yes, you'll be heartily rewarded for your efforts.

Day-Care Service (Child or Adult)

Start-up cost:	$3,000
Potential earnings:	$25,000–$40,000
Typical fees:	$80 per child per week or $125 per adult per week
Advertising:	Referral service, bulletin boards, classified ads, networking with teachers in your local school district and senior centers
Qualifications:	Most states require a license and insurance
Equipment needed:	For children: cribs, toys, movies, and games; for adults: arts/crafts supplies and some form of entertainment
Staff required:	No (but many states impose a limit on the adult-to-child ratio; for example, in Ohio you may have no more than six children to one adult)

Hidden costs: Insurance, possible adjustments to your house for adult day care, such as a wheelchair ramp and a bathroom on the first floor

What You Do

The day-care business has been growing in direct relation to the rising number of women choosing careers in addition to families. There is a need to care for both seniors and children. A few innovative entrepreneurs have integrated both at their care centers, so that the two groups can enjoy and learn to appreciate one another. You can easily start a day-care center in your home if you meet the necessary zoning requirements of your community. It works best if you have a large yard and extra room (perhaps a finished basement) so that there is plenty of room to play. You'll need to be clear in your rates/policies, especially about regular hours, vacations, and payment due dates. And be careful not to let the parents treat you like a babysitter. Be assertive about protecting your personal time with your own family.

What You Need

Your main start-up cost will be getting the word out about your service. Classified advertising, bulletin boards, and mothers' groups are a good way to build word of mouth. Your larger expenses will likely come from updating your home to meet zoning regulations; your home may have to pass inspection before licensing. If you decide not to license or not to carry insurance, be sure to let the parents/families know this, because you will be held liable in the event of a disaster or accident if you don't disclose it. Along these lines, be sure to familiarize yourself with safety procedures in case of an emergency.

Keys to Success

If you love to be around little people or seniors, you'll enjoy the opportunity to do so daily. Also, if you have children of your own, you can get paid while watching them play with others, which is not a bad deal. On the downside, although you are responsible for the children you watch, you are not their parent—a fact the parents themselves may constantly remind you of. Be sure to meet with the parents of children or the families of seniors on a regular basis to keep communications straight.

Desktop Publisher

Start-up cost:	$15,000–$25,000
Potential earnings:	$20,000–$100,000
Typical fees:	$500 (newsletter) to $20,000 (for a large-run book or magazine)

Advertising:	Direct solicitation, Yellow Pages, local publications, word of mouth, networking, advertising in writers' magazines, Web site with samples of your work in an online portfolio
Qualifications:	Computer, design, writing, editing, and communication skills
Equipment needed:	Computer with scanner, laser printer, digital camera, desktop publishing software, fax, office furniture, business cards, letterhead, envelopes
Staff required:	No
Hidden costs:	Marketing, keeping up with changes in software

What You Do

Desktop publishing (DTP) enables people who understand graphic design and typography to offer a range of services to clients. If you are skilled with computer software, you will be able to produce everything from books to flyers. Many small DTP businesses succeed by specializing; for example, they might create newsletters for a specific type of business. Others produce entire books or focus on annual reports. Most will provide only the camera-ready master and subcontract the larger printing jobs to a commercial printer. The DTP field includes many small and large businesses, but there is room for people who do excellent work, produce it on time, and focus on their clients' needs and expectations. Although most desktop publishers handle design and production work for their clients, it would be helpful to provide additional services such as writing and editing, if possible. This will give your customers one stop for most of their production needs.

What You Need

The computer equipment required can be very expensive, depending largely on the graphics capability you need. Macs will be your best bet for design work, and your files can be made viewable by PC-based clients with conversion software or by .pdf creation. You must have a work space that supports the complex nature of some DTP tasks. Figure marketing costs, too, of $1,000–$2,000 in the financial section of your business plan. Your income will be dependent upon how many clients you can win in a short period of time, so you'll need to advertise your services (unless your former employer has become a major client). Billing can be done hourly ($50–$75 per) or, more typically, on a per-job basis. Smaller jobs can net $50–$300; larger ones can bring in $5,000 or more.

Keys to Success

Although working on several different creative projects at one time can be interesting and challenging, the pressure can be unbelievable. In the days of instant information and twenty-four-hour turnaround, everybody expects their work done today. This can be a problem when you have ten or more clients you're juggling. Try to set realistic deadlines with your clients to avoid all-nighters and stress-filled days.

EXPERT ADVICE

What sets your business apart from others like it?
"We produce healthy recipes and a common-sense approach to healthy living," says JoAnna M. Lund, President and CEO of Healthy Exchange, Inc. in DeWitt, Louisiana. "We appeal to the average person and offer quick, healthy recipes that taste good using easy-to-find ingredients."

Things you couldn't do without
A computer and laser printer, plus a fax machine.

Marketing tips
"It's challenging to stay on top of changes in your field, but it pays well to do so," says Lund. "Make sure you're an expert on that which you're reporting."

If you had to do it all over again . . .
"Nothing. I'm quite happy where I am."

Digital Imaging Service

Start-up cost:	$20,000–$40,000
Potential earnings:	$25,000–$45,000
Typical fees:	$15–$45 per scanned-image product
Advertising:	Yellow Pages, mall kiosks and other high-volume locations, banner ads on print-related Web sites, your own Web site with online gallery of your work
Qualifications:	Training in equipment
Equipment needed:	Computer with scanner and video imaging capability
Staff required:	No
Hidden costs:	Insurance, equipment maintenance and upgrades

What You Do
The digital craze is on, and it's not limited to musical instruments or compact disks. You can cash in on the trend by starting your own digital imaging service.

It can be either on-site at a retail shop or kiosk or completely Web-based by allowing customers to upload their favorite photos for you to place on T-shirts, mugs, mouse pads, and so on. You've probably seen such businesses in your local shopping mall or at a community flea market. The proprietor simply takes a video image of a person and places it onto a computer screen for printing on a color printer. The image is then transferred to a product and a personalized gift has been created. It's that simple, and the service generally sells itself if positioned in a high-traveled area. You can buy a franchise or start from scratch if you are familiar enough with the equipment and can work with product vendors. Expect to market your service aggressively; you'll need to talk to people and have excellent sales ability to make enough money to cover your expenses. Still it's a fun method of gift-giving for many consumers.

What You Need

You'll need $20,000–$40,000 for your equipment and space rental, slightly more if you buy a franchise. Your equipment will include a computer with color printer, video camera, and software that permits image transfer from video to computer screen to printer. Thermal transfer equipment will also be necessary to produce those personalized coffee mugs and T-shirts. On the plus side, you might see as much as $45,000 for little effort on your part.

Keys to Success

Your business will fluctuate according to season. Expect slow times in the fall and spring and a busy time each Christmas, complete with long hours and heavy volume.

☞ Disability Consultant

Start-up cost:	$2,000–$4,000
Potential earnings:	$50,000–$75,000
Typical fees:	$60–$80 per hour
Advertising:	Direct mail, referrals, membership in business organizations, Web site with testimonials about how you've helped save companies money
Qualifications:	Extensive experience in field, college degree in related area, ability to communicate well with employers and employees, good writing skills
Equipment needed:	Cell phone, computer, printer, office furniture, business cards, letterhead, envelopes

Staff required: No

Hidden costs: Insurance, association dues, conferences and seminars

What You Do

As a disability consultant you will advise corporations on disability claims and assist them in meeting the requirements of all government and regulatory bodies. Nothing is cut and dried about the disability field, and rapid changes have left even the best-intentioned employers confused about what they must do to be in compliance. Disability claims made by employees are a major cost in some industries, and your recommendations for alterations in the setup of the workplace or refinements in work processes could be seen as extremely valuable.

Managing medical claims is another important function. The conflicts arising from the most common worker problem—back pain—need expert management, both for medical treatment and for the maintenance of good relations with the employee. The third aspect of this field is the requirement to make reasonable accommodations for disabled workers. Creative consultants can often find ways to make small alterations in the workplace, such as lowering the height of a counter to enable a wheelchair-bound person to fill a position at the company.

What You Need

Most of your work will be carried out at the companies for which you are assessing and handling claims, but you will need your own office for writing reports and possibly for client meetings. Expect to spend $2,000–$4,000 for your computer system and Web site. Charge $60–$80 per hour for this service, which can save a company thousands of dollars per year.

Keys to Success

If you have experience in this complex field and can communicate with both sides, the disabled and the employer, you can build a business as a disability consultant. In fact, some disabled people do just this, using their own perspectives to enrich the services they can offer to other organizations. Enabling people with disabilities to hold jobs is an important service, and it keeps employers on the right side of the law as well.

Disc Jockey

Start-up cost: $5,000–$10,000

Potential earnings: $15,000–$25,000

Typical fees: $75–$150 per job

Advertising:	Classified ads, bulletin boards, your own Web site with your music catalog in various categories
Qualifications:	Knowledge of popular music, strong personality
Equipment needed:	Karaoke equipment, turntables, sound/mixing systems, microphone, theatrical lighting (if desired), a large and varied CD and record collection
Staff required:	No
Hidden costs:	Constant upgrade of collection to include current hits

What You Do

Because live bands cost quite a bit more than mobile DJ services, many party-givers book DJs to handle the entertainment needs of their party or celebration. Sometimes they even ask the DJ to play "host" for a theme party. DJs have been around as long as there have been records to play, and they will continue even as equipment gets more sophisticated. For one thing, systems producing excellent sound quality are getting smaller and more portable, making it easier for DJs who travel to several locations in a given weekend. As a DJ, you'll need to develop your own style for building rapport with the audience; study the techniques of professionals you respect and try to emulate them if you can't come up with your own material. You should have a wide variety of music and read industry publications regularly, such as *Billboard* and *Rolling Stone*, to keep up on what's new and what's hot.

What You Need

Your start-up costs are mostly wrapped up in equipment and your music collection itself, because advertising will cost you no more than a few hundred dollars at the outset for classified ads. Look for used equipment and used CDs, which could save you $1,000 or more. Scour garage sales and flea markets for the unusual or obscure. Since you'll be working an average of three to five hours per job, it's not unrealistic to set your fee at $75–$150 per event.

Keys to Success

Your work cycles will be extremely varied, with heavier loads typically in the spring and summer. Most of your work will be done on weekends, cutting into your social life considerably. If you're looking for work that is there when you want it, being a DJ is not for you. On the other hand, if you don't mind the erratic hours and enjoy being with people in a celebrative mood, you'll look forward to each new gig.

⟻ Dog Trainer

Start-up cost:	$1,000–$2,000
Potential earnings:	$35,000–$45,000
Typical fees:	$300 for a three-week session is fairly common
Advertising:	Flyers; direct mail; Yellow Pages; classifieds; networking with vets; free clinics; Web site with free training tips and class offerings, schedules, and fees
Qualifications:	Experience with different breeds, track record of success, patience, and credibility; a permit may be necessary in many states
Equipment needed:	Cell phone; space for pets to roam, eat, and sleep
Staff required:	No
Hidden costs:	Advertising, travel

What You Do

Working dogs need considerable training, depending on the jobs they have to perform. Drug-sniffing dogs, guard dogs, guide dogs, movie dogs, and herding dogs all require specialized training. While these dogs usually receive their training from their breeders or owners, they are sometimes trained by professional trainers who have national reputations for their skill and effectiveness.

A much bigger market is training services for pets. Most pet owners wake up a bit late to the need for training (usually after half of the carpet has been eaten). You can present your service as the solution to those nagging problems that make pet dogs so frustrating at times. Some trainers give classes for owner and dog together while others go to a pet's home and provide individual sessions. Network with veterinarians and pet stores; they are usually the first to hear about animal problems.

What You Need

Your main start-up cost is for whatever marketing and advertising approaches seem best for your community. Somewhere between $500–$1,000 would be an average amount to spend on launching this business. Don't forget to create a Web site and include a "Top 10" list of helpful tips for pet owners. This will help increase your visibility on the Web, but will also bolster your credibility. Since you'll be charging as much as $300 per dog for a three-week session, you could see a tidy profit early in the game. And that's nothing to bark at, is it?

Keys to Success

This job is immensely enjoyable if you love dogs and can tolerate their owners. (Remember, you'll be training them too.) Gaining the trust of an animal is an essential part of any training process, but some trainers find that getting the human side of the equation to cooperate is even harder. Once the pets in your class begin to give up eating the curtains and jumping all over Grandma, however, you will seem like a genius. Then the class can proceed to the really difficult stuff such as coming when called (the pet) and being patient (the owner). For most trainers this is not a route to wealth, but a decent living can be made if you keep up your marketing efforts.

Doll Repair Service

Start-up cost:	$500–$1,000
Potential earnings:	$20,000–$40,000
Typical fees:	Depends on what needs to be replaced and whether the doll is an antique (could be $50–$300 or more)
Advertising:	Yellow Pages, antique shows, specialty shops, hobby magazines, banner ads on doll-related sites with link to your own Web site
Qualifications:	Experience with the art of doll-making and repair, special knowledge of antique dolls
Equipment needed:	Spare parts, precision tools, computer to research and purchase additional doll parts
Staff required:	No
Hidden costs:	Liability insurance, shipping

What You Do

This is a thriving business. As dolls get older, they become more popular to collect. And if they're going to be worth anything later on, they need to be in the best possible shape to command the highest dollars. One early Barbie doll can be worth as much as $500, but only if she's in mint condition. That is where you come in: you repair and restore dolls to their original state. Sometimes this means purchasing used dolls for spare parts. Keep all types of doll parts on hand and network with other repair services to locate spare parts. Pay attention to detail and have the hands of a surgeon. Dolls aren't just made of plastic; there are many different types, such as bisque, china, wax, and mechanical. Know what is special about each doll and what precautions to take when repairing each. Market your service especially hard at antique fairs and specialty shops. Have them keep your business cards by their cash register. You may want to offer related services such as collectibles connections (matching buyers and sellers) and a retail doll shop as well.

What You Need

Advertising will be key to generating most of your business, and will cost about $1,000; the rest of your initial expenses will go to spare parts, about $500 to start. Some may be expensive, so you may want to hold off ordering until there is a need. You will be repairing high-end and antique dolls, so gauge your earnings between $20,000–$40,000.

Keys to Success

Some doll repair services have given the business a bad name. You'll have to overcome this by knowing the ins and outs of doll-making. It is much easier to repair something if you know how it is put together. Take your time and know what you are doing; if you ruin a doll you may have to buy it. Be sure your packaging is secure when you deliver or ship to avoid any damage.

Draftsperson

Start-up cost:	$5,000–$10,000
Potential earnings:	$35,000–$65,000
Typical fees:	$150–$500 per blueprint
Advertising:	Yellow Pages, trade publications
Qualifications:	Degree in drafting
Equipment needed:	Computer with large-screen monitor, computer-aided design (CAD) software, blueprint photocopier, drafting table, related small tools
Staff required:	No
Hidden costs:	Insurance, equipment maintenance and upgrades

What You Do

You're detail-oriented and have a flair for putting the finishing touches on someone else's work. You've also likely studied drafting in college before embarking on this entrepreneurial endeavor, and you have the experience that your customers will eventually come to rely on. As a draftsperson, you will ultimately produce the blueprints that architects and builders need to complete their dynamic new projects. You will make any requested number of copies of each blueprint as well.

Although individuals may hire you for smaller projects, most of your customers will be architects and building professionals, so you'll need to be well connected to get any share of the work that's out there. Set yourself apart by adding additional services or special treatment, such as free delivery to work sites.

What You Need
You'll need between $5,000 and $10,000 to get started in drafting and blueprinting, primarily to cover your equipment costs for such items as your computer and design software, as well as your blueprint photocopier ($4,000 or so) and drafting table with drafting pencils, and so on. You'll likely earn between $35,000 and $65,000 for your efforts.

Keys to Success
It's very precise work you're doing, and often it's a thankless job. (The architects and builders get all the glory.) Oh, well . . . you should always remember that without you, these projects might not have gotten done. Stick close to the builders and architects, since they'll ultimately make up your referral system.

e-Book Publisher

Start-up cost:	$150–$2,500
Potential earnings:	$35,000–$60,000
Typical fees:	$150–$350 for e-book production using e-book creation software; $500 and up if your services include book editing and proofreading
Advertising:	Writers' magazines online forums or chats, banner ads on creative writing Web sites, reciprocal links with complementary businesses (such as e-bookstores and cyber cafés)
Qualifications:	Experience in e-commerce, marketing, and design, as well as Web creation and management and some book editing
Equipment needed:	Computer, e-book creation software, online hosting service with e-commerce capability (to help your clients sell their books), access to graphic design services or a good e-book design program
Staff required:	No

Hidden costs: Corrections can be time-consuming and therefore costly; make sure your customer proofreads the work prior to production or have a policy that there will be charges beyond a set number of corrections

What You Do

Thousands of people believe there is at least one good book in them and that with the affordable technology available today, there's no reason why they can't produce that book. These days all an author needs to do is turn a manuscript into portable digital format (such as .pdf using Adobe Acrobat) and hook up with a printing service that will only print and ship copies as they are ordered. As an e-book or print-on-demand publisher, you will help others to get their words into downloadable, inexpensive electronic books that, if properly promoted, can make both you and the author money while you sleep. You can either go high-end and set up your own Web site to host and promote downloadable books, or you can offer book packaging (preparation) services and guide others through working with more established e-book or print-on-demand publishers such as Xlibris.com, iUniverse.com, Upublish.com, and AuthorHouse.com. You can help others to make their books see the light of day—offering personalized services that large publishing houses no longer offer new authors.

What You Need

All you need to turn dreams into reality is a good computer with high-quality e-book creation software. There are many inexpensive versions on the market, and while you can start with one of these, you will quickly find that there are limitations, such as the inability to design a nice e-book cover. The higher-end versions typically include templates for cover designs, and that will be a very useful promotional tool for the book's sales page in your online bookstore. Spring for the extra hundred bucks if you're really serious about producing highquality e-books.

Keys to Success

In the late 1990s, e-books were not yet considered to be a viable option in the publishing world. Since then, many large publishers such as Random House have launched their own electronic book divisions (Xlibris.com). The competitive landscape is growing larger; the key to success is to identify niche books that have built-in markets and specialized audiences to whom you can promote. Topics that are too broad or that try to appeal to mass audiences don't stand as good a chance, especially when you compare your promotional budget to Random House's.

⌐ Efficiency Expert

Start-up cost:	$5,000–$10,000
Potential earnings:	$35,000–$75,000+ (depending on your market)
Typical fees:	$75–$100 per hour or a monthly retainer of $3,000–$5,000
Advertising:	Trade publications, Yellow Pages, direct mail, business newspapers, banner ads on small-business Web sites and a link to your own Web site with some free time- and money-saving tips plus testimonials
Qualifications:	Ability to spot potential problems and time-wasters before and as they occur; business degree and extensive business experience in operations and management
Equipment needed:	Cell phone, computer, fax, printer, resource materials
Staff required:	No
Hidden costs:	Insurance, under billing for amount of time spent

What You Do

Corporations often have CEOs who want the company run like clockwork, particularly if there are production goals to be met regularly. As an efficiency expert, you will come into a company for a period of about two to four weeks and carefully monitor exactly how things are being done. You will ask workers questions such as, "Why are you repeatedly moving across the room to accomplish one simple task?" and "Is there any other way to minimize the steps involved in your particular process?" You are, in a sense, a detective searching for answers to the big question, which is, of course: "How can this company achieve more in a better and more economical way?" Next, you'll print up a report or make a formal presentation, telling the CEO how he or she can improve operations. You should have a rather broad background in business operations, management experience, and a strong eye for detail. After all, your client companies will be paying you big bucks to figure out what needs to be improved upon at their facilities. You have to convey the idea that you're worth it, so watch your own image and always give 110 percent.

What You Need

Start-up expenses will be relatively low (in the $5,000–$10,000 range), but you should do quite well when you consider what you might be able to earn if you're good at what you do ($35,000–$75,000 or more). You'll need a basic office setup and lots of good resource materials to help workers achieve greater effectiveness.

Keys to Success

While some corporate moguls will hire you to tell them what's wrong with their organization, they may not be willing to actually listen. You'll need to be clear from the beginning that you are offering your professional opinions and advice so that your personal liability will be kept in check.

Electrical Contractor

Start-up cost:	$10,000–$15,000
Potential earnings:	$40,000–$60,000
Typical fees:	$40 per hour for labor plus parts costs (varied)
Advertising:	Yellow Pages, classifieds, neighborhood flyers, community bulletin boards, radio spots, possibly a Web site in more competitive regions
Qualifications:	Skill and experience as an electrician, ability to manage time and expenses, good people skills, license or certification and regular credit hours toward career development in most states
Equipment needed:	Cell phone, tools, parts, and equipment related to the nature of the work, van, marketing materials
Staff required:	No
Hidden costs:	Inventory of parts, vehicle maintenance, insurance

What You Do

Skilled electricians are always in demand, especially ones who can work with homeowners and small business owners. As the general population becomes less handy with tools and wires, your electrical knowledge and expertise will become more and more valuable. This is a classic one-person business, and you may find considerable competition. You will need good estimating skills to assess the cost and complexity of the work you are asked to do. Sometimes it seems as if electricians have to be part detective to interpret the hidden wiring in an old house or to trace the cause of a short "somewhere in the wall." Of course, you'll be familiar with code standards in all the communities in your service area.

What You Need

Costs are relatively high as you must equip yourself to do whatever electrical job is offered. You'll also need to secure certification; and your educational requirements to stay certified may demand that you take regular refresher courses. Set aside at least $5,000 for all of this, then add your equipment, liability insurance, and related costs.

Keys to Success

Many electricians have made an excellent living by focusing on upgrading the wiring in old houses. If your area has a charming neighborhood of old Victorians, twenties bungalows, or quaint cottages that are being restored, you have a golden opportunity to build a client base. Other electricians work closely with an independent builder to install wiring in new structures. For these jobs, getting the work done according to the overall construction schedule will have a big influence on profits for the builder. Your planning and time-management skills can help build you a steady stream of referrals and repeat projects from these builders.

Employee Benefits Consultant

Start-up cost:	$5,000–$8,000
Potential earnings:	$30,000–$70,000
Typical fees:	$25 and up per hour
Advertising:	Direct mail, networking, memberships in business and community organizations, Web site with links to related resources
Qualifications:	Extensive experience in insurance sales, ability to reach business owners, detail orientation, communications skills
Equipment needed:	Office furniture, computer, fax, printer, cell phone, business card, letterhead, envelopes
Staff required:	No
Hidden costs:	Preparation of presentation materials, online fees, errors and omissions insurance

What You Do

An effective employee benefits program is an important factor in building a loyal work force. The challenge is to create a combination of benefits that meets the needs of the organization and also fits its budget. As an employee benefits consultant, you will help growing businesses survey their employees to learn their needs and wants regarding employer-paid insurance. You will work with business owners to design the best combination of benefits for the dollars available. Businesses that have between twenty and 200 employees comprise the best market.

What You Need

Most of your contact with clients will take place at their locations, so your office can be functional rather than impressive ($4,000 should get you started). You'll need to be easy for potential and current clients to reach, and you'll need to produce professional-looking presentations to client companies. You should plan to earn about $30,000 in the beginning.

Keys to Success

Many insurance agents have terrible sales approaches. They seem very eager for their commissions and do not give ongoing service throughout the year. As annual review time rolls around, these agents show up again with a plan to change to new providers for a few dollars less. But implementation and employee education are lacking. You will be able to set yourself apart if your focus is on customer service, not your own profit (at least outwardly). Experience in assisting with claims and with conflicts that arise are also important selling points for your enterprise.

Employee Leasing

Start-up cost:	$15,000–$35,000
Potential earnings:	$60,000–$80,000
Typical fees:	Mark up the going rates by 40 to 50 percent
Advertising:	Direct mail, networking throughout business and trade associations, publishing your own newsletter, Web site with client testimonials
Qualifications:	Knowledge of and contacts in a specific field, excellent organizational skills
Equipment needed:	Office furniture, computer, printer, fax, telephone headset and/or cell phone, business card, letterhead, envelopes, brochure
Staff required:	No
Hidden costs:	Liability insurance against employee misconduct, employee screening costs (background checks and drug testing)

What You Do

While you may not be able to compete with the big, general agencies, you can effectively run a small employee leasing agency. You provide to employers workers with specialized skills, who cannot be reached through the traditional temp services. This business produces good earnings relative to time and materials: you're not doing the actual work, just the organization. Build your database of specialists in a field you have experience with, then begin direct mail, banner advertising or an e-mail campaign to reach your prospective clients.

What You Need

Although the cost of building your initial database and center of operations is not high, you will need a sizable initial investment ($20,000) to cover the delays in cash flow between your clients and your employees. You could see at least $60,000 at the end of your first year.

Keys to Success

You may need to consult an attorney to stay abreast of the laws regarding taxes, workers' compensation, and employment. Some types of temps will need to be bonded, and you will need to measure the advantages of incorporation over the extra costs and red tape involved.

Engraving Service

Start-up cost:	$40,000–$75,000
Potential earnings:	$40,000–$65,000
Typical fees:	40 cents–$100+ per piece
Advertising:	Direct mail, Yellow Pages, networking with business and civic organizations as well as schools, Web site
Qualifications:	Training on the engraving equipment
Equipment needed:	Engraver, molds, stencils
Staff required:	No
Hidden costs:	Insurance

What You Do

For nearly every school, association, or organization, there is a trophy or an award to be given to its members. For many business, there are name badges to be made for the employees. Think of the potential, then, for your engraving business—it's a bottomless cup, isn't it? You'll need to be a strong networker, as much of this business has already been soaked up by those established much earlier than you. But, to compete, you can set yourself apart by offering unique products to engrave or even by reselling recognition products from other sources, such as the retail shop and catalog outfit, Successories™. Sell people on your exceptional eye for detail and customer service abilities and throw in quick turnaround if you can. Your clients will often need an award or trophy to be made on a tight deadline, so you can reap an additional fee for 48-hour service.

What You Need

You could spend anywhere from $40,000 to $70,000 or more on your engraving equipment, depending on how high-tech you get and how large a company you would like. Your best bet is to seek out good used equipment first. In terms of earning power, you could make between $40,000–$65,000 if you work hard and build the right contacts.

Keys to Success

You'll be singled out as a winner yourself if you can keep up with your orders in an accurate, timely manner. The best thing you can do is to send samples to folks with their names or company logos already printed on it, nothing appeals more to a person than a little ego boost. Wasn't it Dale Carnegie who said that there is no sweeter sound than the sound of one's own name?

Envelope Stuffing Service

Start-up cost:	Under $500
Potential earnings:	$10,000–$15,000
Typical fees:	25 to 50 cents per envelope
Advertising:	Flyers and mailings to companies without in-house mailing services
Qualifications:	Knowledge of postal regulations
Equipment needed:	Envelope sealer, letter folder
Staff required:	No
Hidden costs:	Clients who seek to pay one flat fee and then dump extra work on you

What You Do

Companies who use direct mail in their advertising or promotional campaigns need help stuffing the envelopes and getting them properly prepared for the post office. If you're skillful at the manual end of this business (folding/stuffing/sealing envelopes), you'll be amazed at how much you can earn in only a few hours. You'll need to market your services well. And if you find that you have too much business, you'll have the perfect opportunity to hire people with disabilities and retired folks who might be on the lookout for such straightforward, low-pressure work. Make sure you schedule your jobs realistically to allow for quick turnaround, because that is what will likely be expected of you from most of your clients.

What You Need

You may spend a few hundred dollars or so on items such as letter folders and envelope sealers, but this business still shouldn't cost more than $500 to launch. Get the word out by networking with small- to medium-size companies, who usually need help on projects of this kind. Charge between 25 and 50 cents per envelope, and try not to quote a flat rate if you can help it; you may be taken advantage of after the ink is dry on your agreement.

Keys to Success

Let's face it, stuffing envelopes is pretty boring work. If you don't mind the tedium—if you can manage to do your work and still catch *Oprah!* when you want to—this could be a perfect way to either supplement an existing income or build a modest base income. However, remember that your success depends largely on your marketing ability.

Etiquette Adviser

Start-up cost:	Under $1,000
Potential earnings:	$20,000–$50,000
Typical fees:	$15–$35 per one-hour class per person
Advertising:	Newspapers, business publications, networking with community organizations, Web site with some free tips
Qualifications:	Extremely good taste and wealth of knowledge on manners and good behavior
Equipment needed:	Good resource materials
Staff required:	No
Hidden costs:	Networking in high places could set you out some considerable cash in your entertainment budget

What You Do

You've always known the answer to seemingly eternal questions: which fork do I start with and what is that spoon across the top of my plate really for? People rely on your expertise for such sticky situations as who to invite to a wedding, where to place divorced parents in a room together, when not to send a thank-you card, and how long is too long to respond to an RSVP. That's why your talents are needed, but how do you charge for them and still maintain your dignity? Easy. You offer your services in six simple courses. It's too difficult for an etiquette advisor to make serious money handling each question piecemeal, so develop a curriculum and offer your classes to the public or (better yet) the Corporate Confused seeking to become the Corporate Elite. You could offer tips on everything from proper conversation to handling potentially embarrassing situations; for instance, what should you do if your crouton shoots out from your plate to your boss's during lunch?

What You Need

Your start-up costs are so minimal, you needn't worry about whether it is proper to launch this business. Just make sure you have good reference materials for the questions that stump you and leave a little extra cash for entertaining (which could be your main way of bringing in business).

Keys to Success

You'll love the authority and power of being an authoritative expert, but try not to let it get to your head. The last thing any one of your clients wants is a know-it-all. Be matter-of-fact, and try to inject some humor into your profession. Believe it or not, humor is the best teacher in a delicate, personal subject such as etiquette.

☞ Event Planner

Start-up cost:	$500–$1,500 ($5,000–$15,000 more if you need a delivery van)
Potential earnings:	$45,000–$150,000+
Typical fees:	$25–$50 per hour (depending on market and your reputation) for small events; 10–15 percent of total event cost for large events
Advertising:	Community and business publications, Web site, eye-catching marketing collateral, referrals
Qualifications:	Extremely attentive to details, strong project management skills
Equipment needed:	Computer with good event planning software program, cell phone with hands-free accessories (if mandated by your state), e-mail access, a PDA, a good delivery van would be helpful
Staff required:	May need to hire assistants to help occasionally
Hidden costs:	Staffing costs might take a bite out of your profits when you've just begun, since you'll likely need some help from time to time

What You Do

Whether large or small, corporate or intimate, religious or ceremonial, any event requires a lot of planning as well as the ability to execute that plan like clockwork. As an event planner, you will map out themes, strategies, resources, and supplies for events as diverse as bar mitzvahs, birthday parties, retirement parties, weddings, fundraisers, and corporate sales meetings. You will develop a timeline for all of the components of your plan, and will network with key suppliers to ensure that you are getting the best deals on the most innovative elements and points of interest involved in your event. You can probably order a lot online, but you might also look at opening a vendor's account with a local craft supply shop. If you are not 100 percent sure you can make it on your own at first, you might consider doing an online search for a "party business in a box," which has everything you'll need to launch your business successfully, including tips from many others who have launched similar businesses before you. You may also offer to work with another event planner first, serving as a backup and then branching off with the pro's overflow work. That would help you understand all the details involved in operating an event planning business. There's a whole lot of pressure to get everything right, but there's also a whole lot of reward for those who can stand the heat while running the kitchen.

What You Need

You will most definitely need a computer with Internet service and a good event planning software program. Together these will cost around $1,000 to $1,500, but the software program will be well worth the investment, as it will keep you organized and take some of the think-work out of the entire process of event planning.

Keys to Success

Networking with those at churches, rental halls, and party centers will help you to spread the word about your business. You will sometimes need to do events for less money than you might like, but when you do, try to make sure the events become photo opportunities for your local newspaper. Keep a clipping book and scan your own event photos into an online gallery on your Web site. People will enjoy seeing samples of your work, as well as reading testimonials from your happy clients. Do surveys at the end of each event to capture their thoughts, and gain permission to post their comments on your site and in your marketing materials.

Executive Search Firm

> **Start-up cost:** $5,500–$9,000
>
> **Potential earnings:** $40,000–$150,000

Typical fees:	Varies, but often equals 25 percent of first-year earnings of person placed with client
Advertising:	Cold calls, attending trade shows, newsletter to potential clients, direct mail, business and regional publications, Web site
Qualifications:	Excellent people skills, patience, self-confidence, knowledge of specialized fields to be able to select appropriate candidates for jobs
Equipment needed:	Cell phone, computer and office equipment, telephone, business cards, letterhead, brochures
Staff required:	None
Hidden costs:	Phone expenses and advertising costs could exceed budget early on

What You Do

Executive recruiters (also known as "headhunters") are paid by companies to fill management, professional, and technical slots within their firms. Most of a recruiter's work is done via phone and E-mail, so you can do this job anywhere. You will collect as many qualified applicants as you can, gleaned mostly from your vast resume collection and a few friends in high places. Many consultants choose niches in which to specialize; others serve all areas. A sales personality is helpful in this business, as is the ability to be self-motivated. Often finding good people for the positions is easier than finding clients who will hire you to conduct the job search. You will need self-confidence, tenacity, and good networking skills to make it as a recruiter. This career choice gives you a great deal of flexibility and personal freedom, since you can work from any location that has a phone.

What You Need

A computer and printer are essential, as is database, word processing, and communications software and a professional-looking Web site that showcases some of your current job openings. These items will cost from $2,500 to $5,000. You will need a telephone, a headset, and fax, along with office furniture and business cards, letterhead, and brochures to promote your business. These pieces will cost $1,500–$4,500. You'll earn an average of 25 percent of the new hire's salary, so it behooves you to search for the high-end, top-level managers.

Keys to Success

Competition for the best companies and top-notch candidates is stiff, and you get paid only when you successfully match a company with a candidate. But the financial rewards can be considerable, and the satisfaction of helping a good candidate to find a job and your client to fill a key position, makes your efforts worthwhile.

Fan Club Management

Start-up cost:	Minimal, if artist pays for expenses; $3,000–$5,000 if you're totally self-sufficient
Potential earnings:	$10,000–$30,000
Typical fees:	$10–$25 each for memberships; you can also derive a percentage from merchandising products (which may need to be licensed or bought at wholesale cost if you are not working directly for a celebrity)
Advertising:	Direct mail, Web site with e-newsletters and message boards
Qualifications:	Experience in film or television, or as a professional writer; Membership in the National Association of Fan Clubs
Equipment needed:	Computer with fast Internet access; printer; fax; copier; database, label, and desktop publishing software
Staff required:	No
Hidden costs:	Postage and printing costs; server space might become more costly as your site's popularity grows and as more content is generated

What You Do

When a celebrity becomes a celebrity, the last thing she wants to do is sit around answering fan mail. Still many celebrities do realize that their fans are the ones who put them where they are, and they don't necessarily want to ignore them. That is why it makes sense for popular artists to hire fan club managers to keep in touch with their many admirers: they recognize the importance of staying at the top by staying in touch with those whose opinions ultimately matter the most. If you have the right credentials (such as having been a professional writer or prior experience in radio or television), then you might be able to convince a celebrity to let you take charge of his or her mail. In addition to opening and answering huge bags of mail, you'll offer services such as producing a quarterly or semiannual newsletter and merchandising, at the celebrity's expense (offering promotional products like T-shirts, posters, and autographed photos for sale and taking a small percentage for yourself). If you are going it alone, you may save money with value-added items on your site such as a Weblog or an e-newsletter, and seek permission to link to the celebrity's site. If you manage the celebrity's Web site, you can suggest similar such items, along with media clips, interviews, and reviews. Like the celebrity, if you're in the right place at the right time, this could be a golden opportunity for you.

What You Need

You won't need very much at all to get started if you can convince a celebrity to foot the bill for his or her fan club; some celebrities actually do see the value of paying someone else to handle the mail and requests for signed photos. However, most fan clubs operate on their own (with or without celebrity endorsement, but obviously it's easier with). This would leave you with a start-up cost of $3,000–$5,000 if you operate on a shoestring. You could sell memberships for $10–$25 each and offer incentives for joining, such as a free T-shirt or baseball cap. At any rate, you'll be producing e-newsletters a few times per year at a low cost to you (basically time and server space). If all goes well, you could make $10,000–$30,000 per year doing something enjoyable and high-profile. It may not be enough to make you rich, but certainly enough to make you smile.

Keys to Success

This seems on the surface to be a glamorous job, and it is until you get barraged with unreasonable requests, tight deadlines on newsletters, and ego-maniacal celebrities who think treating "underlings" accordingly is the path to greater success. It might help if you continually remind the celebrity just how much more money the fan club is ultimately making them in boosting record or ticket sales. If you're going it alone, you might consider teaming with another fan club manager who knows the ropes and can offer you guidance as you proceed.

EXPERT ADVICE

What sets your business apart from others like it?

"We are an authorized fan club management company and I have a highly specialized background in radio," says Joyce Logan, President of Fan Emporium, Inc., a Branford, Connecticut-based firm representing entertainers such as Michael Bolton, Carly Simon, John Mellencamp, and Mariah Carey. "I put myself in the fan's shoes and give every fan the personal touch . . . we produce newsletters, answer fan mail, sell authorized merchandise, and even have a 900-number service for fans to get concert updates and messages from their favorite superstars."

Things you couldn't do without

Computer with a good database management program, printer and labeling program, Internet access, and fax.

Marketing tips

"Start with just one celebrity, and know that you can't just run a fan club for a little while. This is a serious commitment to the celebrity and the fans. You're dealing with people's emotional links to their favorite celebrity . . . you are a 'merchant of emotions.'"

"I would have made contracts with the artists a little bit differently, so that they would assume all the costs of printing and mailing. We are a public relations firm just like any other, and we need to be recognized as such to stay profitable."

Fax-on-Demand Service

Start-up cost:	$12,000–$15,000
Potential earnings:	$20,000–$50,000
Typical fees:	$150–$300/month to cover incoming calls, with unlimited responses, or lower monthly fees with charge for each response
Advertising:	Trade journals, direct mail, direct solicitations to local businesses, seminars and banner ads on small-business Web sites, your own Web site with available packages and pricing options
Qualifications:	Knowledge of technology and software, marketing ability
Equipment needed:	Modified computer with special fax board, customized software, scanner, office furniture
Staff required:	No
Hidden costs:	Additional phone lines

What You Do

You will provide the technology that allows smaller companies and professionals to match the fax-on-demand systems being set up in-house by large organizations. Your clients will make information available to their customers or employees around the clock. These people call to ask for information, and your automated faxing system instantly sends them the newsletter, data sheet, or restaurant menu they have requested. Automatic broadcasting can reach sales reps or members of an interest group. Once businesses understand how their marketing efforts can be supported by fax-on-demand, they will form an ongoing clientele and a source of steady income for you. But your first task will be to help them see the possibilities inherent in this technology, since most people aren't aware of its options or capabilities. How will what you do be different from e-messaging? You will offer companies the ability to send information about their products and services to people who "opt-in" but want to see it on paper. Believe it or not, the fax is still in demand.

What You Need

This is an expensive business to get into, with start-up costs averaging $15,000. Getting the funding to set it up may present quite a challenge, since it is a relatively new type of business. However if you're creative, you'll find ways to purchase the equipment you need economically; and you'll be billing $150–$300 per client per month, so you will have decent income once your customer base is well established.

Keys to Success

You're going to need a silver tongue and a genius for marketing to get a fax-on-demand service off the ground. Finding organizations that need to send up-to-date printed materials in high volume will be the first step. Creating possibilities that click in with your prospects' needs and assumptions will allow you to get your message through to the people who can see advantages to cutting-edge approaches.

Feng Shui Consultant

Start-up cost:	$500–$1,500
Potential earnings:	$40,000–$65,000
Typical fees:	$100–$150 per hour consultation fee
Advertising:	Local business and real estate publications, networking with interior designers and architects, Web site, referrals, teaching community college courses
Qualifications:	Training and certification from a bona fide school of feng shui would be helpful
Equipment needed:	Compass, cell phone, possibly a computer for research if desired
Staff required:	No
Hidden costs:	Subscriptions and membership dues, continuing education

What You Do

A feng shui consultant uses the ancient Chinese art of feng shui (which means "wind and water") to help businesses and homeowners recognize the most ideal directions and placements for items in their personal space. The thinking behind this is that if your belongings are in perfect alignment with unseen forces of nature, allowing the positive flow of life-giving "chi" energy throughout, then you will have a healthy and prosperous life in that space. To achieve the most positive flow of chi, you'll need to first help your clients identify and remove clutter, so that you can actually see where the best locations are for the remaining "intentional" possessions. This can be a fun and very challenging business for those who enjoy improving other people's lives. You can really make a difference in the way they live, simply by advising them on the best configurations for their meaningful possessions, as well as the virtues of a clutter-free life!

What You Need
You really don't need much to be a good feng shui consultant, since most of your trade depends squarely on your knowledge and ability to convey that wisdom effectively to clients. You might benefit from having a computer to help you stay on top of feng shui news and trends. If you follow the traditional school of feng shui, you will be using a compass much of the time to determine ideal directions for furniture placement.

Keys to Success
Referrals will be a significant source of income for you, especially in your start-up phase. You would do well in the beginning to network as much as possible with architects and interior designers, but you may also consider offering yourself as a speaker at local libraries and events as a way of getting your name out there. Many feng shui consultants are also teachers of this ancient art, so you should definitely consider offering courses through community centers or adult education programs.

Financial Aid Consultant

Start-up cost:	$2,000–$4,000
Potential earnings:	$15,000–$40,000
Typical fees:	Flat rates of $150–$500
Advertising:	Yellow Pages, classified ads, direct mail, membership to and participation in community organizations related to education, seminars and speeches for community groups, networking, Web site that's easily located via search engines
Qualifications:	Experience as a school guidance counselor or college admissions officer, extensive knowledge of the field, ability to relate well to college applicants and their parents
Equipment needed:	Office with conference table for meeting clients, computer, suite software, Internet access, fax, printer, business cards, letterhead, envelopes

Staff required: No

Hidden costs: Subscriptions, Internet Service Provider fees, association dues

What You Do

The cost of higher education continues to escalate. And while one often hears that many types of financial aid are available, finding them is quite another matter. Families need guidance and assistance in finding the sources to which they can apply and in preparing the paperwork. Your services as a financial aid consultant will be in great demand once your name gets known to the community at large. Word of mouth from students you have helped and from their parents will bring you new business regularly. You will need a lot of familiarity with financial aid options to make a success of this type of consulting, and you will need excellent people skills as well. Some financial aid consultants research options on the Internet, while other specialize in aid for private secondary or even elementary school tuition. The bulk of the market, though, is for students entering college.

What You Need

Keeping your own knowledge up-to-date and providing a suitable place for interviewing clients are your two main expenses ($2,000 to start). Part-time work could earn you $15,000; rates could range anywhere from $150–$500 per job, depending on both complexity of paperwork and your geographical location.

Keys to Success

Many parents experience major shock when they first realize how much having one or more children enrolled in the ivied halls is going to set them back. And even the "simple" financial aid forms for determining basic financial need are far from easy to cope with. You can also provide vital help in finding the multitude of special scholarships available for students with a certain heritage, a special academic interest, or some other specific characteristic.

Financial Planner

Start-up cost: $5,000–$8,000

Potential earnings: $40,000–$60,000

Typical fees: Set fee depending on investments, typically $250–$500 or more

Advertising: Networking, memberships in community and business groups, local magazines and newspapers, programs of fundraisers, Web site with some free tips

Qualifications:	Certification is becoming essential; familiarity with financial issues; marketing skills; ability to inspire trust
Equipment needed:	Computer, printer, suite software, Internet access, fax, online account, furniture, business card, letterhead, envelopes
Staff required:	No
Hidden costs:	Subscriptions to newspapers and financial periodicals, errors and omissions insurance

What You Do

The market for financial planning services is becoming very large, especially as the baby boom generation draws close to retirement. In fact, some of them are already there, but they haven't planned as well as they could have for the inevitable. Your biggest difficulty in establishing your business will be that so many others are competing with you. The financial planning business is just one piece of what a full-service investment company does for its clients, so you'll have to position yourself as a more personalized service than your competitors. You'll probably also need to be part of a close network of family, friends, and acquaintances who will work with you and refer you to their friends. This is a very personal business, and your ability to inspire confidence will be vital. Creativity in helping your clients plan their financial future and skill at helping them achieve those goals will set you apart. Is there an underserved group you can target? Can you design plans for self-employed people, the elderly, or investment clubs? Can you work in association with related businesses such as accountant firms to add your service onto their offerings?

What You Need

Your office needs to give you the up-to-the-moment information you need for proper service to your clients (around $3,000 to start); however, you could earn upward of $40,000.

Keys to Success

Most people manage their money very poorly, if at all. They don't plan well or budget, and they haven't faced up to the question of how to provide for retirement. All of these are difficult topics, and dealing with these sensitive issues makes people uncomfortable. You can smooth things over with a reassuring attitude, and by paying attention to the details of your client's finances that they overlook.

EXPERT ADVICE

What sets your business apart from others like it?

Dianne Winnen, a Certified Financial Planner in Akron, Ohio, says she is different because her business caters to middle-income people rather than focusing on seniors with retirement funds. "I'm one of 31,000 CFPs in the country, and I'm proud to be a part of a select group."

Things you couldn't do without
"I couldn't do without my computer, telephone, and copier."

Marketing tips
"You really have to want to be in this field to make it successful for you. Read and educate yourself about business matters."

If you had to do it all over again . . .
"I would've gone in with more realistic expectations about what it would take to survive the first couple of years."

First Aid/CPR Instructor

Start-up cost:	$300–$500
Potential earnings:	$15,000–$20,000
Typical fees:	$10–$20 per participant
Advertising:	YMCA, hospitals, churches, associations, schools, swim clubs
Qualifications:	American Red Cross or American Heart Association certification required
Equipment needed:	"Annie-are-you-okay" dummy for practice
Staff required:	No
Hidden costs:	Educational materials could cost you more than expected; you'll find out what you really need and what you don't from your training instructor

What You Do
Many of us have been given CPR training at schools, churches, or swim clubs, and if you've always been interested in teaching people to save lives, this could be your calling. It is not particularly profitable since volunteers from many associations offer similar courses, but it could provide you with some extra cash. Set yourself apart by adding on a related service, such as a speakers bureau that offers tips on CPR on people with illnesses, disabilities, and so on.

What You Need

It really doesn't cost much to instruct others on the benefits of life-saving techniques; your biggest up-front cost will be for the practice dummy and related resource materials such as models and diagrams. You'll find out from your instructor what educational materials you really need and what you don't. One innovative place you could offer your services is at restaurants. Their staffs always have diagrams of what to do in an emergency, but do they really read them and have they actually practiced on anyone? Not likely. Offer them a group discount!

Keys to Success

The challenge of setting yourself apart from competing services offered free of charge can seem overwhelming at first, but get creative. You can make a small, yet profitable, business for yourself. Be positive and look for the big guys who can help provide a steady flow of business, such as health clubs, restaurant associations, and human resource managers at large corporations.

⊨ Food Item Manufacturer

Start-up cost:	$500–$5,000 (depending on the food product)
Potential earnings:	$30,000–$75,000
Typical fees:	As high as $50 for some items, but most range $2–$25 each
Advertising:	Mail-order catalogs, brochures, direct mail, groceries, farmers' markets, Web site with testimonials about your products and an online store with a secure server for safe ordering
Qualifications:	Knowledge of how to manufacture and market the item
Equipment needed:	Depends on the item
Staff required:	None
Hidden costs:	Legal advice

What You Do

The sky is the limit in food production. Anything from eggs and bottled water to candy and organically grown tomatoes can be manufactured by a home-based entrepreneur. What's involved in such a business varies greatly, depending upon which product you choose, but either offering a unique food item or marketing a tried-and-true favorite in a new way spells success. A package of pasta, for example, can be produced for as little as 46 cents and sold for $3.50 or more. How about pizza? Everyone loves pizza, it's easy to make and, with your own marketing or recipe twists, you can make a tremendous amount of money. Want more ideas? How about food by mail order, a food-preserving business, specialty breads, sassafras tea, holiday cookies, or maple syrup? If you are willing to learn the ins and outs of producing and marketing a particular food product, you can establish a profitable business.

What You Need

Start-up costs depend on the food product you choose. If you need ovens or an assembly line to manufacture your products, it may be relatively expensive to begin. On the other hand, a product such as soup can be started on a shoestring. Packaging and marketing costs for any product must be carefully considered. Explore your market area, examine packaging of similar products, and research the costs.

Keys to Success

Your livelihood is greatly affected by weather and the seasons if it requires growing a crop. You may need considerable knowledge about fertilizers, plant diseases, and so on. You must have a consistent supply of ingredients and a consistent manufacturing method to ensure that your products always taste the same. Any food product is subject to safety and health regulations. The good news is that many food manufacturing operations are quite simple, requiring few ingredients and no great technical skills. Everyone loves to eat, so food products are always in vogue.

Framing Service

Start-up cost:	$40,000–$60,000
Potential earnings:	$40,000–$50,000
Typical fees:	$15 per hour for custom work plus materials; materials only for frame-it-yourself
Advertising:	Yellow Pages, local newspapers, coupon books
Qualifications:	Understanding of operating a retail business plus skill in framing and training a staff, ability to teach customers to frame
Equipment needed:	Framing supplies, special cutters for glass, wood, mats, cash register, retail space
Staff required:	No
Hidden costs:	Insurance, materials

What You Do

This business is lucrative because many people buy prints and other artwork or want to frame their own pieces. Some people don't have the time or patience to frame, so the custom aspect should not be ignored. Take into consideration, however, that about 60 percent frame their own, while 40 percent request custom framing. Material costs fall somewhere around 26 to 32 percent and gross profits about 68 to 74 percent.

What You Need

You'll spend at least $30,000 launching a frame shop, primarily because you'll need lots of storage space and work area with sufficient lighting. More than likely, you'll rent space somewhere close to an art gallery. Charges will vary according to size and make of frame.

Keys to Success

Be mindful that this is a retail establishment, so take into consideration the size of the shop, location, and rent. You might want to sell some ready-made frames and prints to supplement the custom framing business.

Freelance Writer/Copyeditor/Illustrator

Start-up cost:	$2,000–$5,000
Potential earnings:	$22,500–$50,000
Typical fees:	$50–$150 per hour, depending on area and experience level
Advertising:	Personal contacts, trade publications, Web site with links to your online portfolio and a well-planned contact form that enables potential customers to quickly tell you about their project
Qualifications:	Attention to detail and organizational ability; Writing and communication skills for freelance writing and copyediting, sense for graphics and design for freelance illustrating
Equipment needed:	High-end computer (Mac-based would be best for designers and illustrators) with light pen or graphics tablet and a high resolution graphics video card (for illustrating), scanner, printer, word processing, design and contact management software, fast Internet access, fax, office furniture, reference books, business cards

Staff required: No

Hidden costs: Maintaining personal contacts (business lunches, etc.), memberships in trade organizations, software upgrades

What You Do

Many people have made careers out of freelance writing, copyediting, and illustrating—and many more are trying. Success will come for you when you can distinguish your services from those of others who will work for much less; remind clients that they get what they pay for. Excellent communication skills are required to discover exactly what your clients want and need. You then turn those skills around to produce the corrected materials, written texts, or illustrations that will support your clients' needs. This business is built entirely on your abilities, and that requires building up trust slowly and carefully before you can obtain the big projects that bring in enough income to make you financially successful. Using your creativity and focusing on goals are both essential. No detail can slip by your eye. But successful projects will bring you referrals, and each small step can lead to a bigger one.

As a writer, you will work on special editorial projects for clients ranging from small business owners to universities to newspapers—and, if you're a copywriter, you may even be lucky enough to snag a corporate client or two in-between. Your projects might be as specialized as an article for a trade journal or a corporate history; then again, you could be a generalist who writes articles on a wide variety of topics for various magazines and newspapers. Your best bet, at least in the beginning, is to produce brochures for small businesses.

As a copyeditor, you will focus your energies on making sure everything that you see goes back to the publisher as mistake-free as is humanly possible. You will correct grammatical errors, spelling and punctuation mistakes, and even poor sentence flow. Your job is to ensure that all the words on the page make sense and have a certain rhythm to them, so that the reader is carried along through the book logically and comfortably. You may end up copyediting thousands of projects, from annual reports and menus to book-length manuscripts.

As a freelance illustrator, you will market your work to various publishing houses, ultimately in search of a regular contract with at least one. If you do secure a contract, you may design and produce book covers as well as artwork to accompany the text. This area of expertise is particularly lucrative for those who can produce lively, entertaining illustrations for children's books.

What You Need

You'll be spending a lot of time in your office, so whether you plan to meet clients there or not, you'll need to make it an effective workspace. The high-end computer equipment needed to produce professional results is costly, averaging $2,000–$5,000. Your hourly rates should cover all of your overhead, so price yourself competitively in the $50–$150 per hour range. For designers and illustrators, a Mac is a must.

Keys to Success

You can indulge your love of words and/or graphics to the max in the freelance world. You will be learning something new with each project, and you will have the satisfaction of seeing everything you produce be published. Working to support your client businesses can result in a satisfying partnership. However, pricing your services can be very difficult. Nonwriters often do not appreciate the time and effort that goes into producing an effective piece of writing, and there are many writers out there in the marketplace who are likely to undercut you. Deadlines are always too short, and sometimes it can be difficult to obtain the background information needed from a client.

Any way you look at it, freelance writers, copyeditors, and illustrators are typically driven, hardworking people who have earned the circles under their eyes the hard way.

EXPERT ADVICE

What sets your business apart from others like it?

Ruth Dean, owner of The Writing Toolbox in Akron, Ohio, says her business is unique because she listens well and helps clients clarify their ideas and plans. She specializes in technical marketing communications and gets her best results by writing to appeal to the client's intended audience, not just to the client.

Things you couldn't do without

"The fax is essential. Clients want instant communication." A computer and laser printer are also necessities.

Marketing tips

Dean markets by networking. "I just ask clients about their business and listen. That's all it takes. It's important to have writing samples available in simple 'packages' so that clients who are not accustomed to working with writers can figure out how to hire you."

If you had to do it all over again . . .

"I wouldn't have waited so long to go out on my own."

Gardening Consultant/Landscaper

Start-up cost: $5,000–$10,000 (more if you need to purchase a vehicle)

Potential earnings: $40,000–$60,000

Typical fees:	Varied; can be as low as $125 or as high as several thousand per project (depending on whether you're working for an individual or a corporation)
Advertising:	Yellow Pages, community newspapers, city magazines, direct mail, bulletin boards, networking, speaking to community organizations, Web site with free seasonal gardening tips
Qualifications:	Extensive knowledge of plants, growing seasons, and regional climates
Equipment needed:	Gardening tools, hoses, seeds, perhaps a van or pickup truck
Staff required:	Yes (1–5 people to work on several projects simultaneously)
Hidden costs:	Liability insurance and workers' compensation

What You Do

There's nothing lovelier in the springtime than a perfectly planned garden in bloom. If you've always been the type who can effectively plan such perennial pleasures, you would likely be well-suited to this line of business, especially if you don't mind working outside in the dirt for long periods of time during the warmest times of the year. As a gardening consultant, you will meet with either homeowners or business owners to work out the details of what will bloom where. Develop a portfolio of your best work, then reel in more business through speaking engagements or presentations to community organizations. Be sure to always be clear on what your services entail; many well-meaning folks may confuse your services with those of professional landscapers. If you don't cut grass, say so.

What You Need

If you've already been involved in gardening, you likely have many of the tools you'll need to start. However, keep in mind that you'll probably be adding a staff once the phone starts ringing, so you'll need to double or possibly triple the number of tools you have on hand. Also, if you need a vehicle, such as a van or pickup truck, consider leasing and applying a magnetic sign to the door advertising your services. All said and done, you'll shell out between $5,000 and $10,000, more if you add staff. But your fees, which will vary from $125 to several thousand dollars, should offset any costs.

Keys to Success

Plan your speaking engagements and other forms of promotion during the off-season; chances are, you'll be too busy during the spring and summer months.

Genealogical Service

Start-up cost:	$500–$1,500 (depending on whether you have a computer)
Potential earnings:	$15,000–$25,000
Typical fees:	$25–$125 per search; $200–$500 per written family history
Advertising:	Magazines with a historic slant, newspapers, Yellow Pages
Qualifications:	Experience doing genealogical searches; knowledge about the field
Equipment needed:	Computer with family tree software program and high-speed Internet services (for constant research)
Staff required:	No
Hidden costs:	Possibly subscriptions to online databases such as Ancestry.com

What You Do

Everyone would like to know their roots, and what better way to find out than through a genealogical service? By hiring such a service, one will learn about past generations of your family, including the black sheep that every family seems to have. As a family history writer, you would meet with family members to obtain every known detail about a family, do further research on your own, and then compile the information into a family tree diagram or a written report. Mind you, not all is known about every member of every family, but the Mormon church has an extensive genealogical service that you could use to find seemingly obscure bits and pieces. And this service is provided for everyone, not just for Mormons. There are also subscription-only Web sites that specialize in genealogical databases, as well as census reports at major metropolitan libraries to assist you with your search. If you aren't afraid of a lot of research and detail-oriented writing work, this could be a great business for you. Every family has a different, yet fascinating, story to tell.

What You Need

You'll need to have a good computer system and genealogical software to produce the kinds of detail-oriented reports necessary in the family history writing business. Expect to spend anywhere from $500–$1,500 on those items alone, then factor in your advertising costs at around another $350–$500 and up (depending on the size of the publication you advertise in). Be sure to factor annual costs of Web site subscriptions, etc., into your fees.

Keys to Success

Your work is much in demand in these nostalgic times. Although there is not a high upfront investment, your time is worth money and you could spend more of that than you are paid for. Make sure you budget your time accordingly or you could easily (and quickly) come up short.

Gerontology Consultant

Start-up cost:	$500
Potential earnings:	$25,000–$40,000
Typical fees:	$20–$40 per hour
Advertising:	Direct mail; networking with psychologists and medical professionals; speaking engagements; Web site with links to case studies, recent research and related resources
Qualifications:	Background in psychology or sociology
Equipment needed:	No
Staff required:	No
Hidden costs:	Possibly mileage

What You Do

Since the year 2000, the population over the age of 60 risen to as high as 65 percent of the total population. Life expectancy has been rising due to improved health care, exercise, and genetics. With more folks than ever before living past the age of 80, the need for skilled professionals to help all of us understand the process and effects of aging is more apparent. As a gerontology expert, you will work in conjunction with hospitals and psychologists to help elderly patients and their families adjust to the many changes and challenges of growing older. You will counsel them on issues ranging from health care to assisted living programs, and may be called on frequently as a resource person for hospitals and the community at large.

What You Need

Assuming that you have the necessary credentials (i.e., a college education in health and human services or a related field), your start-up costs should be minimal. The first thing you'll need is professional-looking stationery and business cards, so allow about $500 for that and some preliminary advertising. A gerontology consultant works primarily on-site; that is, at the place where his or her services have been contracted, so you won't need to rent office space.

Keys to Success

You will probably enjoy the favorable attention you'll receive from people in need of your services, but you should also keep in mind that many of your clients are under unbelievable stress because they are balancing their careers, children, spouses, with the need to care for aging relatives. They simply can't be in two places at once, and they may be difficult to deal with at times as a result.

Gift Basket Business

Start-up cost:	$5,000–$15,000
Potential earnings:	$25,000–$45,000
Typical fees:	Baskets are individually priced anywhere from $25–$350
Advertising:	Local newspapers, flyers, bulletin boards, direct mail to busy executives, Yellow Pages, banner ads on florist and gift-related Web sites, your own Web site with e-commerce capability
Qualifications:	Natural creativity mixed with a strong business sense
Equipment needed:	Baskets and gift materials, glue gun, shrink wrap machine, delivery vehicle, computer and credit-card processing system or service (such as PayPal.com)
Staff required:	No
Hidden costs:	Shipping costs

What You Do

There's nothing nicer to receive than a basket full of goodies meant especially for you, which is why gift basket businesses have been cropping up everywhere. Some are even offered as franchise opportunities. On the surface, this business seems so simple anyone could do it: you just round up a bunch of neat items, place them in a basket, put ribbons and shrink wrap around all and voila! But there is much more to it than that. You must also be a gifted buyer to get the best bargains on gift items and materials and a real go-getter of a salesperson to bring in the constant flow of business needed to stay afloat. In other words, you should have all the marketing skills of a seasoned retailer in addition to a dynamic and creative mind. If you can handle all of that, you will likely succeed if your market area isn't already saturated. Be sure to set yourself apart from the others as much as possible. Since there are so many others in this trendy business, the competition is fierce. You'll lose out if you don't carve an interesting niche for yourself. Perhaps you could fill your gift baskets with only a particular type of product, such as those manufactured only in your state or those related to a special theme.

What You Need

Your start-up costs hinge on whether you're renting a storefront and whether you're investing in a delivery vehicle or merely using your own car or van. A storefront could generate some walk-in business, but rent is steep for straggler-type businesses. You really should try to keep this business lean and mean for as long as you can, having your clients shop from a catalog rather than at a shop. You'll need to advertise heavily in places your customers are most likely to think of needing your services, and that will run you in the neighborhood of $500–$3,000. Your money will come from the gift baskets you sell, minus production and commission costs. Most gift basket businesses offer an array of baskets for a wide range of prices, anywhere from $25 to $300.

Keys to Success

Since the national recognition of an enormously successful gift basket business named Longaberger, everyone is trying to get into this seemingly easy business. If you feel you can create a gift basket business that truly stands apart in some way, you stand a good chance of earning a living. If you're not sure, think it over or (better yet) write your business plan. It's so competitive that you have to have a niche to survive in a city or suburbia, and if you're in a remote part of the country your customer base will be limited. However if you're creative about gift baskets, you'll be creative in coming up with a way to sell them.

Government Contract Consulting

Start-up cost:	$3,000–$6,000
Potential earnings:	$40,000–$65,000
Typical fees:	$50–$150 per hour or a flat rate of $175+ per project
Advertising:	Trade journals, association memberships, direct mail, networking, referrals, Web site
Qualifications:	Experience in obtaining government contracts, contacts in Washington D.C., writing skills
Equipment needed:	Computer, suite software, fax, copier, printer, cell phone, office furniture, business cards, letterhead, envelopes
Staff required:	No
Hidden costs:	Internet Service Provider fees, telephone bills

What You Do

As companies downsize, they no longer employ people who can thread their way through the complex world of government contracts. Yet these contracts can be a source of business growth to many companies. Potential clients should not be ignored on the grounds that the governmental requirements seem too difficult. Rather, you will guide these organizations into the land of business opportunity that government contracts represent. Your experience with the special language that government agencies use (and the red tape involved in each transaction) plus your contacts in different departments and agencies will help you help your clients in doing business with the government. This is a specialized field, but it can be a very rewarding one. Often, success in gaining one contract will smooth the path for future work. If you can produce the contracts and/or help carry them out successfully with project management skills, you have a very large potential market of companies that would love to hire your services.

What You Need

Equipping your office is the main expense; expect to spend at least $3,000–$6,000. Considering that some government contract consultants charge as much as $150 per hour for their valued service, your expenses will be minimal in relation to your earnings.

Keys to Success

This is an insider business, so you'll need to sell yourself as an insider if you aren't one already. Don't worry—as you begin to achieve success, you will become more of a real insider. The other factor here is a good business sense. What approach to obtaining a government contract would be most appropriate for each of your clients? How can you guide a specific business organization through the process? You are doing a lot of good for your clients each time you are successful, and that should make up for the frequent need to work under time pressure.

Grant Writer

Start-up cost:	$1,000–$2,000
Potential earnings:	$45,000–$100,000
Typical fees:	$500+ per project or an hourly rate of $25 or more
Advertising:	Networking, direct mail, Web site with references or testimonials

Qualifications:	Knowledge of the regulations governing formal proposals, knowledge of technology and industry, ability to write clearly and logically
Equipment needed:	Computer, office suite software, high-speed Internet access for research, laser printer, fax, office furniture, business cards, letterhead, envelopes
Staff required:	No
Hidden costs:	Printing documents

What You Do

Organizations that want to do business with the federal or state government, cities, counties, and special districts often must respond in writing to a request for proposal (RFP). Writing an effective proposal is a highly skilled activity, and often businesses must contract out the work. Charitable organizations also hire grant writers to help them establish their relationship with private foundations. In either case, the piece of writing must conform to the specifications in the RFP, outlining the methods to be used, the needs to be met, and the financial background and expected outcomes of the project.

Some proposal writers are generalists, while others focus on one field, such as education or health care administration. The emphasis, though, is on good writing skills applicable to any field—clear organization, logical exposition, and excellent grammar. Aptitude with numerical data in graphs and spreadsheets is required. Business savvy is also necessary to work with the client's staff who are planning the bid or funding request.

What You Need

You will need to be able to produce professional-looking documents that may include graphs, charts, and tables. Buy a computer and printer with high-resolution and graphics capabilities (around $2,000–$3,000). Your physical office needs to function well as this is a desk-intensive job. Buy a comfortable chair, around $200. You can bill hourly ($25–$50 per hour) or on a per-job basis ($500 and up).

Keys to Success

A skilled grant writer provides the essential link between the client and the funding, whether it is a grant for a nonprofit organization or a contract for a business. It's challenging work that involves constant learning and creative solutions. It can take a long time to gain enough experience to be effective and have enough contacts to keep the work flowing in. Pricing is always a challenge unless you set a sliding scale that reflects the complexity of each job.

🖝 Graphic Designer

Start-up cost:	$6,000–$10,000
Potential earnings:	$30,000–$75,000
Typical fees:	$75–$100 per hour or average retainer fees of $1,000 per month
Advertising:	Business publications, promotional mailings to people in the advertising industry, referrals, Web site with impressive online portfolio
Qualifications:	Art/design background, communication and marketing skills
Equipment needed:	High-end computer (Mac-based) with quality graphics design software, color scanner, large-screen monitor, laser printer, fax, office furniture that includes a light table, business cards, letterhead, envelopes
Staff required:	No
Hidden costs:	Training in new software programs, acquiring new software suites as they become available

What You Do

There is a lot of competition in this field, but skilled, creative graphic designers stand out above the rest. Experienced graphic designers who want to work independently can make an excellent living in a home-based setting producing work for a range of clients. Freelance graphic designers work for a variety of different businesses, including book publishers, newspapers, consumer product manufacturers, and even other small start-ups. Eventually you may decide to set up a studio and employ others to work with you. An ability to communicate well with clients is essential. It is not enough to create designs that appeal to your own aesthetic sense. You need to be part marketer and part psychologist to produce the designs your clients want and need.

What You Need

The computer equipment required is very expensive. You will need the latest software as well, in addition to an efficient and comfortable work space. Figure your charges to be in the $75–$100 per-hour range. Be careful of bidding on a per-job basis; many companies will demand that you do only to take advantage of your time later.

Keys to Success

You can make an excellent living as a graphic designer once you distinguish yourself from the competition and build up a reputation for excellent and on-time work. Good working relationships will lead to a satisfied group of clients that return to you again and again. It can be difficult to bid jobs accurately, and sometimes a few clients will be very slow to pay. Working under rush conditions seems to be the norm, and occasionally you will encounter a customer who is impossible to please.

EXPERT ADVICE

What sets your business apart from others like it?

Kelvin Oden, owner of Oh Snap! Design in Brooklyn, New York, says he's had to pay his dues to get where he is. "On the positive side, I have a young company and can work without limitation or restriction. I can go against the norm."

Things you couldn't do without

A computer, laser printer with at least 600 dpi, and clients are all Oden says he needs to survive.

Marketing tips

"The most important thing is to build really good relationships with your clients. If they're comfortable with you as a person, they'll come back to you."

If you had to do it all over again . . .

"I wouldn't change anything. . . . I'm extremely happy doing what I'm doing."

Hairstylist

Start-up cost:	$12,000–$20,000
Potential earnings:	$20,000–$45,000
Typical fees:	$20–$40 per haircut, $50–$70 for coloring, highlighting or perms
Advertising:	Local or community newspapers, flyers or business cards on bulletin boards, referrals, and a shingle or small sign in front of your home if permitted
Qualifications:	State license; may also require zoning ordinance or variance (check with your city or county zoning board)

Equipment needed: Stylist's chair; mirrors; sink; cabinet for hair coloring and permanent solutions; baskets for curlers, brushes, combs, and related hair supplies; professional-quality clippers and scissors; capes; washing machine; a good broom or vacuum

Staff required: No

Hidden Costs: Liability insurance, zoning permits

What You Do

One of the oldest home-based businesses, particularly for women, is the hairstylist. Hundreds of these businesses can still be seen as you drive around the older suburbs in your community. While many stylists prefer to align themselves with more established or high-profile salons, you can have a solid home-based business if you plan to set yourself apart from the beginning. If you have reliable transportation, you can offer in-home services to clients. Just think of all those who could take advantage of this convenient service—busy executives, stay-at-home moms, nursing home residents, and hospital outpatients. You'll have to figure in travel time. As a home-based hairstylist, you can set your own hours, work with a small or preferred clientele, and take breaks between clients in the comfort of your own home. Do a few haircuts, highlights, and perms per day, five or six days per week or just two to three days per week, and know that all of the profits from your business will go directly to the pocket of your smock. You can decide how hard you want to work and how often, but at the end of each day, you are responsible for the success or demise of your business. Making your clients look their best will be the easiest way to secure referrals and keep your business growing faster than the hair on your clients' heads. Also, you would do well to include add-ons such as professional nail technician services or even makeup consulting. The more pampering and personalized your services, the more likely you will develop a strong referral base.

What You Need

You will essentially need all of the same hairstyling equipment and supplies as a full-service salon, and this will cost you anywhere from $12,000 to $20,000. Your start-up list will include everything from clippers and scissors to styling chairs and hair dryers. You will need also capes, cotton, a supply cabinet full of coloring and perm solutions for a variety of clients, and of course, mirrors galore. Don't forget to invest a little in some business cards and signage to advertise your business; these will likely cost under $250.

Keys to Success

If you work a particular niche, such as wedding party hairstyling or on-call services where you travel to your client's location for personalized hair services, you will find that you fare much better against large chains. Many of those take walk-ins, which, as a home-based business, you may not be as inclined to do. That's why it pays to know your customers—and your niche—from the start.

Handbill Distribution

Start-up cost:	$200–$500
Potential earnings:	$15,000–$20,000
Typical fees:	$5–$10 per dropoff
Advertising:	Flyers or classified ads
Qualifications:	Marketing sense, time-management skills
Equipment needed:	None
Staff required:	Yes
Hidden costs:	Spot-checking the distribution crew

What You Do
Businesses are moving beyond the traditional marketing avenues (magazine and newspaper advertising, radio spots, and so on) to use less expensive, more effective alternatives. In many areas there is a focus on the reliable advertising method of handbill distribution. If you live in an area with a high concentration of people on foot, near a mall or in a large city, you can create a handbill distribution service that forms a significant part of your clients' marketing strategies. You will need a crew of people to do the actual distribution, and you should carry out spot checks to see that they are actually handing them out and not dumping them. If all goes well, you will be able to earn some extra cash.

What You Need
The flyers with which you advertise your own business are about the only cost for a handbill distribution business, aside from what you pay to your crews. You may need to carry insurance for work-related mishaps; check with your agent. Expect to bill between $5–$10 per dropoff or location; add extra for those jobs involving more time and effort.

Keys to Success
The simplicity of this business has great appeal. It's person-to-person, face-to-face. Creating a business that is an almost pure service can be very satisfying to those who love to make something out of nothing. A lot of your energy will be consumed in marketing your operation, however, and more will be needed to hire and manage your crew.

Handyman Network

Start-up cost:	$500–$1,000
Potential earnings:	$20,000–$45,000
Typical fees:	10 to 20 percent of the repair cost; $45–$55 per hour if you are also providing handyman services yourself
Advertising:	Yellow Pages, community newspapers, coupon books, banner ads on community-oriented Web sites, your own Web site with testimonials
Qualifications:	Good communications skills
Equipment needed:	Cell phone, van well stocked with tools if you're going on calls, too
Staff required:	Yes (stable of handymen willing to work on-call)
Hidden costs:	Workers' compensation, tool maintenance costs, liability insurance

What You Do

A handyman network is the perfect way to find employment for the retired tinkerer. You'll run a business similar to a referral service, where you get the call and then match a fixer-upper to a customer in distress. You will dispatch one of your dozen or so handymen to a caller, then sit back and let the work happen. When it's done, the handyman will bring you a completed work order and a check for the service rendered. At regular intervals (typically twice per month), you'll cut a check to each handyman for his percentage of each completed job. You'll be handling everything from dripping faucets to deck-building or possibly even roofing. The possibilities are limited only by your staff's capabilities. Make sure to hire a wide variety of specialists, so that you have enough workers to cover any anticipated project. If you are handy yourself, you can pick and choose which jobs you most want to work on and refer out the rest.

What You Need

If you already have a van for carrying your tools and equipment to house calls you make personally, or if you are simply offering referral services, you'll need only $500–$1,000 to get started in this business. With some hard work and heavy promotion, you can turn a profit of $20,000–$45,000. One tip: make sure you advertise on your van; it's surprising how many handyman networks get referrals that way.

Keys to Success

It's a win-win situation . . . you're helping out retired and possibly displaced workers who need to do something to make ends meet, but you're also helping a customer solve a problem in his or her home. The income is not fantastic, but it's respectable, and there's always room for you to make a few extra bucks if you personally take on jobs.

Home Business Consultant

Start-up cost:	$5,000–$10,000
Potential earnings:	$30,000–$45,000
Typical fees:	$40–$50 per hour
Advertising:	Direct mail to entrepreneurs, networking with entrepreneurial assistance organizations (such as Service Corps of Retired Executives), Yellow Pages, newspapers, banner ads on entrepreneurial Web sites, your own Web site with some free tips and links to related resources
Qualifications:	Business degree or previous entrepreneurial experience
Equipment needed:	Computer, printer, fax, copier, pager or cell phone
Staff required:	No
Hidden costs:	Slow payment for your services as many beginning entrepreneurs have cash-flow problems

What You Do

Home businesses are a large part of the burgeoning entrepreneurial marketplace, and you can cash in on the ground floor if you have the expertise needed to help a home office get off on the right foot. Your biggest challenge will likely be in locating those thinking about working from home, although there are a few directions that may prove helpful. One excellent way to find clients is through online services and work-at-home forums, where you can offer your expert advice free of charge in an effort to get your name and company information out there. You can also comb the business, professional, and entrepreneurial groups that meet in your community for potential clients. Once you get a client base going, you will work with each client on projects that range from advice on computer systems and office ergonomics to marketing strategy. You really need to be well-rounded in your realm of experience, as you'll be giving advice on a wide variety of topics. Make sure that you focus heavily on the types of equipment a home office might need, as well as on tips for balancing home and family. The likelihood of having repeat customers is very low, so be on the lookout constantly for new prospects, many of whom will come via referral.

What You Need

Your launch expenses ($5,000–$10,000) will mostly cover your basic office setup and some preliminary list rentals so that you can send some direct mail pieces to folks who work from home. A Web site with some free tips would be a good way to reach new entrepreneurs, as they will likely be searching for consultants like you. Expect to earn $30,000–$45,000 once you get established; charge $40–$50 per hour for your services.

Keys to Success

While it may be interesting and even exciting to be part of an innovative young company's beginning, it may take awhile to secure payment for your services. If you can charge up-front, and particularly if you accept credit cards, you'll have a much better chance of collecting what your services are worth.

Home Entertainment System Service

Start-up cost:	$10,000–$15,000
Potential earnings:	$35,000–$50,000
Typical fees:	$20–$45 per hour plus parts
Advertising:	Classified ads, entertainment magazines and newspaper sections, referrals, neighborhood flyers, direct mail, Web site with links to related resources
Qualifications:	Electronics skills, knowledge of entertainment systems operation and setup
Equipment needed:	Tools, cell phone
Staff required:	No
Hidden costs:	Vehicle maintenance, phone bills

What You Do

Home entertainment systems can do wonderful things, but only if they are operating properly. Simply getting them installed is beyond the skills of many people, and taking one component out of all the wiring so that it can be delivered to a store for repair seems impossible. All those jokes about not knowing how to operate a DVD player really aren't funny. What they do is highlight your market:

the owners of home entertainment systems that need help getting them together and keeping them running right. Becoming a home entertainment system service person means that you have a large but very focused market. Each successful job ought to lead to referrals.

What You Need
You'll need tools and possibly an inventory of parts.

Keys to Success
Referrals from individual customers will take you far, and a relationship with a dealer for service and repairs would also be an excellent marketing tactic. Many homes have the makings of entertainment centers. If the components were purchased at a mass market outlet, or even by mail, the owner may well have no one but you to do the setup and repairs. Your electronics know-how ought to find a ready market.

Home Health Care Service

Start-up cost:	$1,500–$5,000 ($25,000–$50,000 plus royalties of 3–5 percent if buying into a franchise)
Potential earnings:	$45,000–$150,000+
Typical fees:	$15–$35 per hour or $175 per day
Advertising:	Local and community newspapers, direct mail to Baby Boomers in your community, bulletin boards, Web site
Qualifications:	Some states require licensing and certification; also, you may need to be bonded, or cleared by a bonding company that checks out your background
Equipment needed:	Computer, cell phone with hands-free accessories (if mandated by your state), dependable transportation
Staff required:	Not initially, but will need additional home health aides once business becomes known in the community
Hidden costs:	Liability insurance, franchise fees if buying a franchise, state licensing, chauffeur's license (in some states)

What You Do
As the Baby Boomers grow older and more of us are living in two-income families, the need for high-quality home health care services for the elderly will continue to rise. Some of this care can be provided on a sporadic, as-needed basis for the

relatively able-bodied folks who just need a little assistance from time to time. But more often, you'll be working as many as four or five days per week with clients who need someone to be with them 24/7—feeding, bathing, dressing, and providing companionship for them as they move through the final phase of their lives. The most profitable way to run a home health care business is to manage other home health aids and take a cut of their pay rather than going out on calls yourself. This route will afford you the most flexibility too. When you employ others, you can make money while you sleep. However the downside is you'll need to pay for their background checks and perhaps to get them bonded. Regardless of whether or not you personally provide care services, your clients will receive the best care from individuals like you who approach their jobs with compassion, understanding, kindness, and the ability to mix friendship with business seamlessly. Not everyone is capable of providing this specialized service effectively and reputably.

What You Need

As a home health care aide, the most important ingredient in your business is compassion for others. However, the second most critical element is dependable transportation, because when your clients need you, they really need you. Keep your vehicle in good working order at all times, and keep your cell phone with hands-free accessories (if mandated by your state) handy and well charged too. You're going to be using it a lot.

Keys to Success

You could decide to join a franchise business in the home health care field. Since it is such a competitive industry, you may find that the name recognition as well as start-up support (which can include state licensing assistance) could really be worth the initial investment.

Home Inspector

Start-up cost:	$30,000–$40,000
Potential earnings:	$50,000–$75,000
Typical fees:	$200–$400 depending on size of home
Advertising:	Yellow Pages, real estate publications, local newspapers, networking with real estate agents, banner ads on Realtor and home-buying Web sites
Qualifications:	Thorough knowledge of home construction and building codes or experience in contracting and building, license or permits in some areas

Equipment needed:	Electrical tracer; circuit tester; gas detector; basic tools such as screwdrivers, flashlights, and ladders; computer; fax; printer; cell phone
Staff required:	No
Hidden costs:	Insurance, telephone bills, association dues

What You Do

In this litigious society, home buyers, sellers, and Realtors are all looking for the best protection they can get. Learning the condition of a home up-front from a third-party professional insures that buyers will know just what kind of home they are purchasing before the sale is complete and, in some cases, even prevents them from making a poor investment. Unfortunately, home inspectors are often targets for litigation, too, so look into certification and licensing requirements in your area and protect yourself by either incorporating or affiliating yourself with a franchise organization. Whichever you choose, your work will change on a daily basis, as you'll be moving from one home to another to inspect everything from the condition of the wiring to shingles on the roof. You'll be checking off items in a large binder as you proceed, and this is what you will leave as a permanent record for the potential home owner. It's a necessary service in this buyer beware kind of market.

What You Need

Mostly, you'll need the funds to either develop your own or secure permission to reprint the information contained in each binder you provide your customers. This business will be much easier to get up and running effectively, and in a shorter period of time, if you pay a franchise fee (anywhere from $30,000–$50,000) to an already established company in this field. That way, you're also protected legally.

Keys to Success

Don't underestimate the value of contact with real estate agents. Many of your best referrals will come from them. Likewise, thorough and honest inspections will result in satisfied home buyers, a valuable source of word-of-mouth advertising. You'll have lots of face-to-face contact with them, so excellent communication and people skills are a must.

Home Preparation Service

Start-up cost:	$500–$1,500
Potential earnings:	$25,000–$50,000
Typical fees:	$25–$50 per hour

Advertising:	Local real estate publications, community newspapers, bulletin boards, direct mail, coupon books
Qualifications:	Handyman skills, an eye for decorating detail
Equipment needed:	General home repair tools, a large enough vehicle to transport ladders and landscaping equipment (if you offer these services)
Staff required:	No
Hidden costs:	Liability insurance, advertising

What You Do

What can you do if you are ready to sell your home, but lack the time and energy to do what's necessary to get it ready for potential buyers? You hire a home preparation service, of course. Such a service can patch the walls and spruce up the paint, improve curb appeal with some quick and easy landscaping tricks, and provide advice on eliminating clutter that might turn potential buyers away. Should you launch a home preparation service, you will likely find customers through advertising in community newspapers under "Home Services" in the classified section. Once you get going, you can do some direct mailings to your local Board of Realtors, who should be able to offer a dozen or so good referrals at a time. Keep in mind that they are often the first to see homes that aren't in pristine selling condition, despite protests to the contrary from the current owners. A good realtor, if he or she knows about your services, can be the perfect "rainmaker" for your business. Make a "home checklist" to help you determine what needs to be done quickly and efficiently. This can also be used to provide the customer with a written estimate of how long the job might take.

What You Need

All you really need, besides some flyers or business cards and a few classified ads, is a general home repair tool kit. Depending on the extent of your services, you may need to add on everything from ladders and gardening tools to cement and paint. Having an account at a local hardware store will help you purchase what you need until your client reimburses you.

Keys to Success

It might be a really good idea to have lots of "before" and "after" photos in a portfolio that can be shown to potential clients so they can see the dramatic difference your service can make. Better yet, put those photos on your Web site, along with free tips on how to get organized for a move. You'll be surprised how quickly your phone will start ringing once people recognize the benefit of using a service like yours.

Homeschooling Consultant

Start-up cost:	$300–$1,000
Potential earnings:	$15,000–$45,000
Typical fees:	$25–$45 per hour
Advertising:	School boards, Yellow Pages, local newspapers, Web site with links to resources
Qualifications:	Degree in education, teaching certificate
Equipment needed:	Books, teachers' guides, monthly planners
Staff required:	No
Hidden costs:	Mileage

What You Do

Communication, organization, and the ability to juggle several things at once are needed in this field. Your job will be to set up the school curriculum and schedule classes for parents who seek to teach their children at home instead of in public or private schools. You could consult for a parent who doesn't want the child in the school system for religious or intellectual reasons or whose child has to be out of school for a long period of time due to illness or injury. If you are establishing a new curriculum, you will need the ability to evaluate the child's skill level. If you are helping the student who will be out for a long period, you will have to communicate with her school on a regular basis.

What You Need

Start-up is low after you have obtained your degree. Be prepared to buy books up-front and be reimbursed for them later. Charging $45 per hour on a regular basis could earn you up to $45,000 per year.

Keys to Success

You may need to join a national, state, or local education association program in order to get a job. This business allows for excellent, high-standard teaching without all the hassles of dealing with a classroom. You don't have to answer to a boss and if you find you don't care for the environment, you can quit. Networking is a definite necessity, but with enough contacts, you could find yourself with year-round work.

☞ Image Consultant

Start-up cost:	$1,500–$5,000 (depending on equipment choices)
Potential earnings:	$20,000–$50,000
Typical fees:	$50–$200 per session
Advertising:	Classified advertising or ads in women's or business newspapers, bulletin boards, coupon books, direct mail, Web site with free tips
Qualifications:	None except to be a good example yourself
Equipment needed:	You may wish to use a computerized video system to demonstrate what your suggestions will look like on your client as well as a cell phone for those "fashion emergencies"
Staff required:	No
Hidden costs:	Mileage

What You Do

How many times have you seen a misguided soul wearing colors that should only be on a flag or makeup that dates back to Cleopatra's time? Did you have the guts to pull that person aside and offer suggestions on self-improvement? Probably not. Yet that is exactly what image consultants are paid to do. Particularly in the business world, people are concerned about the way they come across In fact, aside from brides, your most common clients are likely to be those embarking on career changes or job searches, including recent college graduates. Your mission: to help them make a more positive impact on others through look and attitude. In some respects, you will be like the mother who tells it like it is: "You should wear cool blues instead of muddy browns, which make your face appear yellowish." If you are fashion-minded and have an impeccable sense of balance and color, you are likely to find clients nearly anywhere. You may not know this: Image consultants can also coach clients and lead presentations, seminars, and workshops on etiquette, verbal/nonverbal communication, and "professional presence." These are added-value services that can help you become known as an expert in your field. Once you do that, why not write a book to sell at your workshops, or as required reading for your clients? There's a built-in market potential for you.

What You Need

If you're just starting out, you really needn't invest in much more than mirrors, color swatches, and makeup samples. Once you become a little more established, however, you might add on innovative pieces of equipment such as a computerized video system that "morphs" changes on a picture of your client. A good place to set up shop in a heavy-traffic area would be a mall kiosk. Carts can be rented for $300–$500 per week, but the attention might be worth it. Also, wouldn't it be interesting to form a cooperative marketing venture with a related (but non-competing) business, such as a hairstylist or resume service? You could each offer discounts for the other's service as an incentive for clients to buy your own.

Keys to Success

It is fun to play "dress-up" with people who are in the mood for a change, but keep in mind that these people are probably going through some emotional changes that prompted them into action. Be careful, then, of hurting their feelings. Coach and encourage rather than criticize.

EXPERT ADVICE

What sets your business apart from others like it?

Janet Neyrinck, Image Consultant and Certified Color Analyst in Akron, Ohio, says her business is set apart by the fact that it offers many services. "We're not just trying to sell makeup; our goal is to create a total harmonious image, including everything from dress and makeup to hair color. We believe in 'personality' dressing."

Things you couldn't do without:

"I need to have my makeup kit and, most important, my fabrics (for color draping). These are the basis of everything I do."

Marketing tips

"Be out there, be everywhere you can and introduce yourself. Also, be prepared to do a lot of research before buying your equipment."

If you had to do it all over again . . .

"I think that before I'd commit to one method or company's approach to image consulting, I would investigate all of the options out there. I would check the Directory of Image Consultants and ask others what's worked for them."

Incorporation Service for Businesses

Start-up cost: $500–$1,000
Potential earnings: $25,000–$45,000
Typical fees: $175–$300

Advertising:	Yellow Pages, business publications, direct mail to entrepreneur groups, classified postings on online services, banner ads on entrepreneurial Web sites, your own Web site with information about why incorporation is a good idea for business owners
Qualifications:	A good working knowledge of incorporation law
Equipment needed:	Computer, cell phone, fax, legal forms, business cards
Staff required:	No
Hidden costs:	None

What You Do

With more business start-ups than ever before, the need for quick, inexpensive help in forming a corporation is greater than ever. Many people who consider starting a business simply have no idea which form of business is more advantageous for them. A nice benefit to incorporating is that you are personally protected from any lawsuits filed against the company. In other words, you probably won't lose your house or car. You'll be networking with entrepreneurial groups to find clients in need of your services or fielding calls from your advertisements, then meeting with the client(s) to fill out the necessary, and often straightforward, forms required by the government. You may also have to set up the client's Employer Identification Number. You'll present them with their corporate package, which will include easy-to-fill-out forms such as the Articles of Incorporation, any minutes from board of director meetings, stock certificates, and so on. Essentially, you'll be getting a company started on the road to greater growth potential.

What You Need

Advertising will be your largest out-of-pocket expense (between $500–$1,000). It would also help you to have business cards for networking (add another $100–$200). But you could charge as little as $175 and as much as $300 for your services, depending on your area or the size and complexity of the client company.

Keys to Success

If you like working day in and day out filling out the same forms, this job could be just what you're looking for. If, on the other hand, you thrive on excitement and variety, perhaps you should look into starting a business that specializes in putting together business plans.

Insurance Agent

Start-up cost:	$10,000–$15,000 (more if you buy into a franchise)
Potential earnings:	$45,000–$60,000
Typical fees:	Commissions range from 20 to 35 percent
Advertising:	Cold-calling, membership in community groups, radio, newspapers, community publications, billboards, your outdoor sign (of course), Web site with some free tips
Qualifications:	License, experience, outstanding selling ability, affiliation with a particular company
Equipment needed:	Office furniture, computer, cell phone, suite software, printer, business card, letterhead, envelopes
Staff required:	No
Hidden costs:	Membership dues, errors and omissions insurance

What You Do

As an independent agent, you will need to develop a focus or specialty to set yourself apart in the crowded field of insurance sales. One possibility is business insurance, with a special focus on insuring home-based businesses. Dedicated service to your customers is essential in distinguishing your business from the competition. You will be working closely with individuals and small organizations, and you will depend on your financial expertise and your ability to listen to the wants and needs of the buyer. If you can find a way to help people and companies manage their risk appropriately without making them feel pushed or confused, you will be performing a useful service. You will be earning your agent's commission many times over.

What You Need

Knowledge and experience are far more important than equipment, although you will need a computer system that can be networked to your corporate headquarters if you're affiliated with or own a franchise. In that case, your start-up costs will be considerably higher (potentially $50,000–$75,000 for training, licensing the company name, and heavy advertising), but you'll get the support you need instead of having to go it alone. However, should you decide to go it alone, you can expect to spend between $10,000 and $15,000 for your basic office setup, some advertising, and the fees you'll use to take your exam. Either way, your commissions should net between 20 to 35 percent and ultimately lead to an income potential of between $45,000 and $60,000 or more.

Keys to Success

Once you become established, you will have an excellent business that can support your family and possibly make you rich. Being successful in this type of enterprise requires excellent selling skills, up-to-date information on financial issues, and long hours of hard work. You're using people skills and numerical facility intensively. Most of all, you're unwilling to be discouraged if the first 100 sales calls are "no's."

Interior Designer

Start-up cost:	$3,000–$5,000
Potential earnings:	$30,000–$50,000
Typical fees:	$50 per hour or a flat, per-job rate
Advertising:	Yellow Pages, newspapers, networking with builders/contractors, Web site with extensive gallery of your work
Qualifications:	Some states require certification; you should be a member of at least one professional association related to this field
Equipment needed:	Swatches, sample books, catalogs, computer, cell phone or pager
Staff required:	No
Hidden costs:	Phone bills, which can run high in the beginning as you get set up with distributors and manufacturer's representatives

What You Do

As more people buy older homes with fix-up potential, there is more work for interior designers who are skilled at filling spaces with dynamic statements. Do you read *Metropolitan Home* regularly? Are you addicted to the latest home fashions and accessories? If so, you may make a fine interior designer. But the work is more than plaster-deep; you'll need the ability to work with builders and contractors if a room is being redesigned with a specific aesthetic effect in mind. If you apprentice with an interior designer first, you'll gain much more detailed knowledge about the intricacies and nuances of this business. Personalities are the most difficult aspect of the job; getting others to cooperate and work as a team with a unified vision is probably your biggest challenge. Keeping up with fast-changing trends is another. But if you like meeting with people and creating the home of your clients' dreams, you'll enjoy the challenges and learn to overlook the difficulties.

What You Need

Your start-up costs for an interior design service will be in the $3,000–$5,000 range, primarily to cover your first six months of advertising. You'll need classy business cards and brochures about your service, so set aside between $500 and $1,000 for these items alone. Set your fees at $50 per hour (or a per-job basis for larger work), and re-evaluate your prices after your first year of business. The more clients with money, the higher your prices.

Keys to Success

If you truly like working with people in their most intimate surrounding, this is the job for you. However, expect there to be challenges. One might be getting too many clients at once. Another might be clients who request too many changes, which could wind up costing you money. Set some policies in writing ahead of time to avoid this situation, such as adding a surcharge for any work that goes above and beyond your initial agreement.

EXPERT ADVICE

What sets your business apart from others like it?

"I seem to be the remedy person," says Linda Chiera, President of Studio Space Design in Akron, Ohio. "People usually come to me after they've experienced a problem elsewhere . . . I'm working on getting them to think of me first!" Chiera feels that her business is unique in that it provides expert service and assistance with complex projects. "We learn a person's work style and incorporate that into whatever we do for them, whether it be redecorating a home or redesigning their office space."

Things you couldn't do without

Chiera couldn't do without a computer and CAD system, fax, phone, sample books/resources, tape measure, scale, and business cards.

Marketing tips

"Get sales training and get out there . . . join networking organizations such as the Chamber of Commerce. And if there's a mentoring program available in your area, enlist in it. Offer yourself as a speaker, advertise wisely (knowing your exact market), and hire seasoned professionals to do the things you can't." "Finally," says Chiera, "don't be afraid to make mistakes."

If you had to do it all over again . . .

"I would have been wiser about target marketing and advertising. I should have been more careful about selecting the right niche and also should have tried to become more comfortable earlier on about the selling aspect of my job. I'm trained as a designer, and sales and self-promotion have been a bit of a challenge for me until recently."

≡ Jewelry Designer

Start-up cost:	$500–$1,000
Potential earnings:	$25,000–$75,000
Typical fees:	Some pieces sell for $50–$75; others for thousands
Advertising:	Jewelry trade shows, newspapers, jewelry retailers, craft shows, Web site with e-commerce capability, online auctions such as eBay and Yahoo
Qualifications:	Geological Institute of America (GIA) certificate may be helpful but not required; some formal art training and knowledge of jewelry
Equipment needed:	Vices, pliers, jeweler's loop, magnifying glass, molds, melting equipment
Staff required:	No
Hidden costs:	Travel expenses

What You Do

For those who like to create intricate detail with their hands and have an artistic flair, this business is ideal. Some people just jump into this with their natural ability; others who really make it big have some form of formal art training and have also been picked up by a major distributor. Hit the jewelry trade shows, craft shows, and antique shows with a vengeance and take a lot of business cards with you. Having earned a GIA certificate will be helpful in that you'll have studied different types of precious and semiprecious stones and you'll be able to price your pieces appropriately. This certificate also allows an additional income potential as a licensed jewelry appraiser, where you assist jewelry owners in assessing their collection's worth for insurance purposes.

What You Need

Jewelry has one of the highest markups in the retail world at 100 percent, minimum. So with a $500 investment, a lot of imagination, and some smart marketing, you could be well on your way to a first-year income of $25,000. Try to get noticed by the press, and you'll nab more business than you can handle because people really appreciate having one-of-a-kind jewelry.

Keys to Success

Ever hear of the expression the "small but mighty"? Jewelry has been known to bring in thousands of dollars for a single piece. Here's your opportunity to cash in on your one-of-a-kind creation. Since not everyone's tastes are the same, you can create until you're out of ideas (which, hopefully, will never happen). The only problem with the GIA certificate is that it's a six-month program and offered only in New York and California.

Knitting/Crocheting Instructor

Start-up cost:	$100–$300
Potential earnings:	$3,000–$15,000
Typical fees:	$5–$10 per student per class
Advertising:	Craft shows, local library, flyers
Qualifications:	Knowledge of knitting and crocheting
Equipment needed:	Needles, thread, yarn, fabric and scissors
Staff required:	No
Hidden costs:	Fluctuating materials costs

What You Do

Beautiful baby blankets, sweaters, and booties have an heirloom quality in addition to their warmth factor. After all, you don't buy or make a special, handmade blanket merely for its practicality. You choose such items for their sentimental value. And what better way to earn some extra cash if that's what you already enjoy doing? You could teach others your craft if you have patience and an eye for detail. You already know how much time is involved with each project and you can read intricate patterns. If you can also teach others without winding up doing it all yourself, this job is for you. Marketing yourself at craft shops and networking with related fields will be two of the most effective ways to reel in students. Sell some of your work at art and craft shows to showcase your abilities. Always have plenty of business cards on hand.

What You Need

If you are giving lessons, you most likely have all the equipment you need. Keep some extra supplies on hand. Have your students purchase their supplies before they come to class, which relieves you from making any up-front purchases. Plan on grossing an average of $10,000 per year for a great sideline business.

Keys to Success

This can be a very relaxing venture to do in your home. You get to be creative and pass down these centuries-old techniques to others. Be prepared to hold class at hours convenient for your students, including weekends and evenings. On the downside, there is always the possibility that a student may drop out without notice. Try to fill your classes with more students than you think you need.

⟱ Lactation Consultant

Start-up cost:	Under $1,000
Potential earnings:	$25,000–$40,000
Typical fees:	$40+ per hour
Advertising:	Doctor's offices, Yellow Pages, visiting nurse centers
Qualifications:	State licensing or certification; nursing degree is required in most states as well
Equipment needed:	None
Staff required:	No
Hidden costs:	Mileage

What You Do

The womanly art of breast-feeding is not always an easy one to master for new mothers. For one thing, many new mothers are frightened by the prospect of having to be completely responsible for another human being; for another, many hospital professionals are simply not well trained in teaching new moms how to breast-feed properly. As a result, there are many young women out there who are breast-feeding incorrectly—and quite painfully so. Your prospects look good for this consulting business if you are patient and caring enough to show them the way, and with hospitals increasingly being forced to release mothers and their newborns in a short period of time after the birth, there will be plenty of room (and need) for outside professionals. Since many new moms like to share their positive experiences, word-of-mouth could bring in quite a few referrals.

What You Need

Your start-up costs are minimal; mostly, you'll need to make sure you have an adequate amount of resource materials and dependable transportation. For marketing materials, invest in professionally designed business cards—something that gives off a warm, caring feeling. Your fees should start at $40 per hour, collected at time of service.

Keys to Success

It can be stressful dealing with frightened new mothers and helpless fathers; you'll need a cool head to deliver this service. On the bright side, once you've taught the mother how to feed her baby properly, the stress level will sharply subside. And you'll have at least three happy customers.

What sets your business apart from others like it?

Service is what sets apart International Board Certified Lactation Consultant Barbara Taylor's Breast-feeding Specialties in Lake Jackson, Texas. "I offer the added bonus of breast pump rental services as well as one-on-one work with new moms. Also, I have an extremely high referral rate."

Things you couldn't do without

"My own business line with an answering machine; also, my own office space in my home for professionalism and confidentiality."

Marketing tips

"Network with other professionals . . . being in a small town, I often feel cut off. Most of my networking involves a long-distance call! Also, you need to find out what mistakes other lactation consultants have made and share ideas with them about how to promote your businesses as an industry."

If you had to do it all over again . . .

"It would be much easier to succeed in this business if I had been a registered nurse."

Laundry Service

Start-up cost:	$100–$1,000
Potential earnings:	$20,000–$30,000
Typical fees:	$10 per pound of clothes for wash, dry, and iron
Advertising:	Local papers, bulletin boards, flyers, Yellow Pages
Qualifications:	Knowledge of fabric do's and don'ts
Equipment needed:	Extra-large capacity industrial washer and dryer, ironing board or a professional press
Staff required:	No
Hidden costs:	Insurance or "mistake money"

What You Do

Have some business cards handy for this profession and lots of happy customers to refer additional business to you. You should especially seek out professional women who simply don't have the time for laundry detail. There is no other business where word of mouth can make or break you as much as this one. You'll need to be a perfectionist and pay attention to every detail. You should have a room especially devoted to this venture. Have on hand special laundry soap, softeners, starches, and clotheslines for drip-dry. If you don't invest in a professional steam press, have more than one iron available, just in case. Be sure to keep all of your warranties up-to-date on your machines, since they are the lifeline to your business.

What You Need
Overhead may be low (under $1,000) if you already have the machines. Any washer or dryer in good working condition will do, but the extra-large capacity will cut your time in half allowing you to do more laundry in a shorter period of time. The large capacity also allows you to do big-ticket items such as comforters. Since your start-up cost may be low, you could easily make $20,000 or more annually in 40-hour work weeks.

Keys to Success
You either love or hate to do laundry. Since this is a home-based business, you still have time to catch a soap opera or talk show and feed your baby. Be prepared to correct any mistakes, even if they are not your fault (i.e., replace missing buttons, fix a shoulder pad, or totally replace the garment). For this reason, keep some extra "mistake money" on hand. If you make small repairs at no charge, it tends to be good for business. The word will spread about your caring, personalized service.

⋿ Lawn Care Service

Start-up cost:	$500–$1,500
Potential earnings:	$15,000–$25,000
Typical fees:	$12–15 per hour or a flat rate of $50–$75 per job
Advertising:	Flyers left in front doors, ads in local or community newspapers, word of mouth
Qualifications:	Love for working outdoors and some knowledge about lawn care
Equipment needed:	Power mower, rakes, power trimmer and spreader, pickup truck or station wagon
Staff required:	No
Hidden costs:	Insurance, transportation, some equipment rental

What You Do

Most people can squeeze in time to mow their own lawns, but it's the weeding and trimming, fertilizing, aerating, and leaf removal that takes up the extra time. By providing these services, you can rake in profits for yourself. Don't try to compete with neighborhood youth who mow lawns or with professional lawn services that include landscaping and related services. Plant your seeds, develop your niche, and cultivate the business.

What You Need

You'll shell out at least $300 for basic equipment, more for a power lawn mower. Double or triple those costs if you decide to have a team of workers mowing a lawn simultaneously (as is often done). You'll make roughly $50–$75 per job in a residential lawn care business; more if handling corporate accounts in addition. However, your income isn't limited to what you charge, because many happy customers also include a tip for your trouble.

Keys to Success

By scheduling some or all of these services with the same customers in the same neighborhoods, you will save on transportation, time, and rental costs. One day you might be mowing lawns and another you'll be aerating. You might have to rent an aeration roller for $25 a day. But if you schedule aerations in one neighborhood for the same day, you'll easily recoup the investment.

Lawyer

Start-up cost:	$15,000–$30,000 (less if sharing space and resources)
Potential earnings:	$50,000–$80,000
Typical fees:	$125 per hour outside the major cities; $175–$250 per hour in major metropolitan areas
Advertising:	Yellow Pages, networking, association memberships, Web site with your specialty areas highlighted; many legal restrictions on attorney advertising apply
Qualifications:	Law degree, persistence, people skills
Equipment needed:	Office space decorated in a professional (not necessarily ostentatious) manner, access to law library, computer with Internet access, fax, software, laser printer, business cards, letterhead, envelopes

Staff required: No

Hidden costs: People wanting free advice, insurance, Internet Service Provider fees

What You Do

Abraham Lincoln did it, so why can't you? It has been fashionable to mock the "single shingle" lawyer, but opportunities to join huge firms right out of law school—and make huge bucks—have just about vanished today. One way to use the degree you have just suffered through is to start your own business. You create the clientele, you develop the specialty, you do the billing, you reap the rewards. Can you find a way to show total commitment to the success of small businesses in your area? Are you able to disentangle the affairs of wealthy individuals and help to keep them in control of their lives? Can you deal with the anguish of divorcing people and help them manage the separation process through mediation and negotiation? If you answered yes to any of these questions, you can make a go of your single-shingle.

What You Need

Many solo practitioners share office space, support staff, and other necessary costs of setting up in business. You'll need an appropriate and professional-looking space in which to meet your clients, and you must produce and store the paperwork. Spend at least $5,000 on your office and its contents. Include an extra $2,000 for a high-power computer to make online searches less time-consuming and, hence, less costly. Bill out at around $125 to start. After your reputation is as good as old Abe's, you can start charging like the big boys (and girls) at $200 to $300 per hour.

Keys to Success

Probably the most important factor in your success will be your connections to the community you hope to serve. The average Joe tends to have a negative view of all lawyers, and you're going to need to keep struggling against this stereotype. Building trust is so challenging that you will have little chance for success unless you start with a network of people who know and like you. Eventually you will become known as the helpful, skilled lawyer to go to when a need for work in your specialty arises. Another challenge is that you will be constantly asked to work for free. Everyone needs a lawyer from time to time, but many people are reluctant to pay for a lawyer's experience, expertise, and legal skills. It will be your job to track hours, send bills, and make sure the funds are collected. This is a tedious, time-consuming process. Consider offering prepaid legal services, which works much like insurance.

What sets your business apart from others like it?

Stanford M. Altschul, sole practitioner based in Long Island, New York, says he picked a niche and set about servicing it with free information in the form of marketing materials such as brochures and newsletters. "I market myself regularly to my clients, keeping my name in front of them via newsletters, brochures, and other direct mail pieces I produce myself."

Things you couldn't do without

Altschul could not do without a computer and laser printer, telephone, copier, and fax machine.

Marketing tips

"You should definitely be networking with certain industries that will bring you referral business, such as accounting, real estate, and banking. All of these professionals are in regular contact with those who need your services."

If you had to do it all over again . . .

"I made a mistake in being in a partnership that wasn't a good partnership . . . It took me over twenty years to figure out that I prefer working alone."

Licensing Agent

Start-up cost:	$3,000–$6,000
Potential earnings:	$50,000–$100,000
Typical fees:	15 percent of the deal
Advertising:	Association memberships, networking, Web site with client list and testimonials
Qualifications:	Sales ability, outgoing personality, confidence, ability to communicate with technical people, the business types, and the manufacturing specialists; extensive experience and contacts in the field
Equipment needed:	Computer with Internet access, fax, copier, laser printer, office furniture, business cards, letterhead, envelopes
Staff required:	No
Hidden costs:	Insurance, attorney's fees to draw up contracts

What You Do

The licensing agent acts as a go-between, helping a technology-driven company find a manufacturer for its invention. In addition, you help manufacturers or service companies find organizations that offer the technology they need. The service provided by a licensing agent is often transnational. For example, you may be finding technology for Chinese companies that cannot develop it locally. Licensing agents usually specialize in one industry—shoe products, electronic products, and so on—in which they have developed extensive experience and contacts. This way they already know many people on both sides of the street before they start. Some technical competence in the field is required, but this can be gained through experience. The other important quality for a licensing agent is patience. You may work for a long time on several deals, only one of which may pay off.

What You Need

Equipping your office to produce professional-looking reports and to keep in touch with the rest of the world is the main start-up cost; expect to spend at least $3,000 on that alone. However, considering that your 15 percent is spread across a wide range of potential projects, your earnings could be as high as $100,000.

Keys to Success

Becoming a licensing agent is an excellent way for a new entrepreneur to use his or her contacts from a previous line of work. If you have the sales skills, the contacts, and the ability to communicate with the "techie" dreamers as easily as the hard-nosed business types, you can build a successful enterprise. Keep in mind that you will be paid a percentage of the final deal. This can take a long time to bear fruit, and it is essential to have the agreement in writing from the start. There tend to be a lot of disputes if that percentage turns into big money.

Literary Agent

Start-up cost:	$500–$1,500
Potential earnings:	$20,000–$60,000+
Typical fees:	15 percent of gross commission on domestic sales, 25 percent on foreign rights, 20 percent on film rights
Advertising:	Listing in the *Guide to Literary Agents* and *Art/Photo Reps*; ads in *Writer's Digest* and *The Writer* magazines; networking at writers' and publishers' conferences; Web site with client list, recent sales, and current newsletter
Qualifications:	Should know a good book a mile away

Equipment needed: Computer with Internet access, printer, fax, copier, phone system

Staff required: No

Hidden costs: Insurance, copying, postage, long-distance phone calls

What You Do

The literary life is indeed a glamorous one, especially if you're a literary agent. Imagine entire days filled with power meetings at large publishing houses, where you're negotiating for the best deal for one of the many writers you represent. You'll be offering everything from the right to publish to film and foreign rights. Your business may also extend to book promotion, as you could negotiate book tours and publicity for your client in addition to the sale of the book project itself. Of course, you would hope to represent that one unknown client who could really score big in the publishing industry, such as Robert James Waller with his *Bridges of Madison County*. Look everywhere for talent, even in remote cities or small rural towns. No matter how hard you try, realize that not all literary agents can represent a Stephen King. You should go in with an open mind whenever you look through the piles of manuscripts and queries on your desk. The successes could really surprise you.

What You Need

Your start-up is relatively low ($500–$1,500) and mostly covers your initial advertising costs and basic office equipment setup. You stand a good chance of earning an income of at least $20,000 with you commission, but look forward to making as much as $60,000 or more if you get that big break.

Keys to Success

On the one hand, you'll be making a good piece of change hanging around the best media minds in the business. On the other hand, you'll have to know when to give up on a particular project, even if it seems worthwhile. Often in the publishing world, trends take over and dominate what's likely to be published. (Remember, for instance, the mafia book craze a few years back?) You'll need to constantly stay on top of what's hot.

EXPERT ADVICE

What sets your business apart from others like it?

Marie Dutton Brown, President of Marie Brown Associates literary agency in New York City, says her business is unique because her agency primarily represents African-American authors. "We connect clients to the publishing industry and provide counsel for writers . . . we focus on black life and culture as well as books of general interest."

Things you couldn't do without
Phone, fax, copier, and computer.

Marketing tips
"Start small, think big, and follow your niche," says Brown. She enjoys the process of bringing an interesting creative project to fruition and thrives on positive publicity. She has been profiled by the Associated Press, and that has certainly been a profitable marketing tool.

If you had to do it all over again . . .
"I would have started with more capital. As it was, I started at home with only $1,000. It takes more than that to get things rolling."

Litigation Management Service

Start-up cost:	$5,000–$10,000
Potential earnings:	$40,000–$75,000
Typical fees:	$125–$175 hour
Advertising:	Local business associations, advertising in trade journals and business publications, referrals, Web site with testimonials and links to related resources
Qualifications:	Law or accounting background, experience in case management and billing assessment, litigation experience
Equipment needed:	Business office, computer with Internet access, fax, software, printer, business cards, letterhead, envelopes
Staff required:	No
Hidden costs:	Insurance

What You Do
For years, Congress has been working to curb excessive litigation with tort reform acts and related legislation. The astronomical costs of litigation are being monitored closely. For business organizations with a small in-house legal staff or none at all, you can provide this important cost-management service. Assessing ongoing billing can spotlight waste, such as duplication of services, under billing, and incorrect entries. This is painstaking work, and often busy in-house lawyers do not have time to comb through the bills their organization receives from outside counsel. The economic benefit of having an outside service perform this function should far outweigh its cost to the organization.

What You Need

Equipping your office to be functional and to present a professional image will be expensive, between $4,000 and $10,000. You will not be able to run this business from a corner of your dining room table. You'll be able to charge around $125 an hour for your services, so you should be able to afford a decent office.

Keys to Success

This service is a creative way to utilize a background that combines legal training with financial and accounting skills. More and more lawyers are competing for a shrinking number of jobs, but few have the combination of expertise and experience that will make you a success in this tightly focused service niche. Marketing your services will be challenging as the concept is new. One success will lead to referrals, though. You will need to allow yourself considerable time to build the business. A thick skin is necessary to deal with negative reactions you may receive from some lawyers whose accounts you are reviewing for accuracy in billing; some lawyers are notorious for double- and triple-billing.

Magician

Start-up cost:	$500–$1,000
Potential earnings:	$6,500–$20,000 or more
Typical fees:	$50 per two-hour children's party, $300 per two-hour adult event
Advertising:	Yellow Pages; entertainment section of newspapers; bulletin boards; networking with civic organizations; Web site with lots of photos, client testimonials, and an online booking method for customers
Qualifications:	Ability to perform magic tricks convincingly, outgoing personality
Equipment needed:	Magic trick equipment, business cards, computer for Web site management and e-booking
Staff required:	No
Hidden costs:	Advertising

What You Do

To be a good magician, you must have the ability to perform magic tricks quite convincingly, despite the audience's willing suspension of disbelief. You can buy kits from party centers or entertainment retailers or possibly take a continuing education course from your local college. Working as an assistant for an established magician is also a good way to learn the business. Having a good personality and the ability to work well with people is a strong selling point.

What You Need
Start-up should be minimal. Visit the local library to find books on magic for an inexpensive way to learn the art. Investing in magic kits from retailers will cost you a little more. The most expensive start-up cost would be to take a class.

Keys to Success
Perform for free at your friends' parties or children's school functions to get exposure. Once your name gets on the streets, start charging for your services. Attempt to work with your city's parks and recreation department for leads or a convention center to get jobs at conferences. Working with an events planner or advertising agency is another good way to get your own name pulled out of the hat.

Mailing List Service

Start-up cost:	$5,000–$9,000
Potential earnings:	$40,000–$100,000
Typical fees:	15 to 25 cents per entry (name, address, city, state, zip); about $1 per entry per year to maintain the list. Mailing 10,000 pieces of mail could cost your client $800–$1,200
Advertising:	Contacting local stores, associations, churches, clubs, etc. to offer to maintain their lists for them; networking in business organizations; Yellow Pages; direct mail; banner ads on entrepreneurial Web sites; your own Web site with testimonials and e-commerce capability (so that customers can purchase and download lists)
Qualifications:	Detailed knowledge of postal regulations for bulk mailings, computer expertise, fast and accurate typing skills, ability to meet deadlines
Equipment needed:	Computer, printer, specialized software, database, post office permits, office furniture, business cards, letterhead, postage machine
Staff required:	None
Hidden costs:	A backup for your computer system in the event of a disaster

What You Do

Although we all deplore the amount of "junk mail" that is dumped in our mailboxes each day, the amazing growth of direct mail is going to continue. The opportunity to succeed in running a mailing list service for the companies sending those materials is tremendous. Start-up costs are low, skills needed are easy to acquire, and money is there to be made. Your service can include list maintenance, mailings, creation of lists, list brokering, and even teaching others about mailing lists. Staying on top of the changing regulations of the U.S. Postal Service is perhaps the most challenging part of the job. However, software, pamphlets, and seminars abound to bring you up to speed.

What You Need

You will spend from $5,000 to $9,000 on the equipment and supplies needed for this business. Depending on your specialty, you may be able to begin for less, especially if you lease a postage meter machine and some of the other equipment. Charges will vary for your services, but you'll need to set two rates from the get-go: a per-entry fee (usually 15 to 25 cents per name and address) and an annual list maintenance fee of $1 per entry.

Keys to Success

Mailing list businesses are relatively easy to start and to promote. You can have as large a customer base as you wish, rather than relying on just a few key clients. The actual work of creating and maintaining the lists is routine, although it does require attention to detail and great accuracy. A thorough understanding of postal regulations is vitally important, and the regulations are constantly changing.

Makeup Artist

Start-up cost:	$500–$1,500
Potential earnings:	$20,000–$40,000
Typical fees:	$20–$30 per thirty-minute session
Advertising:	Newspapers, beauty salons, bridal consultants, funeral homes, department stores, Web site with lots of "before" and "after" photos
Qualifications:	Eye for color and contour
Equipment needed:	Makeup samples and kits, brushes, cotton swabs, a director's chair, computer with Internet access
Staff required:	No
Hidden costs:	Insurance

What You Do

Your services are needed in extremely diverse areas, from the life and action of the stage to the stately composure of the funeral home. You could offer makeovers for brides-to-be, new moms, college graduates, and those simply in the mood for a new look. Or, you could specialize in helping those who are disfigured due to accident or illness. Whomever you choose as your clientele, you will need to be familiar with all skin types and problems, matching your products carefully with each client's basic needs. With an astounding array of cosmetic products currently available (even at wholesale prices), you could produce professional and fabulous-looking results for just about any client in no time. Study facial structure to know where to shade and what to hide, and you'll be on your way to a beautiful new beginning!

What You Need

Your costs are relatively nominal. Start out with some makeup kits and samples, supplies, and a sturdy chair for your clients to sit on, then add your brochures, business cards, or flyers. All of this should cost you no more than $1,000. Add a little more if you decide to sell the products you're using, because you may need to secure a vendor's license. Of course, if you're aligning yourself with companies like Avon or Mary Kay, you will just need to be sure you cover sales tax when you sell products.

Keys to Success

While you may enjoy the freedom and creativity of being a professional makeup artist, you may also find the lack of predictable income unnerving. Try to offer your services to groups to maximize your marketing moments, because the one-customer-at-a-time philosophy doesn't cut it with this business.

☰ Management Consultant

Start-up cost:	$5,000–$15,000
Potential earnings:	$30,000–$60,000 (average); some make as much as $300,000
Typical fees:	Varies by market and client needs; average of $500–$1,500 per day (can also charge by hour or job)
Advertising:	Networking, referrals, creating audio- or videotapes and CD-ROMs showing your skills, ads in professional organizations' magazines and newsletters, brochures, direct mail, Web site with forecast of future business trends or free management tips

Qualifications: Technical knowledge, expertise, and experience in business management and operations, good problem-solving skills, good people skills, excellent communication skills (written and oral)

Equipment needed: Computer with Internet access, printer, appropriate software, fax, phone, office furniture, reference books

Staff required: No

Hidden costs: Possibly special insurance, such as errors and omissions coverage; continuing education

What You Do

The Institute of Management Consulting has members handling more than 250 specialties. Professional consulting is a fast-growing field that is only going to increase in size, and management consulting is the biggest segment of that field. U.S. companies rely heavily on management consultants, especially in the areas of compliance (with many government agencies), the introduction of new technologies, and to take the place of permanent staff as companies become leaner. Consultants provide many services, from strategy-planning and implementation to analysis and problem-solving. Many who choose to become consultants are those with top-level skills and experience. They want the freedom and greater variety of working for themselves and recognize the world of opportunity that exists in assisting small, entrepreneurial companies get their businesses off the ground—not to mention the opportunity to work as a consultant for much larger companies.

What You Need

Start-up costs will vary according to the requirements of the specialty you choose. No matter what you decide, however, you will require the basic office and computer equipment, which could cost as little as $2,500 or as much as $12,000, depending on the quality and extent of computer equipment needed. You will also need to budget between $800 and $1,800 for continuing education, association dues, and reference books.

Keys to Success

To succeed in this business, you must first analyze yourself; decide what sorts of problems you can solve for a client based on your experience and expertise. Research the companies or types of companies to which you want to offer your services to help you discover needs you can fill. Network with every contact you have in your target areas. Remember, though, that not everyone with good technical skills can be a successful consultant. You need excellent listening and counseling abilities as well as patience. Not only does it take time to grow your business, but often it takes considerable time to determine if your efforts have paid off for the client. Meeting the challenges of working as a consultant can be financially rewarding. You will have the opportunity to work on a wide variety of projects and enjoy helping clients find creative, successful solutions to their problems.

EXPERT ADVICE

What sets your business apart from others like it?

Norma J. Rist, owner of The Boardroom Group based in Akron, Ohio, says her business assists women business owners to become clear about their goals and to achieve them in a shorter period of time and in an easier way than they otherwise could have by providing resources and business information in a group setting.

Things you couldn't do without

"A business phone line, fax, copier, and personal computer. Also, a meeting/conference room is useful for generating group discussion and participation."

Marketing tips

"Segment your niche . . . I started 'Spirit Groups' for home-based business owners at the same time so that I could serve a broader population of women owners and generate more income potential simultaneously."

If you had to do it all over again . . .

"I would have segmented much earlier."

Manicurist

Start-up cost:	$5,000–$10,000
Potential earnings:	$15,000–$35,000
Typical fees:	$50 per set of nails (for length additions) and $15 for a simple manicure or pedicure
Advertising:	Newspapers, coupon books, bulletin boards, Yellow Pages
Qualifications:	Certification in cosmetology or as a nail technician often required
Equipment needed:	Manicuring table with a strong light, credit card processing equipment (if you decide to accept plastic), and nail enhancement or beautification products
Staff required:	No
Hidden costs:	Liability insurance and materials

What You Do

Luxurious nails are no longer for the rich and famous only—brides want them, society mavens want them, young women want them. You'll definitely make money from this business if you are a licensed professional with a strong following, mainly because there are simply not enough really skilled nail technicians to go around. You will, however, be competing with "nail factories" in local shopping malls; these service businesses typically employ large numbers of technicians so they can turn around a great deal of business at a low cost. Position yourself on personal service and attention to detail. At any rate, you'll be providing a timeless personal service for those who appreciate the finer things in life. (Translation: don't be afraid to charge a little more than you're worth.) You'll create beautifully crafted nails that would make Jessica Simpson green with envy or you'll simply clean and shape nails for everyday folks who are in the limelight often (even if it's only before a board of directors). Yes, men and women alike use the services of a manicurist, so try not to forget that in your marketing pieces.

What You Need

Essentially, you'll need a good, strong table and a bright enough light to work with, in addition to your nail polishes and assorted nail maintenance equipment. All of this could cost between $1,000 and $3,000, but add on more if you're planning to rent space somewhere. Charge at least between $40 and $60 for acrylic, fiberglass, or gel nails; $20 for a simple manicure. For silk wraps or tips, charge between $25 and $30.

Keys to Success

If you like working with people from different walks of life, this could be your kind of business—hands down. However, the community gossip might leave you with information you'd rather not know.

⟟ Manufacturer's Representative

Start-up cost:	$2,500–$9,000
Potential earnings:	$45,000–$150,000, depending on your sales ability
Typical fees:	Commission basis, usually 5 to 15 percent of product price
Advertising:	Cold-calling, networking, presentations, reference publications
Qualifications:	Sales experience or expertise in a particular field, good people skills, an ability to negotiate

Equipment needed:	Computer, fax, phone, cell phone, office furniture, business cards, letterhead
Staff required:	No
Hidden costs:	Mileage and costs associated with travel

What You Do

Companies are operating with slimmer sales forces these days, creating a need for outside help with marketing and selling their products. Independent reps can take on an interesting variety of products to sell, everything from gifts and sporting goods to chemicals, adhesives, and heavy machinery. Many experts recommend that manufacturing agents handle eight to ten lines of goods in order to make a nice profit. In addition to a thorough understanding of your product's features and benefits, you also need a solid customer base for each line and enough money to carry you while you get established, which can take up to a year. Having a background in the product(s) you represent is the easiest way to succeed. Look for opportunities with emerging companies, such as those profiled in entrepreneurial publications and business newspapers. Be sure to include a client list or background sheet on yourself when approaching new companies. They appreciate and often require this level of professionalism.

What You Need

Costs start at approximately $2,500 for computer and office equipment. You may also need a laptop, preferably with wireless Internet capabilities, cell phone to use while on the road; if so, tack on another $5,000 to $6,000. At 5 to 15 percent commission, it could take awhile to earn a profit. But one good customer with the potential for repeat business is all you need to start building a business that can grow.

Keys to Success

Sales can be one of the most lucrative home businesses of all. Meeting and working with people can be very rewarding, as can the freedom of choosing the companies you will represent and setting your own hours. On the downside, repping for a living can mean long periods of travel and, sometimes, a long wait to be paid for your services. Also, sales in some fields will require you to be aggressive and highly competitive to succeed.

Can you swim with the sharks—or will you be eaten alive?

Marketing Consultant

Start-up cost:	$5,000–$10,000
Potential earnings:	$60,000–$150,000

Typical fees:	$50 to $200 per hour; $2,000–$4,000 to lead a workshop
Advertising:	Referrals; Web site with key marketing trends and links to related resources, plus testimonials and your client list
Qualifications:	Broad expertise in marketing or specialization in one area, business savvy, high energy level, excellent written and oral communications skills, creativity, persistence
Equipment needed:	Laptop, high-speed Internet access, laser printer, fax, copier, office furniture, business cards, letterhead, envelopes
Staff required:	No
Hidden costs:	Membership dues, phone bills, Internet service provider fees

What You Do

Customers are the lifeblood of all businesses, and marketing is how companies attract them. Sales are the end result of the entire marketing process. Developing ads, writing printed materials and letters, gaining publicity, and designing sales strategies are all facets of marketing. Just developing a focused marketing plan is a demanding activity, let alone carrying out the plan. Most executives need the services of a marketing professional to produce effective results. Marketing consultants supply these services to small companies and fill in the gaps left by downsizing at big organizations. Even though this is the second largest category of consulting after management consulting, opportunities abound if you can produce results. If you're a brand marketing specialist, you can virtually name your price.

What You Need

Marketing materials require a sophisticated and flexible computer setup ($4,000–$6,000). You'll need to be able to produce drafts even if the client's art department or an ad agency creates the final versions. You'll spend an equal amount on marketing efforts of your own, including joining associations in which you can build a strong network. If you're persistent and have the kind of personality that draws customers in, you can earn as much as $150,000 a year.

Keys to Success

Above all, effective marketing takes imagination. What do potential customers want, and what kind of message will enable them to see that your client's product is that very thing? Knowing how to create these interactions will make you a success as a marketing consultant, if you combine that expertise with an ability to scope out your client company. To prove your worth, try to highlight strengths that they may not have realized they had. You may need to structure the goals for the marketing plan and get buy-in from the executives before the ads, promos, or sales letters are developed. Be sure to get a contract with payment milestones in writing as these projects can take many months to come to fruition.

Massage Therapist

Start-up cost: $1,000–$5,000

Potential earnings: $15,000–$35,000

Typical fees: $45–$60 per hour-long session

Advertising: Newspapers, Yellow Pages, bulletin boards, direct mail to corporations

Qualifications: Must be state-certified in most states

Equipment needed: Massage table, oils and other products, relaxing music

Staff required: None

Hidden costs: Possibly liability insurance

What You Do

If you can't keep your hands off of anyone, being a massage therapist could bring you immediate (financial) satisfaction. Seriously, massage therapists are finally entering their own as certified professionals. They must study human anatomy as clinically and carefully as a paramedic would and must have the ability to make people relax enough to enjoy the service. With many of us leading increasingly stressful lives, such professionals should be welcome almost anywhere, from health clubs to wellness centers and even metaphysical bookstores. Many massage therapists offer their services to harried executives and visit them on-site to work out the kinks in their backs and necks. Still others work out of their homes or in small, quiet offices.

What You Need

If you decide to lease a small office, you can expect to spend at least $350 and up per month on rent alone. Add to that your massage table (about $500) and some relaxing music, soothing oils, and clean towels (allow another $250 or so for these). Finally, you must get the word out by advertising to individuals or corporate clients, so expect to spend about $500 to $1,000 on marketing too.

Keys to Success

Working in a relaxing atmosphere while helping others relieve stress can be positively exhilarating for you, but it can also be tiring. Are you sure you can stand up to the physical demands of this business, which usually leaves you on your feet most of the day? If the answer is "yes," the rest will fall into place.

Meals to Go

Start-up cost: $1,000 or more

Potential earnings: $25,000 and up

Typical fees: $5–$10 per "run" plus cost of meal

Advertising: Brochures in office buildings, newspaper ads, Web site with menu options or banner ads on restaurant Web sites

Qualifications: Ability to create attractive, healthy, portable meals, foodservice certification from your state

Equipment needed: Kitchen, cooking supplies and equipment, food packaging, cell phone (with or without hands-free accessories, depending on state laws)

Staff required: Part-time delivery person, if needed

Hidden costs: Mileage and other costs associated with travel; check out legal and health requirements

What You Do

Food delivery to the home or office is an idea whose time has come. Delivering lunches to office workers is especially lucrative. Busy people will love seeing your delicious dinner brought to their door as they arrive home after a long day at work. The menus need not be extensive, which simplifies the operation. You can "pick up" from a variety of local restaurants or prepare your own meals. Challenges include safe food handling practices "on the road," keeping foods hot or cold, as appropriate, and maintaining on-time deliveries.

What You Need

This business isn't costly to start up, especially if you opt to offer a lunch-only service. If, for instance, you offer only sandwiches, soups, salads, rolls, beverages, dessert, you will need very little equipment to prepare the meals. You will need to invest in packaging for the foods, such as disposable plastic bowls, cellophane or foil wrapping. The cost will vary depending on the foods you're selling. Create a flier that can be posted in heavily populated office complexes to get started. Always deliver the next day's menu with each meal as you drop them off. Make sure your insurance policy will cover your vehicle while it is being used for deliveries and, if you are hiring a delivery person, make sure your insurance covers that employee in your car.

Keys to Success

Most people in the food delivery business get up early in the morning to bake and/or cook; night owls may not survive! Expect a long day of work, especially if you deliver at dinnertime in the evening. You'll need an ability to deal successfully with vendors and suppliers to keep costs down and the food quality consistently high. On the upside, the future is bright for food delivery businesses. More and more people have less and less time to cook; everyone is tired of the typical fast food. Start-up costs in most cases are modest, and you can net $70–$100 a day right from the start. The sky will be the limit after that, as you add more routes.

Mediator

Start-up cost:	$5,000–$10,000
Potential earnings:	$40,000–$65,000
Typical fees:	$75–$300 (usually split between the disputing parties); fee typically includes up to three sessions
Advertising:	Yellow Pages, newspapers, bulletin boards, networking with legal groups, Web site with some free negotiating tips and links to related resources
Qualifications:	License required in some states
Equipment needed:	Office with comfortable furniture, phones, computer
Staff required:	No
Hidden costs:	Some cases are more complicated than others; try to see the writing on the wall when it comes to the bigger jobs. A skilled mediator will know how to cut to the chase and keep things moving within the timeframe for which he or she is getting paid.

What You Do

The wave of the legal future is the mediator, especially with the rising cost of attorneys. While attorneys are paid to reach an eventual settlement, a mediator looks for ways to settle any disputes with compromise and without going to court. Because so many marriages end in bitter divorce, mediators have their ripest ground in the domestic sector. It is in this arena that they can save the parties literally thousands of dollars in litigation and get to the heart of the matter through mutual conciliation. Identifying what each party truly wants out of the deal is the most critical part of successful mediation. Are you skilled at helping people to stop hurling pointless accusations at each other and at bringing them back to the issues at hand? Can you help them to see the big picture? If so, you would make a fine mediator. You're essentially being paid to help fighting folks stay out of court. It's an admirable profession, and it's getting to be increasingly profitable.

What You Need

You'll need a nice, comfortable office, so expect to lay out at least $3,000 for your "digs." Next, spend some money advertising in places potential clients typically look for help (namely, the Yellow Pages). You'll charge $75 to $300 per job (which typically includes up to three one-hour sessions) and more if the work extends beyond that timeframe.

Keys to Success

While this is an admirable and respected profession, it's still a personally challenging one. Can you listen all day to folks fighting over trivial and petty things (like who gets the washing machine)? If you're able to keep them focused on the goal of an amicable settlement, you'll do well. But do take time for yourself—you'll need it.

Expert Advice

What sets your business apart from others like it?

Albert H. Couch, a Family, Divorce and Community Mediator for Akron Family Mediation in Akron, Ohio, says three things set his business apart from others like it. "We have a full-time commitment to mediation, and a lot of mediators don't have that. Second, we cap our fees so that our customers know there's a limit to what they'll spend with us. Finally, we have experience in our field and are aggressive in promoting mediation in general. When I'm not mediating, I'm talking about mediating somewhere."

Things you couldn't do without

Couch says he couldn't do without a computer, phone and, most important, the training he's had in his field.

Marketing tips

"Learn mediation inside and out, that's first and foremost." But the second most important thing you can do, according to Couch, is to talk mediation with just about anyone who'll listen. "This is primarily a word-of-mouth business."

If you had to do it all over again . . .

"I'd spend less money up front on advertising, since so much of my business comes from referrals. I advise others to get involved in their community and give as many speeches as you can to promote your business."

Medical Claims Processing

Start-up cost:	$5,000–$12,500
Potential earnings:	$12,000–$48,000
Typical fees:	Monthly rates of $800–$1,500 per client
Advertising:	Direct mail, networking, telemarketing
Qualifications:	Knowledge of insurance billing including CPT coding, Medicare and Medicaid regulations, capitation, changes in legislation and subsequent forms
Equipment needed:	Desk, computer with Internet access, printer, medical billing software, fax, typewriter, CPT coding manual
Staff required:	No
Hidden costs:	Attending seminars and training sessions if new to the field

What You Do

As regulation of the medical field continues, the number of businesses that simplify the claims process will also grow. Due to an aging population and a 1990 federal law requiring physicians to submit claims for all their Medicare patients, many medical offices are inundated with paperwork. These trends have created a great need to hire outside billing services to process the claims and provide various other services such as invoicing, collecting any co-payments required from the patient, tracking past due and un-collectible accounts, and answering all patient questions regarding their claim. A minimum of four to six doctors or practices is required to remain reasonably profitable. If you are looking for a challenging opportunity that utilizes computer technology and sharp interpersonal skills, you will find it in this very promising field.

What You Need

Access to a computer and the Internet and updated medical billing software is a must to really compete in this market. (These expenses will range from $3,000 to $5,000.) In addition, allow for hourly wages of additional staff as your business begins to grow. Be sure to shop around for the best rate on phone service since it will be used extensively.

Keys to Success

Medical claims processing requires patience and attention to detail. The work is often challenging and interesting due to the ever-changing nature of health insurance and Medicare. Although selling your services may be difficult at first, good communication skills and persistence will result in lasting relationships with those doctors whom you service. Once your business is established, processing claims electronically takes little time and can be done at your convenience. Most importantly, a successful medical billing service can be quite profitable.

Medical Transcriptionist

Start-up cost:	$5,000–$9,000
Potential earnings:	$60,000–$80,000 (billing 2,000 hours a year)
Typical fees:	$30–$40 per hourr
Advertising:	Publications of local medical societies, direct mail, telemarketing, networking
Qualifications:	Excellent listening skills; good hand/eye coordination; ability to use word processing, dictation and transcription equipment; understanding of medical diagnostic procedures and terminology; good typing skills; impeccable spelling; one or two years of higher education
Equipment needed:	Computer, high-speed Internet access, transcriber, word-processing software, reference books, business cards, letterhead, envelopes
Staff required:	No
Hidden costs:	None

What You Do

According to the American Association for Medical Transcription (AAMT), there is a shortage of qualified transcriptionists. This job is in demand for two reasons. First, many insurance companies are requiring transcribed reports before they will pay doctors or hospitals. Second, transcribed copy provides health care professionals with the necessary documentation for review of patients' history, legal evidence of patient care, data for research, or to render continuing patient care. Since turnaround time of transcription is a primary concern for health care providers, increase your competitiveness by offering pickup and delivery, seven-day-a-week service, same-day service, and phone-in dictation service.

What You Need

As many as one or two years of education may be required if you have little or no experience. Computer hardware and software will run you anywhere from $1,900 to $5,000 and a transcriber unit from $200 to $800. Do not forget that this job requires hours of sitting in front of a computer; a good chair and a desk at the proper height are smart investments.

Keys to Success

Medical transcribing can become somewhat monotonous. You must possess high levels of self-discipline and focus as you work. In addition, the demand for faster turnaround times occasionally necessitates working nights and weekends. On the other hand, medical transcription work is steady and resistant to recession! This field is still expanding; there's always work for trained transcriptionists.

Meeting Planner

Start-up cost:	$2,500–$6,500
Potential earnings:	$25,000 to start; possibly as high as $100,000 once established
Typical fees:	$40–$60 per hour or $400–$500 per day; planners handling large events such as conventions may get 15 to 20 percent of the overall projected budget for the entire event
Advertising:	Networking with convention and visitors' bureaus, caterers, and travel agents; ads in meeting trade publications; Web site with tips, resources and testimonials
Qualifications:	Excellent organizational and negotiation skills; attention to detail; good business background; good communication and troubleshooting skills
Equipment needed:	Office and computer equipment, high-speed Internet access (for using online meeting resources such as WebEx. com), fax, cell phone, PDA, reference books, business cards, stationery, envelopes
Staff required:	No
Hidden costs:	Phone calls

What You Do

You can have a great career as a meeting planner if you like handling the myriad of details involved in planning formal events and if you have the organization, negotiation, and communication skills necessary to pull it off. Corporations, associations, conventions, and trade shows are all potential sources of business. As companies become leaner, employees can no longer be spared to plan meetings.

Also, meetings and events are increasingly viewed as great sales and marketing opportunities. Therefore, creative, talented meeting planners are in demand. You will need to be knowledgeable about many areas, everything from hotels and catering to travel. You may need to negotiate a block of hotel rooms, find exotic locales for company meetings, book speakers and entertainers, set up promotions, and handle all the many small and large details that make for a successful event. In return, you may get to travel and stay at exclusive resorts and hotels, you will meet interesting people from many walks of life, and you will have the satisfaction of seeing people enjoy the event.

What You Need

A computer will cost from $1,000 to $3,000. Additional software, printer, telephone, and fax will add from $900 to $3,000 or more. Office equipment, reference books, insurance, letterhead, and so on will bring the total costs to $2,700–$8,500. Fees are typically $40–$50 per hour or $400–$600 per day. To get more assignments from the get-go, you should do a few "free" events to give potential clients a good idea of how spectacular your meetings really are.

Keys to Success

Meeting planning can be very rewarding, but it often requires long days and hard work. If you are good at handling details, you're halfway to success already, because all of those little pieces of the puzzle are crucially important. To hear about conferences and conventions, plan a civic or charitable event on a volunteer basis to gain experience. In addition to making sure you have adequate money for your start-up, bear in mind that a meeting planner's livelihood is often tied to economic conditions, since companies may tighten their meeting budgets to cut costs. However small they may become as a result, meetings and conventions will always be around, and the trend toward outsourcing them to professional meeting planners will continue—good news for you!

Message Retrieval Service

Start-up cost:	$15,000–$25,000
Potential earnings:	$20,000–$35,000
Typical fees:	$50–$75 and up per month per client
Advertising:	Networking and referrals, Yellow Pages, business publications
Qualifications:	A pleasant phone voice

Equipment needed:	Computer with word-processing and contact management software, phone headsets
Staff required:	Yes (usually 1–5 employees)
Hidden costs:	Additional phone lines to handle more clients, staff salaries

What You Do

Answering services have been around for a long time, but the explosive growth in small service businesses has made them even more important than ever. You can take your pleasant phone manner and your good listening skills and create an excellent business opportunity. Some software allows keyboard entry of caller information; other newer cell-phone pagers can immediately connect you to the plumber or consultant who has hired you to be his "home office." A higher-tech approach is a voice mail system, with an options menu and the capability of recording and sharing long messages.

What You Need

Equipment required depends to some extent on the level of service you plan to offer. If you're using a phone system including a switchboard with headsets, you'll spend at least $2,000 on equipment in the beginning. If you opt for the high-tech voice mail system, you'll shell out $5,000 or more. At any rate, you will be billing a healthy monthly fee of $50 or higher, so the equipment and cost of paying your staff could pay for itself in a relatively short period of time.

Keys to Success

You have a pleasant voice and care about people. You know how to filter out what is important from the background chatter. No one is better at keeping track of things than you. What can we say? You're a natural for this business. On the downside, this business does tie you down to your desk and phones. You will also have to work hard at marketing to develop enough customers.

Messenger Service

Start-up cost:	$20,000–$45,000 (including liability and accident insurance)
Potential earnings:	$45,000–$60,000
Typical fees:	$35–$50 per delivery run
Advertising:	Yellow Pages; business publications; promotional items (such as pens, magnets, or notepads); company name and number on delivery vehicles, employee T-shirts and jackets

Qualifications:	Driver's license (if delivering by car)
Equipment needed:	Fleet of delivery vehicles, bicycles or (yes) Rollerblades; some companies require delivery persons to provide their own means of transportation
Staff required:	Yes (you can't be everywhere at once, after all)
Hidden costs:	Insurance such as liability and workers' compensation (this is a high-risk profession, particularly for bicyclists and Rollerblade delivery people in large metropolitan areas)

What You Do

What happens when you have an important message or document that absolutely, positively has to be there that day? You call a messenger service to run it over to the appropriate local business. Maybe the messenger service is made up of a small fleet of vehicles or maybe it's comprised of a bunch of college students on Rollerblades, skateboards, or bicycles. However you determine to power your own fleet, you'll be wise to invest in safety gear and perhaps even first-aid training for each of your employees. It's a dangerous world out there, particularly in the big city. Even though it is definitely faster to deliver an envelope via bicycle as opposed to a vehicle in a large, congested city, the high cost of personal injury may make this business a little more costly than you'd anticipated.

What You Need

You'll need a good fleet and lots of delivery people to make this one work profitably. Ideally, you'll have a small staff that works quickly enough to tackle several runs per hour, making your profit margin higher than most of the larger, better-known delivery services. You'll charge $35–$50 per delivery (and may have a surcharge for speedier runs), so you can expect an income of $45,000–$60,000 per year.

Keys to Success

Make sure your staff is physically fit, able to handle multiple tasks, and just plain be quick about it. You'll make lots of money if your staff can manage to get through the streets safely and are required to use their own vehicles, Rollerblades, bikes, and so on.

Mobile Paper-Shredding Service

Start-up cost:	$15,000–$18,000
Potential earnings:	$20,000–$40,000
Typical fees:	$30–$50 per office visit

Advertising:	Local business periodicals, direct mail, possibly a Web site that details the geographic area your services cover and that includes tips on how to avoid identity theft
Qualifications:	Marketing skills, excellent time management and scheduling ability
Equipment needed:	Paper shredder, computer, printer, fax, cell phone
Staff required:	No
Hidden costs:	Vehicle maintenance and repair

What You Do

Mobile paper-shredding services are quite popular in major U.S. cities. It has always been important to certain types of businesses to maintain security; but this is becoming increasingly difficult to accomplish as valuable information becomes increasingly easy to access. Some banks, for example, have suffered great losses when criminals obtained and analyzed their discarded paper trash. Computer codes, product information, even customer records are essential to keep confidential. The value of your service is that it guarantees security; shredding is completed on the client's premises so that no possibility exists for loss of data and information. Shredding can be done by staff, but it is time-consuming and messy. You are saving time and trouble by bringing your shredding machine to your client's site on a regular schedule to perform this necessary but tedious task.

What You Need

You will need a heavy-duty shredder as well (about $300). Charge $30–$50 per office visit; offer a monthly rate to more regular clients, such as attorneys and government officials.

Keys to Success

Try to get into this business fast if you intend to do so at all, before the crush of competitors limits your opportunity to make a fair profit by your labors. Marketing will need to include considerable education so that your potential clients become aware of the advantages to their organization of this service.

Modeling Agency

Start-up cost:	$5,000–$25,000
Potential earnings:	$45,000–$250,000+

Typical fees:	10–15 percent commission on modeling jobs; $150–$1,500 to train models (depending on your market and your experience/reputation)
Advertising:	Local newspapers, Web site, schools, bulletin boards, direct mail, participation in local events
Qualifications:	Experience in training models for runway and portfolios, connections in the world of media and advertising
Equipment needed:	Professional-looking home office, video equipment, music equipment, photography and portfolio books, business cards, Web site with extremely high-quality photos
Staff required:	Yes, a receptionist/scheduler and perhaps more trainers (who can work on a commission basis)
Hidden costs:	Liability insurance, equipment upgrades, TV/radio ads, business travel

What You Do

Do you think you can spot the next Gisele or Tyra Banks? Do you have an eye for that "special something" in child, female or male models? You might be able to launch a successful modeling agency. Since there are many so-called modeling agencies out there that try to lure wannabe models into huge fees and even illicit activity, you will want to work hard to set yours apart as professional and legitimate. Having a home office in a nice, safe location will go a long way toward accomplishing just that, but so will a high-quality, detailed Web site that showcases your agency and its personal, professional service. Such "down-home" touches will quell the fears of many worried parents—and win over skeptical clients. You will spend some of your time soliciting new models to join your agency, supervising photo shoots, and helping your models to build their portfolios. But you will also spend some time schmoozing with the best advertising agencies in town in order to secure auditions and well-paying gigs for your models. So plan to be in and out of your home office a lot.

What You Need

You will likely want to partner with a good photographer to help your models build strong portfolios, and this may cost you a retainer fee (some of which you can charge back to the models as part of their sign-up fee with your agency). Since yours is a people-oriented business, comfortable chairs in your office are also a must. Don't forget a computer with digital camera and photo-editing software; you may also want to design and/or update your own Web site. All said, you could spend anywhere from $5,000 to $25,000 on starting your modeling agency.

Keys to Success

In addition to networking with ad agencies, you might also consider partnering with event planners and promoters who specialize in fashion shows. Be sure that you carry your marketing materials with you everywhere you go. All the world is a runway, as far as you are concerned.

Monogramming Service

Start-up cost:	$5,000–$15,000
Potential earnings:	$20,000–$50,000
Typical fees:	$3.50–$100 each piece (depending upon items chosen and number of units/volume discounts)
Advertising:	Yellow Pages, local school districts, direct mail to companies
Qualifications:	Some sewing skills or ability to operate monogramming equipment
Equipment needed:	Monogramming equipment, business cards
Staff required:	No
Hidden costs:	Insurance

What You Do

Baseball caps, sweatshirts, and jackets with company logos on them . . . you've seen them everywhere. You have a knack for knits and for transferring a company's identity to the appropriate material. Or maybe you simply want to monogram initials onto towels, blankets, and other home accessories for the marriage-minded. Whatever your specialty area, you'll need some equipment and marketing savvy to get your business off the ground. Silk screening is a good place to start; check your local art supply shops for information and creative options. For the more advanced monogrammer, research thermal transfer devices or computer-aided sewing machines in business and trade publications before making an expensive purchase.

What You Need

This business can be started on a modest budget. However, depending on the equipment you invest in, you could spend as much as $15,000 or more to get started. You will most likely need to insure any equipment purchased, plus any supplies. Expect to earn back your initial outlay in about two to three years, based on an income potential of $20,000–$50,000 per year.

Keys to Success

Advertising and marketing skills will play an important role in making this business a successful venture. Monogramming is much more than just initialing towels, and you'll need to convey that in every piece of literature you send out, particularly on your business cards.

Mortgage Loan Broker

Start-up cost:	$3,000–$10,000
Potential earnings:	$15,000–$50,000
Typical fees:	Commission equal to 4 percent or less of the value of the mortgages placed, paid by borrower
Advertising:	Classified ads; real estate magazines; newspapers; referrals; banner ads on Realtor or home-hunting Web sites; your own Web site with current rates, online application via secure server, testimonials and links to related services (such as title companies, etc.)
Qualifications:	Extensive knowledge of real estate finance, license (in some states)
Equipment needed:	Business cards, letterhead, envelopes, computer with online access to current mortgage packages and rates, cell phone
Staff required:	No
Hidden costs:	Advertising, mileage and time making a lot of cold calls

What You Do

Borrowers, both individuals firms, who want second mortgages come to you to find a lender. Third, fourth, and even higher levels of mortgages are possible in certain cases. You may operate entirely independently or work as a subcontractor with a real estate agent or attorney. You will need to keep putting your message before the public because, for the most part, each transaction will be with a new client. Occasionally mortgage brokers find borrowers for lenders, rather than the reverse.

What You Need

Costs to start can be relatively low ($3,000–$5,000) if you know what you are doing. All you'll really need to get going is a good mortgage program and a license to provide mortgages for hopeful customers. You could earn your first $15,000 easily enough, charging only 4 percent of the total mortgage.

Keys to Success

Once you develop a good reputation, you may find that repeat business from one or more lenders will bring in an excellent income. But most mortgage brokers focus on finding potential borrowers and then linking them with the dollars. You'll need an ability to inspire confidence and to speak the language of people on both sides of the transaction. Patience and active listening are also very valuable in this type of enterprise.

Mover

Start-up cost:	$1,500–$3,000 (if you already have the truck)
Potential earnings:	$20,000 and up
Typical fees:	$35+ per hour
Advertising:	Classified ads; radio spots; direct mail; flyers; community bulletin boards; referrals; simple Web site with contact information, testimonials and packing tips
Qualifications:	Physical strength, experience
Equipment needed:	Truck, pads, straps, packing materials, computer and printer (for invoices, Web site maintenance and tax records), high-speed Internet access, cell phone
Staff required:	Yes
Hidden costs:	Insurance, truck maintenance

What You Do

To set up a successful small business as a mover, you will need to carve out a niche for yourself. What can you specialize in? What type of moving service is not readily available in your community? The companies that provide enormous trucks to move households across the continent are too expensive for a move within the same community, and they are too hard to schedule. Small household moves are an underserved market, and meeting these needs in a flexible, cost-effective way could allow you to fulfill your entrepreneurial ambitions. Other local movers specialize in commercial moving: relocating businesses, office expansions, and so on.

What You Need

The truck is the major expense, but you could start out for as little as $1,500 if you rent one only when needed. And hiring helpers will also cost you. You'll need to purchase a decent computer ($1,000) with software to help you manage the financial and promotional aspects of your business (invoicing, estimating, Web site maintenance, e-mail, and bookkeeping). Your physical endurance will determine your earnings, but you should make at least $20,000 in your first year.

Keys to Success

Your market may well be people who originally plan to do their moves themselves and realize at the last moment that the task is too big. You will need to position your business so that these frustrated, desperate people can find you easily and realize that the cost of your service is far outweighed by the value they will receive: less breakage, no backaches, a faster completion of the move process, and so on. You will need to inspire confidence in your customers so that they trust you with their valuables. An added advantage of doing so is that they will recommend you to others, and word of mouth will eventually carry your business.

Multilevel Marketing

Start-up cost:	$500–$1,000
Potential earnings:	$20,000–$50,000
Typical fees:	10–20 percent of sales, plus bonus for new distributors
Advertising:	Networking, memberships in business and community groups, brochure, direct mail, banner ads on entrepreneurial Web sites, your own Web site with testimonials raving about the profitability of your company; possibly catalogs and leaflets
Qualifications:	Sales skills and experience
Equipment needed:	Basic computer setup, high-speed Internet access, phone
Staff required:	No
Hidden costs:	Marketing materials, membership dues

What You Do

Some products don't seem appealing unless they are demonstrated. The classic example is Tupperware, which just sat on store shelves until the company realized that buyers needed to be shown how the top is burped to create a vacuum seal. Many other products, such as cosmetics or lingerie, are sold as Tupperware is, mostly in group parties. Often a business starts when someone develops enthusiasm for, and commitment to, a product or company. The sales process for that product or company then seems to happen almost naturally. You should consider participating in multilevel marketing of a product that has been especially effective for you, such as a line of cosmetics or a nutritional supplement that has made a difference in your sense of well being. You will be selling not only the product, but the opportunity for others to sell it as well, which is what sets multilevel marketing apart from direct sales. You're aiming to maximize your own income potential by deriving percentages from other salespeople you recruit.

What You Need

This is another business where you begin with nothing but your own energy and commitment (and as little as $500). Soon, however, you'll need a nice brochure and Web site to entice potential sales representatives.

Keys to Success

Do you know that you can sell? More importantly, do you love the sales process? Do you enjoy helping your customers discover products that will improve their lives? If so, you can make an excellent living in the multilevel marketing world. However, far more people have tried it than have made the easy millions that are sometimes promised. You really do have to work very, very hard. You can't give up when your first seventy-four efforts end in no sale. You will have to manage your time well, and you will have to find a company whose products are worth this much of your commitment.

Music Instructor/Professional Musician

Start-up cost:	$150–$25,000 (depending on whether you already own a professional-quality instrument)
Potential earnings:	$15,000–$70,000
Typical fees:	$15–$25 per class per week $150–$500 per event
Advertising:	Community newspapers, bulletin boards at local schools and universities, wedding directories
Qualifications:	Experience as a professional musician; music degree a plus
Equipment needed:	Performance-quality instrument, a piano or tuning fork, music stands, a metronome, and a room dedicated to musical instruction
Staff required:	No (but you could partner with others for a chamber group or quartet and split the take)
Hidden costs:	Travel expenses, extra strings and related musical supplies

What You Do

Moved by Mozart? Driven by Dvorzak? Whether you specialize in teaching piano, voice, cello, violin, flute or any other musical instrument, you will enjoy filling your home with the sound of music when you are a professional music teacher and/or musician. Students are always plentiful, especially when you live near a lot of elementary, middle, and high schools with music programs. Often, there aren't enough good teachers to go around, so when you become known for what you do, your appointment book will fill up rather quickly. Still, the young are fickle, and there will always be lots of turnover with your student roster due to lack of commitment, moves to other cities, or just plain lack of effort. Particularly with the younger set, you will need to work hard to encourage your students to stick with it, to learn how to discipline and "fine-tune" themselves into good musicians. Offer incentives (such as free movie tickets or a free video of their latest recital) to keep your students happy and motivated.

What You Need

You will, of course, need a performance-quality instrument. Some music stands, instruction books, and maybe even a tape recorder would be a good idea as well. Your students may purchase their own instruction books or purchase them directly from you (if you have the space to stock some). A good tuning fork and a metronome to help keep a steady rhythm are the only other items that you will absolutely need to get started. If you already own a good instrument, you won't spend more than $150 to get this business off to a quick start. Just make sure you bill your students for a set number of lessons upfront and at the beginning of each month, as music lessons are often the first thing to be cast aside by busy families or students with wavering commitment.

Keys to Success

Advertising your teaching and performing abilities in community newspapers is often the best way to generate a strong client list in the beginning, along with offering your services through schools and universities. But don't forget to do a little schmoozing with party, wedding, and event planners to get the higher-paying gigs. And always take a full stack of flyers or business cards with you to each performance. Referrals can get you everywhere in this business, and that is a Bach you can bank on.

Mystery Shopper

Start-up cost:	Less than $500
Potential earnings:	$10,000–$20,000
Typical fees:	$25–$50 per shopping experience (generally, per day)
Advertising:	Personal contact with managers at stores, hotels, corporations
Qualifications:	Knowledge of area to be evaluated, being a good actor or actress so as not to be noticed, being highly observant
Equipment needed:	None
Hidden costs:	Mileage

What You Do

Mystery shoppers are used in a variety of settings: retail stores, hotel chains, restaurants, charitable organizations, government organizations, collection agencies, and banks. Their purpose is to observe the business from a customer's point of view and to report to management its shortcomings and strengths for the sake of improving service. A mystery shopper acts like a customer, observing the quality of the service, looking for employee theft, and even shopping the competition for valuable information. One of the benefits to companies of using mystery shoppers is that they are less expensive than electronic surveillance.

What You Need

You won't spend very much at all launching this one, but you probably won't become a millionaire, either. Earning $10,000–$20,000 per year would probably be as good as it gets.

Keys to Success

You might want to stick to a particular industry where you already have experience or knowledge. Chains would provide continuing business and multiple sites to shop without being known as a shopper. Provide a written and oral report of your findings. In some states, mystery shoppers are considered private investigators and therefore must be licensed. Look into your state's laws regarding licensing.

Nanny Service

Start-up cost:	$10,000–$40,000
Potential earnings:	$40,000–$70,000
Typical fees:	$20–$35 per hour
Advertising:	Yellow Pages, newspapers, parents' groups, business associations, Web site with testimonials and information about your fees and services
Qualifications:	Business experience, preferably experience in managing a sizeable staff
Equipment needed:	Computer with high-speed Internet access, cell phone, fax
Staff required:	Yes (about 20–30 nannies)
Hidden costs:	Liability insurance, health benefits and possibly background checks for your nannies (however, some nanny services require candidates to cover that cost)

What You Do

Not just your average babysitter, a nanny provides daily care for children in addition to helping with household chores. Obviously, then, nannies should enjoy being essentially another mom in a busy household. You need to carefully screen your nanny candidates (including running a background check with the police to make sure they have a clean record) and match them carefully to prospective households. Make sure that your client homes fill out a questionnaire detailing their preferences and exactly what kinds of work they expect to have done by the nanny. Also, since many nannies drive kids to soccer practice or other recreation activities, be sure that each nanny has a valid driver's license. Your nannies should be CPR certified as well.

What You Need

Your costs to start a nanny service are generally quite high for a number of reasons, including liability insurance, office overhead, and benefits. Once you factor in your advertising costs (a good-size ad in the Yellow Pages and flyers or brochures for parents' and professional groups), you've spent anywhere from $10,000–$40,000. Nanny services are particularly lucrative in large cities, where most of the need is.

Keys to Success

It is a challenge to match the right nannies to each of your clients' households, but if you ask all of the right questions up-front, your chances of success will be high. Nannies are filling an important void in the lives of working families, and if the two-income family trend continues to rise, your service will be among the most profitable businesses to start.

Newspaper Delivery Service

Start-up cost:	$1,000–$5,000
Potential earnings:	$10,000 or more
Typical fees:	Usually a flat rate of $150–$300 per week, depending on size of delivery area
Advertising:	Cold-calling
Qualifications:	Stick-to-itiveness
Equipment needed:	Van, canvas bags
Staff required:	Yes
Hidden costs:	Vehicle maintenance, fuel

What You Do

You will be providing newspaper delivery on a subcontracting basis within a specific geographic area. With morning newspapers being the norm in many localities, it has become more difficult for newspaper publishers to find reliable delivery people. It is very difficult for the preteens who used to fulfill this role to get up way before dawn, deliver papers, and still get through a full day of school. You take over, delivering one or more routes yourself and hiring a crew to complete the rest.

What You Need

You may need a van to pick up bundles of newspapers and to drop them off at your assistants' routes, but you could get by with just about $1,000 start-up expense if you already have one. For a part-time job, $10,000 a year to start is easy money.

Keys to Success

This is another American classic: a job that depends on hard work (and an excellent alarm clock) rather than on education, social position, or good luck. You'll probably need to have others working with you to earn an adequate return on your efforts, and managing others always requires thought and effort. There's no glamour to the job of delivering newspapers, but it's good, honest work, and you'll get plenty of exercise.

⸺ Notary Public

Start-up cost:	$100–$200
Potential earnings:	$6,000–$10,000
Typical fees:	$10 per requested service
Advertising:	Yellow Pages, local newspapers
Qualifications:	License, usually upon recommendation of two lawyers
Equipment needed:	Seal
Staff required:	No
Hidden costs:	Mileage, if you travel to customer locations

What You Do

Notary publics usually add this service on to a related business. Witnessing signatures and administering oaths will bring you a small fee each time, but you will not become a magnate by this route alone. A surprising number of transactions must be notarized, though, so if you can draw in foot traffic or position yourself next to a business related to your services (such as a photocopy shop, license bureau, or post office), it can be well worth the trouble of obtaining the license. Check the requirements in your area, since they differ from state to state.

What You Need

Start-up costs are minimal and include only the license fee and your seal (not more than $500). A sign directing people to your location will bring walk-ins to have you witness their signatures. Fees are low, but so is the cost of providing the service.

Keys to Success

Why not? What do you have to lose? If people are going to pay notary public fees, why not have them pay you? Creativity in developing an associated service will enable you to make a business enterprise out of the enthusiasm for having things notarized that runs throughout American bureaucracies. Document typing is one possibility. Dreams of glory may pass you by, but the challenges are negligible too.

Online Auction Consignment Service

Start-up cost:	$50–$2,000 (depending on whether you already own a computer)
Potential earnings:	$5,000–$65,000+
Typical fees:	Varies, but is typically 50 percent of list price per item
Advertising:	Local flea markets; garage sales; community newspapers; ads on eBay, Yahoo, and other online auction sites
Qualifications:	Ability to use a digital camera and write sales-generating descriptions
Equipment needed:	Computer, digital camera
Staff required:	No
Hidden costs:	Storage space, time involved in gathering and listing items, specialized selling software

What You Do

With the success of online auctions such as eBay and Yahoo! Auctions growing exponentially, it's easy to see why everybody wants to earn money for items that are simply taking up space in their attics or garages. But who has the time to photograph and write the kinds of descriptions that really sell these items, let alone the patience to manage the sales from listing through purchase and shipping? Even posting feedback can, at times, be a chore. That's why the business of taking in other people's items on a consignment basis makes so much sense. And that is why you can really make a full-time income if you are good at locating unusual or desirable items and setting fair prices that take shipping and packaging into account. If you know your stuff (as well as other people's), you can easily create a solid business for yourself with an "online flea market." Millions of people buy and sell items on eBay everyday, making it a terrific marketplace for your consignee's items. Just be sure they sign a consignment agreement that spells out your contract to sell specific items over a specific period of time for your clients, and what percentage you will take of each sale for your services. Be sure that your customers understand that you will remit funds to them once per month to keep your accounting time from biting into your listing and sales functions.

What You Need
Of course, you'll need a computer and a good digital camera (preferably with zoom). If you want to be able to list several items quickly and efficiently, you might invest in power-selling software as well. Some auction sites will let you store your images on their server for free or at minimal cost, but others will not. In those cases, it may make more sense to sign on with an image hosting service. The technology and service options change rapidly, so it pays to check out any updates or policy changes on your auction site(s) regularly.

Keys to Success
The best online auction consigners have an eye for what sells. Visit local flea markets and collectibles shops to see which items are hottest right now, and keep notes on their asking prices. Scan auctions for similar items online and set your prices realistically. Just because you want top dollar doesn't mean you'll get it.

Online Marketing Specialist

Start-up cost:	$2,000–$4,000
Potential earnings:	$20,000–$40,000
Typical fees:	Hourly rate of $45+
Advertising:	Bulletin Board Services, direct mail, trade journals, business publications
Qualifications:	Knowledge of marketing, business savvy, awareness of the unwritten rules and limitless possibilities out there on the Internet
Equipment needed:	Computer with fast Internet access, printer, fax, office furniture

Staff required: No

Hidden costs: Internet Service Provider fees, time spent educating client

What You Do

Marketing is always creative; online marketing is even more so. You'll be creating the actual marketing approaches for a variety of different businesses to get the word out on the Internet. So if newness is your bag, then this is your game. Even more than with conventional marketing, you will need to deliver more than you promise, to tell more than you sell, and attract the attention of potential customers rather than push products at them. The Internet is the perfect way to inform people about some products and services, but it is still useless for others. You'll spend enough time developing your own markets, but once you do, expect to earn more of a cutting-edge salary for your toils.

What You Need

The ability to create effective Internet messages will require increasing levels of computing power (equipment costs $2,000–$4,000). Expect to spend a pretty penny initially for online services, because you'll likely end up subscribing to all of them in addition to the Internet. You'll need to see what your work looks like on different platforms. Subscriptions to newsletters and magazines on the computer industry are also essential as resource guides; estimate spending at least $2000 per year to keep up-to-date. You can charge $45 per hour until you feel you're experienced enough to command $75 per hour. You may decide to accept MC/Visa over the Internet, so be sure to include in your price the surcharge for such capabilities.

Keys to Success

Experience, good sense, and highly refined marketing skills will make you successful at this new game. You'll need to be persistent in creating your own market before you can begin creating customers for your clients. You'll need a high tolerance for monitor-staring, and you'll need to watch out for the uncharted pitfalls that accompany any cutting-edge activity, such as time spent educating and rewriting.

EXPERT ADVICE

What sets your business apart from others like it?

Tim DiScipio, President of Easton Media Group in Greenwich, Connecticut, says he has a unique niche in the electronics marketplace. "I've got valuable years of experience in this field; something others can't claim in a constantly growing industry. It's attractive to companies that want someone who's been in the industry for a while and knows their way around."

Things you couldn't do without

Obviously DiScipio couldn't do without a fast, powerful computer (or two or three), but he also needs a DSL line, a telephone, and a fax machine.

Marketing tips

"If you're going to thrive in this business, you really need to network and expand your contacts regularly. Everyone in this industry has a different, unique niche . . . align yourself with the real players who can help you expand to where you need to be. Stay within your own niche; don't try to be everything to everyone."

If you had to do it all over again . . .

"I would have relinquished the time-consuming business operations duties and focused on my areas of specialty. It would have simplified my problems and allowed me to remain focused."

Online Message Board Manager

Start-up cost:	$500–$10,000
Potential earnings:	$5,000–$50,000
Typical fees:	Monthly subscription fees typically start at $10 and annual fees at $20–$50; most of your income will come from banner ad sales
Advertising:	Online directories and links
Qualifications:	Online marketing skills
Equipment needed:	High-power computer with fast Internet access, fax, printer, phone
Staff required:	No
Hidden costs:	Increased server space if your list becomes very popular

What You Do

More and more folks are seeking ways to communicate with others who have similar interests. If there is no official online message board or interest group on a subject such as iguana ownership or vintage jewelry collections, your business can provide one. You would advertise the availability of such a listserv, then post as many pieces of related information as possible to generate the number of users tapping into your service. The more information you have online, the more you'll be able to charge individuals for getting to this data—or advertisers for the privilege of enticing your list members with banner ads of interest to them. Checking the messages frequently and removing outdated ones are important aspects of your service. You will need to make sure that messages are arranged neatly and that any inappropriate material is removed on a regular basis. Check with major carriers to familiarize yourself with their message board regulations and any possible charges you may incur from them for use of their online services.

What You Need

All you will really need to start is a computer (about $1,000) and an Internet Service Provider (ISP). Online message boards are widely available; the more popular ones reside at Yahoo.com and Google.com. Be sure you can offer enough to generate a good audience as well as attract advertisers. Check carefully to avoid duplicating another service or you may have some problems. What you earn is directly dependent upon how many people use your service, so make sure your topic is of wide interest.

Keys to Success

Selling skills and patience are the two vital ingredients here. To gain repeat business, you have to keep up with the message boards under your care. A large clientele is needed to make an adequate profit overall. Remember that some competing online message boards are offered for free. Keep your list updated often with fresh messages, and actively pursue related businesses to solicit banner ads.

Online Retailer

Start-up cost:	$50–$2,200
Potential earnings:	$10,000–$100,000
Typical fees:	Varies
Advertising:	Banner ads, reciprocal ads with similar businesses, collectors' magazines
Qualifications:	None; some prior sales experience may be helpful
Equipment needed:	Computer, digital camera, strong inventory
Staff required:	No
Hidden costs:	Storage, shipping preparation, promotions and specials, processing credit cards online

What You Do

Have you ever wanted to own a retail business, but not wanted the overhead of a storefront? An Internet store might be a great option for you. It would be wise to identify a niche first. Do you want to specialize in selling hard-to-find comic books? Or how about vintage jewelry or cosmetics? Maybe it's purses or designer clothing you want to sell? Regardless of your commodity, you'll need to figure out how best to reach your intended audience. Maybe you post regularly on a free electronic mailing list that puts you in direct contact with hundreds of potential customers; if so, remember to use your company name and link to your Web site in the signature line of your postings. (Blatant self-promotion is not acceptable on most electronic mailing lists.) You should also consider promoting your business through paid advertisements on search engines like Google.com to ensure that the link to your store ranks high when customers are searching for the kinds of goods you offer. The money you save in rent and inventory storage will far outweigh anything you spend on advertising, so do invest your start-up money wisely on a nice site that makes it easy for customers to do business safely with you. There are plenty of Internet service providers who can help you set up an online store in literally minutes. And the good news is, you can even run a store as a side business to another one so that it provides a second stream of income.

What You Need
You'll need a computer and a digital camera with zoom and/or a high-quality scanner at a minimum. It might be a nice idea to print up a few T-shirts with your Web address on them, and ask family and friends to wear them around town (even better if you have family and friends all over the country!). You really don't need business cards, but you might consider creating nice-looking invoices and packing sheets with your logo on them. This can be done using your own computer, so your start-up costs are really small.

Keys to Success
Your best bet for success as an online store owner is to align yourself with a supplier of good products that are sure to be appealing to others and that you can offer at a discount. If you can work with a distributor who can help you sell $40 perfume for $15–$20 online, you have a very good chance of scoring high on customers' lists. And repeat business will be a breeze.

Online Services Consultant

Start-up cost:	$4,000–$6,000
Potential earnings:	$10,000–$30,000
Typical fees:	$50–$75 per hour or $150+ per job
Advertising:	Online message boards, flyers, publications, word of mouth, banner ads on general-interest Web sites, your own Web site with computer tips
Qualifications:	Technical knowledge of hardware and software, good written communications skills, marketing ability

Equipment needed:	PC with high-speed Internet access, at least five phone lines
Staff required:	No
Hidden costs:	Internet service provider fees

What You Do

As an online consultant, you will assist those in need of specific pieces of information or directions to a bulletin board service (BBS) or other online services such as search engines, databases and more. You will troubleshoot for them, providing help in areas where the user is not as knowledgeable. Charges may be for the service received (employer/job searcher) or the knowledge gained such as the ability to use a certain piece of software. Some online consultants charge a flat monthly fee (typically $8–$10 per month); others have a low fee and add-on charges for time above a certain amount per month. You may need to send invoices or to obtain credit card capability to receive payments. The easiest way to be certain you're paid for your services is to obtain credit card information early in the process.

What You Need

Your initial investment is relatively high, since this is a very technology-dependent business. A computer, high-speed Internet access are necessary to begin, and a wireless hub would be most helpful—so that you can have many different online services running simultaneously. Of course, if you are very familiar with online message boards, search engines and bulletin board services, you will likely have a good start on your equipment already.

Keys to Success

In this fast-paced e-world, you can take your enjoyment of communicating online and make it into a business. Once you have found a niche, a group of potential subscribers with a strong interest in a topic and an enthusiasm for learning more, you can use your skills to guide them on their way. BBS subscribers often expect immediate, or at least rapid, responses from their sysop (system operator), so you will need to be available several hours each day. Developing a method of charging that is competitive while bringing in enough income can be difficult.

Outdoor Adventures

Start-up cost:	$5,000–$10,000
Potential earnings:	$50,000–$100,000
Typical fees:	$300–$1,000 per person (depending on length of excursion, group size, and corporate versus individual rates)

Advertising:	Magazines with an outdoor or fitness focus, newspapers, public speaking on outdoor and environmental issues, direct mail, banner ads on health and fitness-related Web sites, your own Web site with descriptions of your exciting packages plus client testimonials
Qualifications:	Outdoor leadership skills and experience, knowledge of the natural world, first aid certificate, excellent planning ability
Equipment needed:	Outdoor equipment for yourself and group, van, basic office setup (including computer, high-speed Internet access and fax), cell phone
Staff required:	Yes
Hidden costs:	Insurance, equipment repairs and replacement

What You Do

There are almost as many ways to conduct an outdoor adventure as there are individual personalities. Broadly defined, your business will take groups of people into the outdoors, camping, hiking, and experiencing the vanishing wilderness as participants rather than as mere observers. The supply of popular, long-established organizations offering outdoor programs has not nearly met the demand. Many small organizations have been very successful in offering related services such as corporate retreat planning. Some focus on learning to exist with little material support in a wilderness environment. Others offer opportunities for self-development, self-reflection, or fitness. Another popular approach is to create group activities that build relationships of trust for business organizations, college freshman orientations, and similar groups.

What You Need

Your decisions about equipment will affect the cost of your start-up and of your continuing operations. Advertising will be an ongoing requirement; expect to spend at least $5,000 on that alone each year. However, if you market yourself well, especially via the Web to corporations, you can really carve out a mighty fine living for yourself to the tune of $100,000 or more. Plus you'll have a good time doing it!

Keys to Success

An outdoors adventure business will rely on your love of the wilderness and your creativity in designing effective, appealing programs that allow your customers to encounter it. But not everyone who can build a camp out of hemlock twigs and catch mountain trout for dinner is also people-oriented enough to share their expertise with others. Wet, cold campers with blistered feet are not as easy to charm as day trippers on a short hike. So emphasize that experiencing and surviving the full range of challenges builds self-esteem, group solidarity, and an enduring respect for the power and beauty of nature.

Outplacement Services

Start-up cost:	$15,000–$30,000
Potential earnings:	$75,000–$150,000
Typical fees:	Retainer fees of $1,000–$3,000 per month
Advertising:	Yellow Pages, direct mail to human resource managers, trade shows, promotional items, networking, banner ads on human resource-related Web sites, your own Web site with client company testimonials and your unique selling proposition (i.e., what sets you apart from other outplacement firms?)
Qualifications:	A background in human resources
Equipment needed:	Computer with Internet access, fax, phone, letterhead, business cards, corporate directories, career counseling/skills assessment materials, cell phone
Staff required:	No
Hidden costs:	Insurance, phone bills, and time spent with each client (they'll want more of your time than is profitable for you)

What You Do

The late '90s through the early '00s weren't exactly kind to much of the workforce. Unfortunately layoffs still abound in certain industries. That is why you need to promote your services, which help displaced individuals find new work elsewhere. Read the business pages daily to keep tabs on local companies. Generally, whenever there's a bad quarter, a layoff will follow. Your goal is to be the first (or the best) to approach these companies—at a time just before they actually need you. Your services can be in place before the downsizing is even announced to the employees, which is generally the way companies prefer to handle the layoffs. In this way, it will look like they already have a plan for those employees caught completely off guard.

What You Need

Your start-up costs are likely to be quite high. You'll need to have a computer system with high-speed Internet access for doing online job searches and similar research. Detailed corporate directories alone could run as high as $6,000 per set. A professional-looking Web site would also be a wise investment. Expect to spend between $15,000–$30,000 getting started; expect to pull in between $75,000–$150,000 per year once you've established a name for yourself. It's a business that can be lucrative for those who have a good reputation. Word of mouth travels fast in industry these days (especially via e-mail).

Keys to Success

The best thing you can do in this business is stay on top of things. Keep an ear to the ground, perhaps by networking closely with members of the Society for Human Resource Managers. And always get your promotional materials in front of the vice president of operations or other key decision-makers before your competitors do.

Paging Services

Start-up cost:	$10,000–$15,000
Potential earnings:	$30,000–$50,000
Typical fees:	$10–$30 per month
Advertising:	Newspapers, radio, TV, direct mail, flyers
Qualifications:	Technical skills, organizational and sales skills
Equipment needed:	Computer paging system, office furniture, business cards, letterhead, envelopes
Staff required:	No
Hidden costs:	Phone bills, insurance

What You Do

No longer limited to a few types of professionals, paging services now appeal to many businesses and individuals. Parents use them to keep track of children, and sales people use them to maintain a close link to their offices. In fact, almost everyone who works away from a home office can use a pager to increase productivity and maintain the highest possible level of responsiveness to customers They're more subtle and less disruptive than cell phones. Creative marketing will connect your new paging services business to these emerging markets. Excellent service will keep your clients linked to you for their mobile communications needs.

What You Need

The required communications and phone equipment is quite expensive ($10,000 and up), and you may need an inventory of pagers as well. Set your monthly rates competitively to ensure maximum return.

Keys to Success

It will take determination and responsiveness to your market to make your enterprise stand out from the competition of cell phones that can do virtually anything. Still, there is a market for pagers in professions where subtlety is still a virtue. How many times have you overheard extremely personal cell phone conversations in very public places? Pagers still give users the option to be courteous in an increasingly discourteous world.

Party Planner

Start-up cost:	$500–$1,000
Potential earnings:	$20,000–$40,000
Typical fees:	$300–$500 per party or 15–20 percent of total cost of party
Advertising:	Yellow Pages; direct mail; flyers; networking; banner ads on community Web sites; your own Web site with photos, party themes, and online booking capability through secure server
Qualifications:	Resourcefulness, creative ability, exceptional organizational skills
Equipment needed:	Planning system (hand-held PDA or a good planning book), cell phone, fax, camera or camcorder (to record parties so that other potential clients can see the results of your work)
Staff required:	No
Hidden costs:	Travel expenses, spending too much time on each project for the amount being paid

What You Do

A party planner tends to all the details for any given social function, from hiring the caterer, florist, and musician(s) or entertainer(s) to addressing and sending invitations. Planners should have a creative flair and be able to suggest a variety of party themes to fit the occasion. For instance, you could come up with a Caribbean theme where all the party-goers must dress in tropical attire, all the music is calypso-inspired, and giant papier-mâché palm trees sprout from the corners of the room. Or plan a party that is a surprise for your client's family members, with a little Sherlock Holmes–style caper for guests to solve upon their arrival. Whatever your plan, you'll need to be extremely well organized to maintain a good reputation, and since your business will grow primarily based on referrals, you'll need to keep this uppermost in your mind. More than likely, you'll put in way more hours than you should for each job, but the return will be worth it if your ideas are exciting or innovative and your execution of those ideas is first-class. In other words, the payoff will be directly related to what you put into it.

What You Need

It's a good idea to purchase some party planning guides from a bookstore (or borrow them from the library) and build yourself a Web site that showcases your themes and talents. Advertising costs will be your biggest start-up expense. Be sure to get a Yellow Pages ad ($30–$100 per month, depending on ad size) since this is where many people who don't know you personally will be apt to look. You can charge either on a percentage basis (15 to 20 percent of total party cost) or a flat fee of $300–$500 per party.

Keys to Success

While getting started, you might want to plan some friends' parties for free. This will give you valuable experience and build a portfolio, so to speak, of your successes and innovations. Keep at least a photo album if not a video of your parties so that you have something to show potential clients when you meet them in person or participate in local trade shows. Nothing sells better than demonstrated success. On the downside, expect there to be difficulties in dealing with the personalities involved in planning a party. Remember, too, that even though your tastes may be better than your clients', they will not always be the prevailing ones.

Personal Assistant

Start-up cost:	$100–$1,000
Potential earnings:	$25,000–$55,000
Typical fees:	$10–$45 per hour or a flat rate if the service is on a regular basis (such as weekly trips to the dry cleaners or grocery store)
Advertising:	Local/community newspapers, bulletin boards (especially at grocery stores), community coupon books, referrals
Qualifications:	None (but will need a chauffeur's license if carting people around)
Equipment needed:	Dependable transportation, computer, cell phone with hands-free accessories (if mandated by your state) and/or pager, a Personal Digital Assistant (PDA) or some such tool to keep you organized
Staff required:	No
Hidden costs:	Fluctuating fuel costs, liability insurance

What You Do

You are supremely organized. You can tell people where, when, and how to find virtually anything in your city, and people often look to you as their personal errand service. So why not make a business out of it, offering such services to others in your community? You won't need much to get started, except for a strong desire to help others solve their problems and get things done. How many times have you heard from people that they could get so much more done if they just had the time to do it? You can be quite a valuable person in the lives of many a harried professional, handling everything from picking up laundry and dry cleaning to grocery shopping or assisting with vacation plans. Your work will be different each day, as well as for each client, so the challenges are many and interesting. On the downside, you may need to put in a lot of hours to make a good living, at least in the beginning. Once you become more established and start getting more referrals than you can handle, it's time for the personal assistant to hire a personal assistant.

What You Need

You will need a decent computer with Internet access so that you can use a good search engine to find all the resources you'll need quickly and efficiently. More than that, you'll need a cell phone with hands-free accessories (if mandated by your state) to be in constant communication with your clients. They will almost always want you to do that "one more thing" before the day is done. A PDA would be most handy in keeping your files handy while on the road.

Keys to Success

Stay organized by investing in a good goal-setting or time-management software package. You will always be juggling so many different tasks, and you will wear many hats for your diverse client list. Don't forget to pencil in some time off to de-stress and re-energize, as you are your own best product and service.

Personal Development Coach

Start-up cost:	$1,500–$5,000
Potential earnings:	$50,000–$150,000
Typical fees:	$150–$350 per client per month typically, 1–3 phone calls per month are included, with unlimited client access to you via e-mail
Advertising:	Community and local business publications
Qualifications:	Certification depends on interest area

Equipment needed:	Depends on area of focus, but in general, a computer would be handy for research and to develop resource lists for your clients
Staff required:	No
Hidden costs:	Ongoing professional development courses, liability insurance, Web site maintenance and updating, networking

What You Do

Right now, there are thousands of people who work too hard and don't have the balance they need in life to help them set and achieve their goals. As a personal development coach, you can help them attain new heights as healthy, well adjusted, and more fulfilled human beings. You likely have a background in counseling, education, human resources, or even theology. As a coach, you will offer your clients personalized goal-setting in addition to daily, weekly, or monthly motivation. If you are a licensed counselor, you can also offer psychological or emotional counseling. You will start with a detailed questionnaire to help your clients recognize what's lacking in their lives, and then you will co-develop an actualization plan that seeks to significantly improve their lives. To do this most effectively, you should first go through such training yourself. The International Coach Federation (*www.coachfederation.org*) offers training and professional development and can help you to find a good coach to teach you all you need to know about being a good coach!

What You Need

Training and certification will be your biggest start-up costs, ranging anywhere from $3,000 to $5,000. Certification, although pricey and not yet mandatory, is highly recommended since it will give you instant credibility. Use a search engine with the keywords "coaching certification" or visit CoachU.com to learn more about the process involved in becoming a good personal development coach. Of course, if you've spent a lifetime working as a productivity, financial, or image consultant and feel you have the know-how and reputation, you can forego the certification and hang your shingle out for immediate business. Just keep in mind that the International Coach Federation is pushing for a credentials program with formal training and certification. You may still need to do it at some point in your career.

Keys to Success

The best way to break into this field is to first find your own coach, a good one who can serve as a teacher and mentor. Keep in touch with your coach as you develop your new business. Even psychologists visit other psychologists after they establish their practices, and it can always help you to stay on top of your game.

As a personal development coach, you may find that you have a tendency to be a sponge that absorbs your clients' issues and clouds your own. Having someone else to talk to will help you keep your head on straight, which will only allow you to offer better advice and guidance to your clients. Take care of yourself as you help others learn to take care of themselves.

Personal Instructor/Fitness Trainer

Start-up cost:	$100–$1,000
Potential earnings:	$20,000–$65,000
Typical fees:	$50–$75 per hour
Advertising:	Business cards, brochures, flyers, bulletin boards in health clubs
Qualifications:	Experience, physical fitness, knowledge of equipment and CPR
Equipment needed:	Membership to a gym or your own equipment if you want to work out of your home
Staff required:	No
Hidden costs:	Mileage and travel time needed to meet clients where they work out, liability insurance

What You Do

Do you keep yourself physically fit, have a great personality, and enjoy teaching others? If you answered "yes" to all three, pull out those business cards and start a personal trainer business. You'll have to market yourself like a pro. Give seminars about being fit and cover the benefits of working out to get your name and face out there in this highly competitive occupation. Experience will be on your side. Remember, you are marketing yourself and motivating others to become physically fit at the same time, so you must be in excellent physical shape and condition. Be prepared to work out alongside your clients if they request it, teaching them all the latest ways to get and stay in shape. Keep a couple of before and after photos of yourself and others whom you've helped tone and shape. Create a video and sell it through local health clubs.

What You Need

Start-up costs can consist solely of a gym membership; or, if you want the client to come to your home, you'll need a full set of equipment including free weights, Nautilus, and weight training equipment. That could send you into the $100,000 range for start-up costs. You have the potential to stay in shape and make a decent living in the range of $20,000–$65,000 or more, depending on how affluent your clients are.

Keys to Success

How many people can say that going to work relieves stress? Not only can you have fun and stay in shape, you get to have a social life on the job. Working out has become very social and everyone can do it, but the downside is, a client may quit without warning. Some people consider working out to be seasonal, so you'll really have to go out there and establish a good client base.

Personal Shopper

Start-up cost:	$500–$1,000
Potential earnings:	$10,000–$25,000
Typical fees:	$20–$40 per hour
Advertising:	Brochures, classified ads, personalized notes to busy executives, Web site with testimonials and rates
Qualifications:	An eye for a great deal and the ability to match gifts to personalities
Equipment needed:	Dependable transportation, cell phone
Staff required:	No
Hidden costs:	Mileage

What You Do

Do you consider yourself to be the "shopping goddess of the universe"? Are you able to consistently choose tasteful and well-received gifts? If so, this business could be your dream come true. Many of today's executives are simply too busy to spend an hour or two shopping for the perfect gift, so you can do it for them by offering your services at an hourly rate. You'll need to make sure that the client provides you with some method to purchase the gifts or arrange for the items to be held for pickup by the client. Build a strong network of places to shop; familiarize yourself with every gift/specialty store, retail store, and florist in your area. You'll need this vast resource (and plenty of catalogs) to come up with refreshingly new approaches to gift giving. Another part of your business might be purchasing items for busy executives themselves; they could provide you with a personalized size (and preference) card, then send you off on a buying odyssey.

What You Need

Brochures and personal notes sent to managers of large corporations are a good way to introduce yourself and your services. Be sure to stress the advantages of using a shopping service (chiefly, the time-saving and money-saving factor), and be clear in the beginning about the way you bill. Then you'll need to start collecting catalogs, visiting malls and unusual shops, and combing the newspapers for sales. Your clients will expect you to know everything possible about shopping, so take the time to prepare!

Keys to Success

If you only want to do this job part-time for individual clients, you won't make as much as you would working full-time for large companies. Be sure that you bill on an hourly rate rather than a per-job basis; otherwise, people may try to take advantage of you. Difficult situations may occur when the client isn't happy with the purchase, but you should be able to return anything you buy. All in all, the joy of spending other people's money is hard to resist—it gives you all the pleasure with none of the guilt.

Pet Grooming

Start-up cost:	$5,000–$10,000
Potential earnings:	$25,000–$40,000
Typical fees:	$30–$60 per pet-priming session
Advertising:	Yellow Pages, direct mail, community bulletin boards, referrals from vets
Qualifications:	Experience, patience, knowledge of animal behavior patterns, familiarity with the grooming standards of different breeds
Equipment needed:	Grooming table, clippers, brushes, combs, bathing tub/shower accessories, shampoos, dryer, detangler, hair bows, business cards
Staff required:	No
Hidden costs:	Supplies could get out of hand

What You Do

You have to really love animals to consider this business. But if you enjoy working with pets—many of whom may not enjoy taking a bath—you can build a decent business providing these services. Pet ownership increases each year in this country, but people have less free time than ever to groom them. What Afghan owners can really manage to comb out their pet's entire coat every day, as the books recommend? White poodles need considerable grooming to present themselves in a clean, fluffy, well-trimmed coat. Aside from the pet's appearance, good health practices dictate cleaning and brushing the coat regularly. Once you establish rapport with Rover, you are likely to have regular repeat business from his owner. Giving cats their flea baths is another popular service (to the owner, definitely not to the feline). As an add-on, consider selling pet supplies and/or specialty products for the pampered pet.

What You Need

Trying to do all this in your family bathtub is a poor idea. To make a go of the business, you'll need the setting and equipment to do a professional job without breaking your back. This may set you back around $10,000, but you stand a good chance of earning it all back in a year or so if there aren't many competitors in your area. Charge between $30–$60, depending on whether you're in the country or in a large city.

Keys to Success

You may not be the only pet grooming service in your community, but you can be the best. You can offer pickup and delivery services, specialize in terrier coat stripping or caring for poodles, and leave each "patient" happy and sweet-smelling. You'll need to make your customers feel that your service is the one that they can't live without. This is hard, physical work, but each grooming session leaves a beloved pet looking better—until he can get outside again.

Political Campaign Manager

Start-up cost:	$1,000–$5,000
Potential earnings:	$30,000–$150,000 or more
Typical fees:	Monthly retainer of $1,500 (if you're a beginner); $5,000–$10,000 per month if you're a seasoned pro
Advertising:	Boards of Election; direct mail to local government officials; Web site with your credentials and testimonials; business cards and effective, well-produced brochure
Qualifications:	Law or strategic public relations background and a love for the sport of politics
Equipment needed:	Cell phone, computer with DSL line, fax, printer
Staff required:	No
Hidden costs:	Errors and omissions insurance, mileage, phone bills

What You Do

Can't get enough of the latest political races? Addicted to campaign media coverage at all levels of government? If your answer is, "yes," you should seriously consider launching a business in political campaign management. A recent survey conducted by the Center for Congressional and Presidential Studies at American University discovered that nearly 50 percent of political consultants made at least $100,000 a year. But you really do need to build a name for yourself first. You will initially spend a great deal of time immersing yourself as a fixture on the local or state political landscape, getting to know everyone who's anyone, and making sure that you stay in regular contact with them as you build your business. Once you've been hired, you can expect to work on crafting a complete campaign plan that includes everything from fundraising to booking and writing speeches and from advising the candidate on how to handle the media to rounding up much-needed volunteers in every area possible (basically, meetings, meetings, and more meetings). At the community level, nearly all of your efforts will be grassroots. However once you begin to build a track record (or become connected to an influential politician who's bound for bigger and better things), you can expect to be hiring others to work on your team as financial, ethics, and media advisors. At that level, you will become nearly as powerful as your candidate.

What You Need

Since this is largely an image business based on your ability to strategize effectively, your biggest expense will likely be wrapped up in your own promotional materials. After all, how can you advise politicians on self-promotion if your materials leave a lot to be desired? Expect to spend anywhere from $1,000–$3,000 on the essentials (cell phone, computer, and so on) and at least another $2,000 on your business cards, brochure, and Web site.

Keys to Success

You are your own best consultant. Be sure all of your materials are top-notch, and that you are above reproach. Many a good political campaign strategist has fallen victim to scandal because they were so busy coaching the candidate, they forgot to watch their own backs. Keep all of your dealings at the highest level of integrity possible.

Pool Maintenance

Start-up cost:	$15,000–$30,000
Potential earnings:	$30,000–$50,000
Typical fees:	$75–$150 per total cleaning/shocking treatment

Advertising:	Flyers at pool sales and service centers, direct mail coupons, Yellow Pages, local newspapers
Qualifications:	Knowledge of maintaining and repairing inground and aboveground pools
Equipment needed:	Pool cleaning equipment (water vacuum, hose, etc.) and chemicals, cell phone
Staff required:	No
Hidden costs:	Insurance, phone, transportation

What You Do

Many people like the convenience of owning and using a pool, but who really likes the maintenance that pools require? You do—and you can earn a living providing this necessary service for busy pool owners who simply don't have the time (or energy) to clean or repair pools. You'll clean, repair, chemically shock, and maintain each client's pool. You're selling convenience and peace of mind to the luxury-minded. Of course, you'll do better if you're located in a part of the country, where pools are common such as the Sun Belt. In cooler climes you may have to offer your services in a wider geographic area to support your business, and that would mean increased travel expenses to and from customers.

What You Need

You'll need the right cleaning equipment and chemical supplies to stock your van with; expect to spend at least $15,000 on all of these items from the outset. However, at $75–$150 per cleaning job, you could stand to make some decent money cleaning and maintaining pools. Spend a few hundred dollars on business cards to leave behind for repeat business and referrals.

Keys to Success

By offering excellent service, you can build a customer base. Remember to call these people back periodically for repeat business. That follow-up could reap you thousands more dollars in the long run.

Printing Broker

Start-up cost:	$1,000–$3,000
Potential earnings:	$35,000–$50,000
Typical fees:	10 to 15 percent commission on sales
Advertising:	Yellow Pages, trade publications, direct mail, cold calls, referrals

Qualifications:	Printing sales background
Equipment needed:	Cell phone, computer, printer, fax, copier
Staff required:	No
Hidden costs:	Insurance, mileage

What You Do

For those who are inexperienced in the world of printing and publishing, a printing broker can be a godsend. Relying on an extensive background in printing sales, a printing broker can actually save the client hundreds or thousands of dollars in printing costs by shopping for the best (and most current) rates. The broker does not work for one specific printer, but represents all of them, in a sense, because he or she will offer a client the best going rate without sacrificing quality. Clients could be anyone from advertising agencies to community newspapers and book publishers. To be successful, you'll need to have a natural sales ability and the technical know-how to get printing jobs accomplished. You're servicing two sides here: the customer who needs a brochure or book printed and the printing house. If ink is in your blood, this could be a terrific opportunity for you.

What You Need

Your start-up costs are only $1,000 to $3,000, because you'll only need to have a basic office setup and some advertising to get things off the ground. With a printing background, complete with contacts, and some heavy shoe action, you could make $35,000–$50,000 per year, especially if you can build a solid reputation with documented savings for your clients.

Keys to Success

Your contacts will make or break you in this business; always be honest and reputable, and you'll reap the benefits threefold. Why threefold? Because your satisfied clients will tell at least two other contacts about your services and how much money you saved them. On the sour side, you could wind up spending a lot of your own time trying to negotiate deals that don't materialize. And that means you'll have to eat the related costs.

Private Tutor

Start-up cost:	$500
Potential earnings:	$15,000–$20,000
Typical fees:	$10–$20 per hour

Advertising:	Classified ads, Yellow Pages, word of mouth (school principals would be a good group to network with), banner ads on sites like *www.craigslist.org*
Qualifications:	Teaching experience or degree in area of expertise
Equipment needed:	None
Staff required:	None
Hidden costs:	Mileage

What You Do

Since classrooms are getting larger and larger, many students' needs are getting overlooked. Your services may be needed to bring a struggling student up to speed. Perhaps the best part about this type of business is that it is recession-proof! As long as there are students, there will be a strong need for capable individuals to guide them to scholastic success. Determine where your area of expertise lies and meet with teachers in this subject to ask for referrals. Once you get a few clients, word of mouth will grow quickly. You may find that you need to network with other tutors to build referral systems of your own. At any rate, as a tutor you will find out the student's needs (probably in a written report from her teacher) and develop lesson plans tailored to those specific needs. Try to make the lessons interesting and empower the student so that each success feels like her own.

What You Need

Purchase a few used textbooks (preferably with teacher's guides) and buy yourself some good books on learning challenges and motivation to succeed. To be a good inspiration to your student, you'll need to demonstrate your own willingness to learn. Your only other start-up cost will be advertising, and that will generally stay under $500.

Keys to Success

Encouraging a young student's success while fostering a thirst for knowledge can be richly rewarding if you are genuinely interested in education. Helping a student overcome what seemed like an obstacle offers you—and the rest of the world— optimism about our own possibilities. Aside from an occasional obnoxious child, what's there to hate about that?

Product Designer

Start-up cost:	$10,000–$20,000
Potential earnings:	$50,000–$150,000+

Typical fees:	Varied according to project; can be as low as $500 for a simple design sketch to several thousand for a complete design/technical layout with product specifications
Advertising:	Direct mail, Web site with photo gallery of your work and links to related services with whom you are affiliated
Qualifications:	Degree in product design
Equipment needed:	Computer, computer-aided design (CAD) software, digital camera or scanner
Staff required:	No
Hidden costs:	Insurance, excessive changes in product specifications (make sure you're clear on what's expected—and get it in writing)

What You Do

Behind every good product is a strong design team. If you have a reputation for quality product design done quickly and within budget, you could offer your services to such a team on a contract basis. If you can accomplish all of that, you stand a very good chance of building lasting relationships with product manufacturers. They'll depend on your flair and expertise to pull off challenging products. Your experience in design for manufacturability (i.e., designing products with the manufacturing team's constraints in mind) will be a valuable commodity among your clients. They appreciate working with professionals who understand that good design isn't just artistic; it's practical, too.

What You Need

You'll need to invest between $10,000–$20,000 in a high-end computer with a large monitor and a computer-aided design (CAD) software package. Mac computers are superior to PCs for designers. Since most of the people you might work with probably use Macs, compatibility issues can be minimized. Your advertising budget will be virtually nonexistent, because your area of expertise depends heavily on word of mouth. If you are successful in building the kinds of contacts you'll need to survive on your own, you'll be making anywhere from $50,000–$150,000 or more. Obviously if you're working for large, well-known manufacturers, your earnings will be on the high end because these companies are more apt to pay big bucks for quality design.

Keys to Success

Your work will not always be your own. Since you'll be working on a contract basis most of the time, you will often be brought in to solve design problems or pick up where another designer left off—not the biggest outlet for your creativity, but an opportunity to be a creative problem-solver nonetheless. The work is solid, it's demanding, and it's profitable for the talented.

Professional Organizer

Start-up cost:	$500–$1,000
Potential earnings:	$25,000–$45,000
Typical fees:	$25–$40 per hour
Advertising:	Write articles for your local newspapers on time management and/or organizing space; WelcomeWagon.com; direct mail coupons; conduct seminars through local community continuing education; network; a Web site with some free tips
Qualifications:	You must be a highly organized person by nature, with drive for efficiency; knowledge of systems, furniture, products, supplies and accessories are a must
Equipment needed:	Pager or cell phone, computer
Staff required:	No
Hidden costs:	Mileage, cell phone bills

What You Do

Most organizers specialize in at least one of five areas: space planning (organizing office arrangement of furniture, traffic, lighting, noise, and leisure space); time management (setting goals, developing action plans, scheduling, and delegating tasks); paper management (organizing the steady flow of information materials by setting up filing and retrieval systems, sometimes with the aid of a computer); clutter control (finding the proper and efficient placement for things to keep clutter to a minimum); closet/storage design (organizing closet and storage space). Choose one or two and market your services accordingly. This business would thrive in highly urban areas with busy professionals who want their home life to run as smoothly as the office. And it's much more fun to organize other people's lives than to run our own!

What You Need

You'll spend at least $500 or so on business cards for networking, but that's almost negligible considering that you'll be charging $25–$45 per hour for your expertise.

Keys to Success

Look into the National Association of Professional Organizers for more information. Hook up with an organization that conducts seminars, and offer your services as an instructor. This can supplement the income of your consulting service rather nicely.

Property Management Service

Start-up cost:	$3,000–$6,000
Potential earnings:	$25,000–$50,000
Typical fees:	$25 per hour or a monthly retainer of $500–$2,500
Advertising:	Classified ads, referrals, memberships in community and business real estate groups
Qualifications:	Experience in the field, related degree helpful, outstanding management skills, good ability to communicate and work with people, knowledge of basic bookkeeping, understanding of building maintenance issues
Equipment needed:	Office furniture, computer with Internet access, suite software and possibly specialized property management software, cell phone, printer, fax, business cards, letterhead, envelopes
Staff required:	No
Hidden costs:	Insurance

What You Do

This is the business for someone who likes juggling a thousand balls at one time, pulling many different pieces together, and keeping track of the people and data that go with the projects. If you're good, you'll become indispensable to the owners of the properties you manage, and you'll have a well-established enterprise that will keep you busy and well rewarded indefinitely. Why are good property managers so valuable? You maintain all the financial records for each property, which include income and expenses, bills, and taxes. Skill at auditing bills is extremely valuable just by itself. The ability to keep repair and maintenance schedules up to date is essential, so you will need to be able to pay great attention to detail and also have the people skills required for relating to the individuals who carry out the work on your buildings. Collecting rents is another central piece of this puzzle.

What You Need

Your own office needs to support you well, especially in communicating to building owners, repair personnel, and tenants. A cell phone will be handy as you travel from site to site. Your computer, which will cost around $3,000 to start, will be the tool used most for tracking all the financial information related to the properties. Depending on your location, you should make at least $25,000 annually.

Keys to Success

The owners of properties—your clients—will need to place great responsibility on your shoulders. Things can degenerate very quickly in a poorly managed building. Once the financial records become tangled, it can be very difficult to bring them into order or even to learn if the expenses are exceeding the income. You are asking your clients to have a large amount of confidence in you, and marketing these services successfully may depend on how well you can engender that sense of trust. It may be, however, that you will only need a few clients. This is one small business where constant marketing may not be necessary.

Public Pay Phone Service

Start-up cost:	$5,000–$10,000
Potential earnings:	$20,000–$30,000
Typical fees:	$50 a day for each telephone installed in high-traffic areas; $25–$30 per day in low-traffic areas
Advertising:	Flyers, bulletin boards, visible installation locations
Qualifications:	Communications technical skills, marketing ability
Equipment needed:	Pay phones, installation equipment
Staff required:	No
Hidden costs:	Insurance, repairs

What You Do

In many locations across the United States, it is extremely difficult to find a pay phone that actually works. Small businesses are finding this niche in the huge telecommunications market. If you have telephone-industry experience, you may be able to ride this trend and create a viable business enterprise as a means of supplemental income. An extremely refined marketing sense and skill at linking your callers to the network of major phone company services will define your ability to make a go of this. Some franchises are available.

To set up a public pay phone service, you need to first contact manufacturers of the phones to secure inventory. Equally important is your contact with the public utilities commission in your state. There may be regulations with which you will have to comply, so do your homework ahead of time.

Prepaid phone cards, which can be imprinted with an advertiser's information, are a related method of building business with a service like this one. For instance, many retail shops offer prepaid calling cards with their logo printed on the card; it's a good way for many companies to keep their name in front of their customers. You can market the same capability to companies, and then contract with a specialized card production house to finish the work.

What You Need

Costs may be relatively high for a small business, depending on the type and configuration of services you plan to offer. Plan to invest at least $5,000 in this start-up; and, if you decide to buy into a franchise, expect to pay an up-front fee of $10,000 or more. Earnings are dependent upon phone location and usage; prepaid phone cards generally retail for $5 and up.

Keys to Success

This business will allow you to express your marketing agility to the utmost extent. It can be a real high to play the game that most people think is available only to telecommunications giants. The risks are significant, though, and there are a large group of businesses out there offering alternative types of communication services, from pager services to online bulletin boards.

⩧ Public Relations Consultant

Start-up cost:	$5,000–$10,000
Potential earnings:	$35,000–$75,000
Typical fees:	$50–$75 per hour; a bid-per-job basis could range anywhere from $500–$15,000 or more; a monthly retainer would be in the range of $1,000–$5,000
Advertising:	Networking and personal contacts, speeches before business or community groups, volunteer work for nonprofit organizations, telemarketing, a high-end Web site with portfolio of client work and glowing testimonials
Qualifications:	Strong communication and telephone skills, assertiveness and persuasiveness, ability to deal effectively with abstract concepts, high energy level
Equipment needed:	Computer with Internet access, printer, fax, desktop publishing software, telephone headset, multiple phone lines with call-forwarding and conferencing features, office furniture, business cards, letterhead, envelopes, cell phone and subscriptions to online press release distribution and tracking services such as Bacons.com and PRNewswire.com

Staff required: No

Hidden costs: Slow starting time; expect two years before profit

What You Do

As with so many other fields, the demand for PR is growing. At the same time, corporations are cutting their public relations staffs down to a few good, but extremely overworked, people. Work is definitely being farmed out, so public relations is ideal for a home-based business. Relationships with clients take time to develop, though, and depend in part on your network of contacts in the media. When a small company has a breakthrough new product, when advertising is too expensive, when an organization needs to get its message across to the public, or when a negative situation occurs that needs a positive spin, your PR services can be invaluable. To attract media attention and interest, you will need outstanding writing and speaking skills, a healthy dose of creativity, awareness of what the different types of media (trade journals, the nightly news shows, and so on) are hungry for, and an ability to put all the pieces together. It's fun, yet tough to do well unless you're an animal at networking with influential media types.

What You Need

A very well-equipped office is a must, and you will need to present yourself and your business at the level of polish and professionalism you are selling for your clients. Expect to spend at least $4,000 on your office and equipment; bill at least $50–$75 per hour for your expertise. Don't forget to reserve some of your best PR work for yourself. Invest in some creatively produced collateral materials (brochure, business cards, and Web site).

Keys to Success

For creative, dynamic, and above all energetic people, public relations is a wonderful field. If you thrive on relationships with many different individuals and organizations and love the stimulation of constant change, you should consider making PR your business. As a solo practitioner, you'll start with small projects and gradually expand your network and contacts to take on more complex projects. Not everyone has the skills and attributes to make a success of PR, although many people are out there trying. You will need to produce results. Realize that your business will take tremendous time and effort to grow. Marketing your own services must be a priority even as you complete one project after another for your clients. Media representatives can be fickle; getting publicity for your clients will require new angles and ideas each time to catch the media's attention.

Publisher of Personalized Children's Books

Start-up cost:	$5,000–$15,000
Potential earnings:	$20,000–$40,000
Typical fees:	$15–$30 per book
Advertising:	Business card, bookstores, preschools, direct mail, flea markets
Qualifications:	Writing capability and computer aptitude
Equipment needed:	Computer with specialized layout and binding software/equipment, color laser or digital printer, digital camera
Staff required:	No
Hidden costs:	Editorial and design mistakes

What You Do

Customized picture books can brighten any kid's day. After all, what could be better for a kid than reading a story with his own name and photo throughout? With these picture books, kids can actually be a character in the book they are reading, and many parents are more than willing to pay money for such a personalized item. You'll produce books using one of a few templates, and then simply drop in the child's name and photo via computer. Then you'll print the books out on the laser printer, bind them, and package them up for your customers. You can get the word out by advertising in community newspapers. Or rent a mall kiosk during weekends or holidays to sell your services directly and in a place where you can produce products on the spot.

What You Need

Your prices will range from $15–$25, depending on the length of the book. There will be an initial investment around $10,000 for your basic equipment setup and paper stock. If you're not great at creating your own stories, you'll likely be buying into a franchise. Expect to shell out a franchising fee of $30,000–$50,000, but if you do, you may be thankful for the support and the ease of production that results from such an affiliation. You'll have to use mockups or prototypes to sell your services, so don't forget to include a few sample books in your start-up plan.

Keys to Success

This is a fun and entertaining venture. Who wouldn't love to make a child smile and get paid for doing it? The flipside of that is the frustration of working with difficult customers. It goes with the territory, since you'll likely be in a retail setting. Be prepared for little tantrums every once in a while.

Rare Book Dealer

Start-up cost:	$5,000–$10,000
Potential earnings:	$20,000–$40,000
Typical fees:	$10–$15 plus a percentage of sale on book (based on your markup)
Advertising:	Yellow Pages, book industry publications, networking with bookstore owners and managers, Web site, and banner ads on book club Web sites
Qualifications:	Good organizational skills and excellent follow-up ability
Equipment needed:	Computer with Internet access, printer, fax, phone with toll-free number
Staff required:	No
Hidden costs:	Internet service provider package, phone bills

What You Do

Some avid readers will go to extraordinary lengths to find a used or rare book that they'd relish having in their private collection. Whether you're providing this service in addition to running a bookstore (as many rare book specialists do) or running it as a separate business, you'll need to be highly detail-oriented and well organized to make this business profitable. The good news is, there are plenty of publications that you can subscribe to, and these provide monthly listings of what books are currently available through other dealers. Sometimes, you'll be lucky enough to work out an even trade (and maximize your own profit on the book you're selling to the customer). Most often, however, you'll derive your income from a search fee ($10–$15 in some areas) and a sales commission on the book itself, which you will have priced accordingly to suit your bank account's needs. The older and more rare the book, the harder it is to locate. But if you can manage to drum up one yellow-paged copy, your earnings could be quite high on just one book.

What You Need

It will take between $5,000–$10,000 to get started with your computer and online searches. Expect to spend $1,000 or so on advertising in your first year. If you are good at what you do, you could earn between $20,000 and $40,000 per year.

Keys to Success

The stress level is actually quite low in this field, and you can search for a book at your own pace for the most part. However, you don't get paid as much for looking as you do for finding. Sign on with Web-based services such as *www.abebooks.com* to expedite your searches as well as to automate your sales.

Real Estate Broker

Start-up cost:	$500–$1,000
Potential earnings:	$25,000–$100,000
Typical fees:	20 to 30 percent commission
Advertising:	Yellow Pages, memberships in local business and charitable organizations, local newspapers, Web site with link to Multiple Listing Service and a showcase area for your own current listings
Qualifications:	Real estate license
Equipment needed:	Cell phone, computer with Internet access, printer, fax, copier, business cards, letterhead, envelopes
Staff required:	No
Hidden costs:	Travel, marketing, subscription to online Multiple Listing Services, franchise fees

What You Do

As a property broker, you will be focusing on only one part of the residential real estate agent's job. You will be doing the basic research rather than carrying out the entire process through to closing. You will develop a range of choices based on the buyer interview. This gives the agent and the buyer an opportunity to plan, clarify wants and needs, and consider the financial implications. It is especially reassuring for families making transcontinental moves to know what choices are available to them within their price range, general preferences for neighborhood type, and so on. Your job, essentially, is to match your clients to their perfect home. You're different from a relocation specialist in that your territory is limited to your own immediate community. You provide information on the homes in your geographic area as opposed to helping clients relocate elsewhere around the country.

What You Need

Start-up costs could be as low as $500, but marketing efforts will be ongoing unless referrals or subcontracting can bring you adequate business. You could earn $25,000 to $100,000 annually.

Keys to Success

You will need to continuously prove that your services add value and don't threaten other agents but rather augment their services. Keeping good records of your effectiveness will support your marketing efforts. Projecting an enthusiasm for your local area, its different communities, and its varied attractions, will enhance your work. This is a good choice for someone who loves houses and enjoys thinking about what type of family would choose each one, but who finds the sale process unappealing. Not everyone wants to spend all weekend showing picky buyers house after house, only to see the sale evaporate. Acting essentially as a home researcher, you can create a service that suits you as well as it does your clients. You will send them links to online photos and tours of homes in their price range, and then connect them with either the listing agent or the Realtor of their choice.

Relocation Consultant

Start-up cost:	$3,000–$6,000
Potential earnings:	$20,000–$45,000
Typical fees:	$25–$35 per hour
Advertising:	Trade publications, networking, memberships in real estate and general business organizations, Web site, banner ads on Web sites for human resource professionals
Qualifications:	Real estate experience; knowledge of your area's neighborhoods, attractions, amenities, schools
Equipment needed:	Office furniture, computer with Internet access, printer, fax, business cards, letterhead, envelopes
Staff required:	No
Hidden costs:	Phone bills, membership dues, entertaining clients

What You Do

Your ideal market will be companies that do some relocations but are too small to provide much assistance in-house to the executives they are transferring to your community. Moving is a challenging experience for almost all families, and enlightened employers will see the value of your assistance in making the transition go as smoothly as possible. You will provide advice as the transferees begin to make decisions: What neighborhood will we like best? Where can we find elder-care or child-care? What sports are played at local high schools? Can we find a house with enough land for trail riding? You work with the employees before they are ready to choose a real estate agent.

What You Need

Equipping your office will be the main expense (about $3,000). You will do some work by e-mail and fax, but most of your time will probably be spent driving to the different areas of your city or having a restaurant meal with a transferee. Bring a cell phone everywhere you go. Annual wages of $20,000–$45,000 can be expected.

Keys to Success

You're doing two kinds of marketing here. First for your own service and second for your community. Many organizations use relocation consultants to help persuade a prospective employee to take the job with that company. How the prospect and his family feel about moving to your area can be a major factor. Your services can offer an unprejudiced look at what the locality has to offer. Hospitals recruiting a certain physician and companies recruiting someone for an upper-management position will both value your service highly.

Repair Services

Start-up cost:	$350–$500
Potential earnings:	$25,000–$45,000
Typical fees:	$25 per hour or quote per job
Advertising:	Yellow Pages, community newspapers, coupon books, bulletin boards
Qualifications:	Trade school may be necessary for electronics repair, but otherwise just the ability to fix things
Equipment needed:	A well-stocked toolbox, cell phone, van
Staff required:	No
Hidden costs:	Possibly liability insurance; while it can cost some money, it can also help protect your own assets should a repair fail and a lawsuit arise

What You Do

Do you have a knack for fixing things around the house—a TV, stereo, computer or even lawn care equipment? If so, you can easily launch your own repair service. You can get your start by offering to fix a few items at no charge for your family, friends, and neighbors, in exchange for their testimonials about your talent for repair. Then put together a nice-looking but simple flyer advertising your services to a larger community group via direct mail or posting on bulletin boards. If you want to partner with others who specialize in different types of repair, you can band together and form your own handyman network. Either way, this is an easy business to break into with little risk. So break out the toolbox and get busy!

What You Need

Elbow grease and a good set of tools are all you'll need in the beginning. Once you start handling several repairs at once, you might invest in a tool bench (or build one yourself). For as little as $350, you can get a repair business off the ground and off to a terrific start if you are a talented fixer-upper.

Keys to Success

Start small, and then build your confidence as well as your clientele by promoting your business through a track record of fast, economical service. Referrals will truly bring you the most new business, but once you have several jobs under your belt you can start to do a little advertising in community newspapers and the Yellow Pages.

Resume Service

Start-up cost:	$1,000–$5,000
Potential earnings:	$20,000–$50,000
Typical fees:	$150–$500 per resume (depending on location)
Advertising:	Yellow Pages, newspaper classifieds, Web site with testimonials, banner ads on job-search Web sites and career boards
Qualifications:	Writing ability, attention to important detail, strong organizational ability
Equipment needed:	Computer with Internet access, printer, fax, paper, extra computer disks or CDs
Staff required:	No
Hidden costs:	Insurance, spending too much time with one client

What You Do

To get a job in a competitive marketplace, people simply must have a dynamic resume. Those who really want to put their best foot forward will come to you for a resume and cover letter that looks professional. Since many of your customers may not have the time or patience to post their resumes in multiple places at once, they may also pay you to do so for them. Regardless, your days will be spent meeting with a wide variety of clients from all walks of life (from foundry supervisors to attorneys), writing down specific job histories, and adding pertinent skill information that will get your clients those sought-after interviews. It's a time-consuming job, but it gets easier with experience. You can add value (and income) with additional services such as cover, follow-up, and referral letters.

What You Need

Your start-up is relatively low ($1,000–$5,000) because all you really need is a good computer setup and a small advertising budget to get the word out. You can expect to earn $20,000 or so in most medium-size markets; in New York City and other large metropolitan areas, you'll be charging much more for your services (up to $500) and could easily make $50,000 per year. But remember—you can do this work over the phone and via the Internet, so the sky is the limit for your customer base.

Keys to Success

If you're a writer, this is an easy way to make a living (or earn an additional income to support your quest for the Great American Novel). However, you do need to enjoy working with people. They will hound you day and night until their project is finished, and possibly even afterward. If you don't like to be hounded, stick to novel writing.

Expert Advice

What sets your business apart from others like it?

Katina Z. Jones has a nontraditional resume service called Going Places Self-Promotions, Inc., in Akron, Ohio. She says that her business is unique because it breaks many of the traditional rules of resume writing. "We do resumes that are not only eye-catching, but also go beyond providing a mere rundown of a client's job history. We like to add a sense of not only what a person has accomplished in her career, but also who she is and how she might fit into an organization. We have a 98 percent success rate in helping clients secure interviews because of that personalized approach."

Things you couldn't do without

"I couldn't do without my computer, laser printer, phone, pager, and fax. My clients want fairly quick turnaround, and these items help me to accomplish that. Also, I need to have plenty of paper catalogs on hand, as I use a ton of specialty preprinted stationery on which to produce resumes."

Marketing tips

"Set yourself apart from the people who are glorified typists . . . recognize that the resume industry is changing rapidly, and the resumes of the past (with cookie-cutter objectives and meaningless buzzwords) are just not getting people results anymore. After you have your niche, network like crazy. Anywhere you go, introduce yourself; you're bound to meet someone who either needs a resume or knows someone who does."

If you had to do it all over again . . .

"I would have started networking much sooner and would also have put together a more meaningful marketing plan. I don't think I strategized nearly enough in the beginning."

Retirement Planner

Start-up cost:	$1,000–$2,000
Potential earnings:	$20,000–$40,000
Typical fees:	$150–$1,000 (depending on scope of project)
Advertising:	Newspapers, publications of local interest groups, membership in community organizations, word of mouth, direct mail, Web site with retirement planning tips and links to related resources
Qualifications:	Expertise in financial planning; certification helpful; experience or a degree in finance or a related field
Equipment needed:	Computer, printer, fax, cell phone, copier, marketing materials, business cards, letterhead, envelopes
Staff required:	No
Hidden costs:	Conferences for continuing education

What You Do

Retirement planners are finding a rising demand for their services, due to widespread fears about the future of Social Security. You will be distinguishing yourself from the hundreds of financial planners searching for customers in every community by your focus on this one vital piece of the financial puzzle. As with lawyers, accountants, and other professionals who operate as small businesses, your challenge will be to gain the confidence of your clients so that they prefer your excellent personal service over the security of dealing with a large institutional business that claims to offer the same type of benefits. You'll sell them on how meticulous you are at developing financial strategies tailored to their own unique financial situations instead of a grid in a book. You'll take a good look at their plans for retirement and work out a sensible budget based on that information. You may also suggest financial products or options, such as mutual funds.

What You Need

You just need adequate materials, costing about $1,000, to present the image of reliability that will make people feel confident in your knowledge and expertise.

A Web site that's plentiful with links and resources will also help position you as knowledgeable in your field. Don't spend too much on furniture and desks because you will be travel to your clients' homes and other meeting sites most of the time.

Keys to Success

Retirement services is a tough sell. While almost everyone needs them, people are afraid to contemplate the reality that they should be saving more, spending less, and keeping to a budget. Your hook for this market may be to find a way to send a reassuring message that it is possible to plan responsibly for retirement without taking all the fun out of today.

Reunion Organizer

Start-up cost:	$2,000–$3,000
Potential earnings:	$15,000–$50,000
Typical fees:	$5–$10 for each classmate who attends
Advertising:	Word of mouth and prospect calling on schools for their referrals to alumni organizations, banner ads on Web sites like Classmates.com
Qualifications:	A big network of friends and acquaintances in your community, patience, determination, organizational ability
Equipment needed:	Cell phone, computer with Internet access, database and suite software, fax, copier, office furniture, business cards, letterhead, envelopes
Staff required:	No
Hidden costs:	Phone calls

What You Do

Reunions have always been popular, since virtually everyone wants to find out how former classmates have fared over the years since graduation. High school reunions are a major focus of this business and finding the "lost" members is an important part of the process. Your persistence and sheer determination need to be applied to the search process, which usually starts one year before the event. Former employees of some organizations also occasionally hold reunions, and there is a niche market in putting together reunions for today's far-flung families. Once you discover everybody's whereabouts, you may turn your attention to the event itself, arranging the catering, photos, band, decorations, and mementos.

What You Need

Basic office equipment ($2,000–$3,000) should get you started, but you will need to get the database program ($175–$300) as soon as possible. Set your charges differently for the time involved and the number of people you're expected to locate. Many charge between $5–$10 per attendee, but others charge a flat rate commensurate with an hourly fee of $10–$15 per hour.

Keys to Success

Most communities are excellent markets for this service, but many people don't know that it exists. Consider the organizations and groups in your locale that have reunions, such as schools and colleges. Do one excellent job to get a foothold, and you will find that the referrals will begin to roll in. Your success will depend to some extent on the material and information you have to work with, but once you refine your people-searching skills, you should have a service to offer that can't be matched by amateurs. One tip: Online phone books or the new telephone directories on disk or CD-ROM can help you locate nearly anyone in the country.

⫢ Roommate Referral Service

Start-up cost:	$500–$1,000
Potential earnings:	$10,000–$25,000
Typical fees:	20 to 50 percent of a month's rent
Advertising:	Yellow Pages, flyers at apartment complexes, Laundromats, supermarkets, newspaper classified ads, Web site with current listings and banner ads from related services
Qualifications:	Excellent organization skills
Equipment needed:	Database management software, computer with Internet access, printer, phone, credit card processing equipment
Staff required:	No
Hidden costs:	Insurance

What You Do

With the rising cost of living in many major cities and the rise in displaced folks who need to share rent (divorced people, students, and those who need temporary living arrangements) you could make a fine living playing matchmaker for live-ins. Ideally, you would have a method for screening each of the candidates (police checks at the very least) and a method for securing your payment ahead of time (credit card processing equipment would be helpful). Advertise in places where people generally look for a place to live, and you'll have found your special niche. Develop a good questionnaire that asks the kinds of questions a potential roommate would want answered. To double your income potential, you could add on other services such as mediation between rumblin' roomies or budget development assistance. The best advice is to focus on one area first, then branch out your services as you move successfully along.

What You Need

Your costs are incredibly low when compared to most other businesses, mainly because you can create your own flyers to post in noticeable, highly trafficked areas. You can also purchase classified ads in community and university newspapers, as well as post online on sites such as www.craigslist.com. You can also build and maintain a Web site of your own, or pay to have one that attracts roommate-seekers. Even though your income potential is on the lower end of the spectrum, so is your overhead; most of your income is sheer profit. For this reason, a roommate referral service would make a fine part-time supplemental income opportunity.

Keys to Success

The only advice is to be sure you carefully screen your applicants—bad matches are sure to strike you if you don't. You could always organize your Web site so that roommates choose each other based on profiles they enter on your site.

Rubber Stamp Business

Start-up cost:	$5,000–$15,000
Potential earnings:	$40,000–$60,000
Typical fees:	$5–$15 per stamp
Advertising:	Mail order, direct mail, newspapers
Qualifications:	Training by a printing professional
Equipment needed:	Computer with laser printer, photopolymer system (you can subcontract the larger orders that need to be made of rubber)
Staff required:	No
Hidden costs:	Materials can run high (as much as $1,000 per year)

What You Do

The rubber stamp business gets the stamp of approval from many experts on entrepreneurship. Why? Because it's a relatively easy way to make steady money from a simple product. The variety of stamps you can produce is mind-boggling. Think of the last time you went into a retail store and saw literally hundreds of choices, from frogs and stars to computers. Now think of the possibilities in the business world. Small businesses need to have return address stamps because they're cheaper in the long haul than labels and more readily available. You can sell wholesale, retail, or mail order with this business. Expect to generate immediate interest if you introduce your company with introductory specials and discounts for new customers. You'll work with printers and graphics people who can provide you with all the background and technical information you need. So what is to lose from a product line so easy to produce?

What You Need

You'll need to invest in some equipment ($3,000–$5,000) at the outset. If you're buying a franchise version of this business, which could provide you with all the training you'll need, expect to spend another $10,000 minimum on licensing fees. Since you'll be marketing your inexpensive product to the masses for $5 to $15 each, you stand a good chance of making a go of this one.

Keys to Success

The investment's not too high and the income potential is great. What more could you ask?

⊊ Sales of Novelty and Promotional Products

Start-up cost:	$1,000–$5,000
Potential earnings:	$30,000–$60,000
Typical fees:	$3–$300 per product
Advertising:	Trade publications, business periodicals, direct mail, catalogs, Web site with e-commerce capability
Qualifications:	Sales ability
Equipment needed:	Computer with high-speed Internet access, suite software, fax, laser printer, business cards, letterhead, envelopes, marketing materials
Staff required:	Probably
Hidden costs:	Inventory, reprinting of catalogs and other sales materials

What You Do

This is the business for you if you know what will amuse people (namely, your clients' customers) and catch their attention. You are providing a facet that is essential to every business: marketing. Novelties and promotional materials put the name and message of a business before the public. They can be an enormously effective way of reaching out to customers. In this business, you are far more than just a writer of orders. You present ideas for the new and different. Promotional materials can take many forms, and fitting the object to the message takes a special kind of marketing insight. You'll need to have an enthusiasm for sales and marketing in your blood. You need to be as creative and offbeat as possible to attract the attention of companies who want to attract attention to themselves.

What You Need

Your relationship with your distributor will determine your need for inventory, which ideally will be kept to a minimum. Demonstration samples and catalogs may be quite expensive, though. Try to secure a good arrangement with your manufacturers and their reps before trying to produce your own. You can earn a living selling these types of products. Just look at how well companies such as Successories are doing, and you'll know that the market is there.

Keys to Success

Your devotion to the needs of your clients will make you stand out from the crowd. There is quite a lot of competition in this field, but many of the other businesses just throw a catalog at prospects and expect them to do the creative work. You, on the other hand, develop a presentation focused on each client's distinctive needs and expectations. You give them several appealing options, and you carry out the detailed ordering and delivery process. It is work, but it's also fun.

EXPERT ADVICE

What sets your business apart from others like it?

"We have not only created a specialty product, but something that has a life and character all its own," says Mark Juarez, President and CEO of Tender Loving Things, Inc., in Oakland, California, which produces tiny wooden creatures with massage capability.

Things you couldn't do without

"Birch or maple wood, drilling machine, glue, smiley-face brander, and office equipment to run shipping, production, art, marketing, customer service, and administrative departments."

Marketing tips
"We turn profits into social responsibility; we donate 10 percent of our product to nonprofit organizations and other groups that might benefit from the caring touch."

If you had to do it all over again . . .
"One of our biggest external challenges has been combating knockoffs and copycats." Juarez suggests protecting yourself as early as possible within federal trademark regulations.

Sales Representative

Start-up cost:	$1,000–$3,000
Potential earnings:	$20,000–$50,000+
Typical fees:	Percentage basis
Advertising:	Word of mouth, direct mail, cold calling, Web site that includes your success stories and testimonials
Qualifications:	Energy, persistence, ability to manage time well
Equipment needed:	Computer, fax, cell phone (hands-free accessories would be best, since you'll be on the road a lot)
Staff required:	No
Hidden costs:	Catalogs and other sales materials for which some of your clients may charge, traveling to meetings, inventory replacement

What You Do
Many people try their hand at direct sales, yet only a few of them make it big. What's the difference? Consider your goals. Do you want to make a few bucks and sell a line of products you like to family, friends, and acquaintances? Is your main goal to make your own purchases at a discount? Or are you planning to put the effort and commitment into direct sales that you would into establishing any other type of small business? Many products are best sold person-to-person because they benefit from demonstration. Finding an excellent product line to work with is vital, and you should feel confident in the company as well. The rest is up to your selling skills and personal drive. Some companies encourage their salespeople to create networks of additional salespeople whose sales then bring a percentage to the person who recruited them. This practice acts as an incentive to everyone in the sales force. It is one way to large earnings, if you can achieve it.

What You Need

Expenses in the beginning are very low (around $1,000), but watch out for hidden charges and fees from the manufacturers. These should warn you off the companies that might exploit you. An income of $20,000 in the beginning is realistic.

Keys to Success

How many opportunities are left in this country in which your own hard work will define your success? Direct sales is one of them. Are you comfortable with cold calling? Are you committed enough to keep yourself going with no one to answer to but yourself? Do you genuinely like people and enjoy helping them find products that will add something to their lives or businesses? Or, on the other hand, would you be satisfied with direct sales as an add-on to some other activity? Be sure you're clear on what you want and what you will need to do to achieve it. If you have big ambitions, you'll need a very big commitment to achieve them in direct marketing and sales.

Sales Trainer

Start-up cost:	$500–$2,500 (for spinoff products, add another $5,000–$15,000)
Potential earnings:	$80,000–$150,000+
Typical fees:	$125–$150 per hour plus travel expenses
Advertising:	Professional sales associations, networking, advertising in local business publications
Qualifications:	Sales training or teaching experience
Equipment needed:	Computer, printer, fax, high-speed Internet access, cell phone
Staff required:	No
Hidden costs:	Liability insurance, travel expenses not covered by client, incentives to help secure new clients (CDs, books, consulting time, or other business-building freebies)

What You Do

If you have a knack for inspiring and motivating others, in addition to a sales or marketing background, becoming a sales trainer could be a fun and profitable business option for you. You will travel all over the country offering high-paying workshops, seminars, and keynote speeches that energize sales professionals and motivate them to peak performance. Once you become better known for your motivational abilities, you will see that the largest part of your job is actually marketing your own best product—yourself—to other companies who might sponsor your seminars. Keeping the calendar full will insure that the money keeps rolling in, so don't forget to get testimonials from each gig in order to continually gain more interest in your services. Forget the tired buzzwords of the past. Develop your own formula for sales success, and you can make yourself a valued resource among thousands of sales professionals everywhere.

What You Need

Most sales trainers have also written books and produced a variety of spinoff products such as cassette tapes, CDs, DVDs, or videos. Expect to spend between $1,000 and $5,000 for marketing materials, including brochures, business cards, and a Web site that is as dynamic as you are. Aside from your self-promotion tools, you really don't need more than charisma and tenacity to get a business like this off the ground.

Keys to Success

In this business, reputation is everything. Inspiring others to reach for their best is a noble profession, but it can only be successful if you constantly promote yourself to more prospects. Having a complete portfolio of "spinoff" incentive products like books, CDs and self-assessments on your Web site is one way to keep customers coming back—and the money streaming in.

Seamstress

Start-up cost:	$500–$1,000
Potential earnings:	$20,000–$40,000
Typical fees:	$5–$75+ per item
Advertising:	Newspapers, bulletin boards, fashion shows
Qualifications:	The ability to create fashions and apparel without patterns would be useful
Equipment needed:	Sewing machine, materials
Staff required:	No
Hidden costs:	Remakes could take up more than an inch of your time

What You Do

If all you need is a needle and thread to design a business you feel comfortable in, then the alterations/sewing business is a perfect match. In this recession-proof business, you will repair or alter your customers' clothing, but you can also offer custom-sewn clothing to busy executives who appreciate fine threads designed expressly for them. Creativity and the desire to make good clothes even better are the only requirements you'll need, and the higher the quality of your work, the more people will hear about your service. Word of mouth is nearly always the best way to grow the alterations business, although you may want to consider posting your business card on all the bulletin boards you can find in your community. Also, leave some extra cards for owners of dress shops, who often refer their customers to good tailors or seamstresses.

What You Need

Your biggest up-front expense will be a good sewing machine, which will cost $1,000 or more. You might look into buying a used commercial sewing machine, because they are more durable and can be purchased for as little as $400. Be sure to invest in a healthy amount of professional-looking business cards, because you'll need a lot of them to spread the word about your service. Use a rate card to keep track of what you're charging per job. Some alterations are simple and inexpensive, ranging from $5 to $10, while others are time-intensive and require you to charge $75 or more.

Keys to Success

If you like to spend much of the workday by yourself, you'll love this type of work. However, the hours can be long and the rewards not as frequent as you might like. Sewing is tedious work except to those who truly enjoy it, so make sure that you enjoy it enough to spend 65 percent of your workday doing it.

⫶ Secretarial Service

Start-up cost:	$3,000–$5,000
Potential earnings:	$20,000–$40,000
Typical fees:	$10–$20 per hour (depending on size of the company you're working for)
Advertising:	Classified ads, Yellow Pages, phone contacts
Qualifications:	Good editorial, typing, and clerical skills
Equipment needed:	Computer, high-speed Internet access, fax
Staff required:	No
Hidden costs:	None

What You Do

The executive stretches in his chair, puts his feet up on his desk, and calls for his secretary . . . only, he's likely to be kept waiting because he's sharing with ten others who are already in line with their requests. The old days when everyone had a personal secretary are gone; many functions have been replaced by small secretarial pools or computers. But the need for personalized service has not gone away. Often a beleaguered company, its small administrative force stretched to the max, needs to farm out work. That is where you come in. You can assist them for a short period of time, typing letters or producing manuals that would simply be too costly to employ a full-timer with benefits to do. Training and/or experience as a secretary will help you understand the types of skills that you need (dictation, shorthand, filing, and form typing are just a few) and who might want your services. There is a lot of flexibility possible with this type of business. You could handle after-hours work for out-of-towners, temporary fill-ins for local companies, contracting overflow, and so on.

What You Need

A computer is the recommended choice for running a secretarial service since it has greater versatility and a variety of available programs (compatible, of course, with your client's). Plus, you can work efficiently with your clients via the Internet. Computers will cost anywhere from $1,000–$3,000. Buying a used or a factory refinished computer only a year or two old will help keep start-up costs down. Advertising in the Yellow Pages for $50–$100 per month, in the classifieds for $10 per week, and leaving flyers at hotels where businesspeople from out-of-town might need some help are some easy, inexpensive ways to get word out about the services being offered. Remember, the amount of time it will take to finish one assignment will vary and is generally unknown at the start, so charging an hourly fee of $10–$15 will prove more profitable than working for a set price per task.

Keys to Success

Since it's likely that this job will involve working with many different people, tolerance of personality quirks will make jobs—and time—go more quickly and smoothly. The hours will be varied, which could become stressful for you (and your bank account) at times. This business needs a high-energy, go-getter type of person. Do you have what it takes?

EXPERT ADVICE

What sets your business apart from others like it?

"I'm incredibly fast, accurate, and affordable," says Jana McClish, owner of Paragon Word Services in Akron, Ohio. "I can offer a quicker turnaround than most of my competitors."

Things you couldn't do without

McClish needs a computer, answering machine, and a 10-key adding machine to run her business effectively.

Marketing tips

"You have to be persistent and market almost constantly. You must be confident and be able to sell that confidence in order to get in the door. You really need to have a special skill that sets you apart, too."

If you had to do it all over again . . .

"I'd research my equipment purchases better. I needed to buy new equipment a year and a half into my business because I did not purchase wisely. Also, I would've started with a much bigger base of prospects . . . I was discouraged in the beginning because I didn't have huge amounts of work."

Seminar Service

Start-up cost:	$5,000–$10,000
Potential earnings:	$30,000–$50,000
Typical fees:	$125–$500 per speaking engagement; service earns 25–40 percent of this
Advertising:	Press releases to newspapers, radio, business/civic organizations, a well-produced Web site that includes streaming audio or video clips from previous seminars that you've produced
Qualifications:	Managerial and marketing skills, expertise in planning and promotion
Equipment needed:	Computer, printer, tape recorder, transcription equipment, business cards, letterhead, envelopes
Staff required:	No
Hidden costs:	Transcriptions and tape reproduction

What You Do

If you have a sense of what trends are catching the attention of the public, you may be able to create a business by arranging for speakers on these topics. If you can organize appealing seminars and publicize them effectively, you can make a good living in this area. You can make some of the presentations yourself, but in order to be very successful you will need to have a list of speakers available who can make amusing or captivating presentations that stay with the audience long after they leave the meeting. Enjoyable seminars have a sense of give and take, with a lively speaker and active participation from the audience. These satisfied customers will be your best advertising; they will return with their friends for future sessions. An add-on business is sales of presentation tapes or transcripts. If you are a bit of a showman yourself and have good event planning skills, this business may be expressly for you.

What You Need

Each seminar requires extensive planning and advertising. You will need a computer ($1,500–$2,500) to prepare materials and flyers and to keep track of your database of effective speakers and satisfied customers. Invest in a Web site that showcases your best speakers via streaming audio or video clips. Mailings will cost you $500 and up for each event. Your speakers can earn $125–$500 or more for each speech they deliver, and your percentage of that could be as low as 25 percent and as high as 40 percent.

Keys to Success

Bringing together a group of people for an enjoyable seminar is almost like putting on a play. There is a sense of excitement when a presentation goes well. You can get satisfaction from enabling people to learn something they need or want to know. You are also providing a service to your speakers, who rely on you to organize and support their work. Not all seminars are well attended, though. You may have chosen the wrong topic or bad weather may interfere with the success of the meeting. It takes a very detail-oriented person to make all the pieces come together in a business like this one.

⟰ Silk Flower Arranger

Start-up cost:	$500–$1,000
Potential earnings:	$20,000–$40,000
Typical fees:	$25–$300
Advertising:	Yellow Pages, newspapers, bridal salons, restaurants
Qualifications:	Some training with flower arranging, creativity
Equipment needed:	Phone, floral accessories (vases, baskets, floral tape, access to a wide variety of silk flowers)
Staff required:	No
Hidden costs:	Materials

What You Do

There's nothing in the world like fresh flowers, but they only last a short while. That is why silk flowers are the mainstays of interior decorating. All you have to do is dust them every once in a while and they retain their beauty forever. You'll always have plenty of customers if you choose to work in this field, from brides who don't want to worry about wilting flowers to mourners who want to give the bereaved family a lasting token of their remembrance. You'll work many hours in your office, putting together the arrangements that have been ordered by your customers. The only problem is that you'll have to work hard to get customers, since there are plenty of others in this business. Think about what makes you different, and let your customers know exactly what your unique marketing point is. Finally, network with funeral homes, churches, and wedding shops for cross-marketing opportunities.

What You Need

Obtain a vendor's license (approximately $25) and buy your supplies at a wholesale store. Check with local craft stores to see if they offer additional discounts if you have a vendor's license. When starting the business, invest a few hundred dollars in floral supplies and silk flowers so you can make arrangements to sell at craft shows. Also, set aside money for booth space rental ($25–$100). Your products will sell anywhere from $25–$300.

Keys to Success

Gain experience by working with florists or taking classes at craft stores. Once you have some knowledge of floral arranging, sign up to sell your goods at holiday craft fairs. Always have plenty of business cards/brochures to accompany each sale, and keep an album with pictures of your work to show potential clients.

Small Business Consultant

Start-up cost:	$5,000–$15,000
Potential earnings:	$50,000–$150,000
Typical fees:	$900–$2,000 per day
Advertising:	Word of mouth, presentations made to business groups, audio-visual materials, professional organizations, Web site with tips for small business owners
Qualifications:	Experience and expertise in marketing, management sense, communication skills, research and planning ability

Equipment needed: Office furniture, computer with Internet access, suite software, printer, fax, business cards, letterhead, envelopes

Staff required: No

Hidden costs: Make sure you get paid ASAP, as many of your clients who launch small businesses have little money to begin with

What You Do

As a small business consultant, you are the one with the knowledge and expertise to assess and solve many of the difficulties facing today's small businesses. Between complying with growing government regulations, integrating new technologies, and competing in a tightening economy, most small businesses are looking for consultants who have proved their ability to solve problems. This position offers variety, challenge, and respect.

What You Need

A sizable time investment and at least $5,000 are necessary to identify and approach your clients. Do research, send letters, and do lunch. Build a Web site that is well visited because of the great information it offers small business owners. Look for ways to add more value to your services by partnering with related businesses. If you work at it, you should make at least $50,000 your first year.

Keys to Success

You must know what you are talking about at all times. While you are selling your experience, companies are buying concrete solutions to their problems. Be able to apply your skills to your own business as well as to your clients'.

Standardized Test Preparatory Services

Start-up cost: $1,000–$5,000

Potential earnings: $30,000–$45,000

Typical fees: $75–$175 per client

Advertising: Yellow Pages, direct mail to students/parents, Web site that offers study tips and links to related resources

Qualifications: Familiarity with all standardized tests (including SAT, ACT, GED, LSAT), teaching degree helpful and required in some states

Equipment needed: Practice tests, pencils, timers, computer with high-speed Internet access

Staff required: No

Hidden costs: Insurance

What You Do

Thousands of students each year must take standard tests for entry into college, and they usually must spend weeks preparing for these all-encompassing tests. There are sections on math and language usage in most of these tests, and you can help students prepare for each by answering their questions and presenting them with similar questions or problems as practice guides. Perhaps you'll choose to work with a more specialized test such as the LSAT, which people must pass before being accepted to law school. Whatever area you choose to specialize in, you'll need to work with groups of students at one time to make it truly profitable.

What You Need

Your start-up costs will be relatively low, because you'll only need some workbooks, pencils, and timers. Since your clients will be paying up front for your services, you don't have to worry about maintaining an inventory prior to accepting clients. It would be great, if you already own a computer, to create your own Web site and give it some value with free study tips and links to related resources. You may have to spend $35 or so per session on space rental; check with local schools for their after-hour rates. At $75–$175 per student, you can easily see an income potential of $30,000–$45,000.

Keys to Success

If you enjoy repetition, this could be a relaxing and comfortable way to make a living. All you have to do is provide the same services over and over, and collect your checks as you do. On the other hand, it could become too repetitious, and therefore less challenging than most entrepreneurs would like. You decide what your comfort level is.

⨎ Stock Photography Service

Start-up cost: $500–$10,000

Potential earnings: $25,000–$150,000+

Typical fees: $25–$250 per customer/per photo/per use (10–15 percent of each sale goes to photographer whose shot has been purchased)

Advertising:	Search engine advertising, reciprocal banner ads with related businesses (such as printers), business and graphics trade publications; a more expensive option that might be worth it is advertising in four-color, hardbound stock photography books sent directly to a mailing list of good prospects
Qualifications:	Photography and digital image editing experience would be helpful
Equipment needed:	Computer, digital camera, photo editing software
Staff required:	No
Hidden costs:	Constant maintenance of Web site (can save significantly if you learn to do this yourself), burning and shipping of CD photo discs

What You Do

A growing number of advertising agencies and corporations are using desktop publishing technology to develop marketing collaterals, print advertising, and Web graphics that promote products and services in a variety of creative ways. One necessary ingredient is economical, ready-to-use, high-quality photography that stands apart from all the tired old clip art out there. A stock photography company can provide these clients with 24/7 online access to an extensive portfolio of great photographs for use in their marketing materials. Whatever your clients' subject matter, you will network with several photographers to build a keyword-searchable archive containing as many varied shots as possible—all at reasonable enough one-time usage fees to make a decent amount of money for both you and your "stable" of photographers. If you are adept at securing interesting, high-quality work and willing to offer it at a reasonable price, you can make a lot of money over and over again from work that is basically done once.

What You Need

To offer stock photography services, you will most definitely need a powerful graphics-oriented computer system with a high-resolution screen on a larger monitor. Most designers use Macs. This kind of system, with photo-editing software such as Adobe PhotoShop, will cost you anywhere from $3,500 to $5,000. Your Web site will cost you another $500 to $1,500 per year to build, host and maintain. Since photographers can e-mail you .jpgs, if the images are small enough, your postage costs will be relatively low unless photographers or customers insist on burning CDs. Just in case, plan ahead for this hidden cost.

Keys to Success

This is a excellent way to get student work out there for mass consumption by agencies and corporations. If you're near a university, you may want to network with students to include their work at a fraction of what it might cost you to represent experienced photographers.

Systems Integrator

Start-up cost:	$1,000–$5,000
Potential earnings:	$37,500–$100,000
Typical fees:	$150+ per hour
Advertising:	Direct mail, publications, networking, Web site
Qualifications:	Technical knowledge and expertise in systems; time-management skills
Equipment needed:	Computer with high-speed Internet access, software, fax, office furniture, letterhead, envelopes, cell phone
Staff required:	No, but subcontracting may be required depending on project needs
Hidden costs:	Time and expense of staying current in this demanding field

What You Do

Computers are wonderful business tools; few organizations can begin to operate without them today. Yet no one would disagree with the premise that the design and planning of computers, both hardware and software, has a long way to go. Operations and compatibility problems are enormous, and as businesses grow, they must resolve issues related to the necessary growth in their information systems. If you have the expertise to be a systems integrator, nearly every growing company in the United States, possibly the world, needs your services. One successful project should enable you to easily move on to another. You will need some people skills to work with the information systems staff at your clients' offices.

What You Need

Most of your work will be carried out at your clients' premises and on their equipment, so you needn't spend too much on your own office and equipment. A cell phone would be ideal for handling computer emergencies while on the road. Keep in mind that you'll need to be familiar with many different types of equipment, some of which you'll own and some of which you can lease. You'll need to be billing at a rate of at least $100 per hour.

Keys to Success

Many businesses need your service, so if you live within commuting distance of an urban area, you ought to be able to create an excellent and profitable business of your own as a systems integrator. A long-term commitment to a single client, necessary to complete most projects in this field, can limit your contacts. But it should provide you with an excellent referral base. This is an extremely challenging field; however, one problem is that the people making the decision to hire you often have little understanding of what their information system needs. Education, then, is a major part of each sales effort. Systems integration is often carried out under high pressure. Bidding jobs is challenging as well.

Tax Preparation Service

Start-up cost:	$5,500–$15,000
Potential earnings:	$40,000–$100,000
Typical fees:	$25–$50 per hour; more if complex
Advertising:	Referrals, networking, ads in local publications and Yellow Pages, direct mail
Qualifications:	An interest in people and their situations, patience, excellent math skills, thorough understanding of tax laws and calculations; CPA certification helpful but not mandatory
Equipment needed:	Computer, phone, high-speed Internet access, fax, office equipment (including copier), specialized tax software, reference manuals, business cards
Staff required:	None
Hidden costs:	Time and money for continuing education, if needed

What You Do

Income tax regulations and their associated forms are often too complicated for the average person to comprehend. Making heads or tails of tax forms, then, is a much-needed service and one that people often don't mind paying for (remind them that income tax preparation fees are tax-deductible, and you'll sell them even more on your service). You obviously need to have a thorough knowledge of tax law, tax preparation, and related forms to succeed, but you don't need to study for a license unless you want certification as a CPA or other designation. This is complicated, detailed work; our tax laws are cumbersome and confusing. It would be quite beneficial to take a training course before you begin. This would not only ensure that your skills are adequate, but would give you a feel for whether this work is for you. Tax preparation can earn a talented, detail-oriented business owner a very nice income.

What You Need

Detailed tax guides, special software, errors and omissions insurance, a good quality printer and copier, and the usual computer and office equipment will be required. You may be saving some ink and paper by e-filing, but you'll still need to print a client copy of each document. Depending on what you need, your office can be set up for as little as $3,500. Charge at least $25–$50 an hour for your services; more if the job looks complex.

Keys to Success

Since people will always have to pay taxes, you will never run out of potential clients. IRS guidelines are complex and confusing to most citizens, so knowledgeable tax preparers are in great demand. However, constant upgrading of skills is required to meet the changes in forms and regulations. Tax preparation is seasonal, which means cash flow can be uneven; you might add other services to fill in the slower months.

Telemarketing Service

Start-up cost:	$6,000–$10,000
Potential earnings:	$40,000 or more
Typical fees:	$30 an hour
Advertising:	Yellow Pages, direct mail, business publications, membership in local business and civic groups, Web site with links to related resources, banner ads on sales-related Web sites
Qualifications:	Experience, persistence, ability to market your own service, writing skills for preparing script and reports
Equipment needed:	Telephone with headset, ergonomic office furniture, computer with Internet access, suite software, printer, fax, business cards, letterhead, envelopes
Staff required:	No
Hidden costs:	Utility bills, marketing time and materials

What You Do

Telemarketing is a specialized and very focused form of marketing. No business can survive without effective marketing. Your challenge will be to reach the organizations that need to develop their customer base and to show them how your service can help them grow. Telemarketing can be informational, a way of doing market research, but the major proportion will be focused on sales. As a small business, you may choose to offer a specific type of telemarketing: pharmaceuticals, commercial photography, wedding services, and so on. Specializing will help you focus on your own marketing.

What You Need

You'll need excellent telephone equipment and reasonably sophisticated computer equipment to track results and produce reports (about $6,000 to start). Once you get the hang of it, you can make $40,000 annually.

Keys to Success

People skills are even more important to success as a telemarketer than they are in other types of small businesses. Listening well, being persuasive, and fine-tuning the message for the receivers of your calls are all essential. You'll need experience writing effective scripts, and you'll need patience and persistence. It will probably take some time to develop the client base for your business. You can distinguish yourself from the run-of-the-mill telemarketers as someone who has experience, a proven track record, and an unquenchable enthusiasm for your clients' projects.

EXPERT ADVICE

What sets your business apart from others like it?

"While there are many marketing and advertising agencies, public relations firms, and telemarketing organizations, my company is a one-stop agency that has the capability of coordinating any and all aspects of a marketing plan," says Cheryl D. Cira, owner of Marketing Dimensions in Columbus, Ohio. "I cannot stress how important it is to be honest and up-front with your customers. Marketing Dimensions looks at each project and account as a long-term relationship."

Things you couldn't do without

"Essentials include telephone equipment and office furniture. It also helps to have computers in order to enter large lists, track calls, pull up records, and run reports. Computers are also used for simple design work, database management, and mail merges," says Cira.

Staffing tips:

"Telemarketing projects depend on the work and devotion of employees. And, because people are people, there are some aspects that cannot be controlled, such as employees quitting without notice, coming in late, and calling in sick time after time. My office manager is very good at juggling schedules and maintaining a strong pool of telemarketers, but it can get crazy at times."

If you had to do it all over again . . .

"I don't think there is any one thing of great importance that I would change or do differently. In general, however, I wish that I had had more hands-on experience in managing a large staff and more working knowledge related to personnel issues."

Temporary Employment Agency

Start-up cost:	$60,000–$150,000+
Potential earnings:	$200,000–$450,000
Typical fees:	$1,000–$1,500 per employee per project
Advertising:	Yellow Pages, direct mail, newspaper ads, billboards, referrals, Web site with current job listings and online registration capability for temp employees
Qualifications:	Previous employment agency experience would be helpful; business background and ability to match candidates successfully are paramount
Equipment needed:	Cell phone, computers (four to six) with printers and fax, Internet access, phone system
Staff required:	Yes
Hidden costs:	Workers' compensation

What You Do

Temporary agencies used to specialized only in clerical types. But since the era of corporate downsizing, there has been an increase in professionals entering the "temp-to-perm" field, from marketing communications professionals to product designers and even attorneys. It's a $33-billion industry, mainly because the large companies that employed thousands a few years ago are now using help only as they need it or are seeking to try out candidates for a few months until they're sure they want to hire them permanently. After all, from their point of view, why pay the huge benefits packages and salaries for work that can be done, even if only temporarily, on a project-by-project basis? From your standpoint, this philosophy makes perfect sense; you're making your money on the fact that both workers and corporations are seeking less permanent commitment. Workers are beginning to see the positive side of nonpermanent employment; they can freelance, launch businesses of their own, and so on. And the companies see the obvious benefit of saving money where possible. It's a win-win . . . all you have to do is match the right temp to the right assignment, and make sure that all of your employees are trained and able to work on short notice. You'll do an extensive background check and insure that each temporary employee has sufficient credentials and/or experience to do a fine job. Then you'll sit back and reel in the money, particularly if you choose to specialize in a hot area such as nursing or engineering.

What You Need

You'll need $60,000–$150,000 to buy into a franchise. If you decide to go it alone, you may need more because you'll have to pay for a comprehensive benefits plan, several computers, specialized software programs (including scheduling and billing) and the placement staff or account executives to manage each account thoroughly and professionally. This is an extremely lucrative field, and you can make anywhere from $200,000–$450,000 if you develop enough contacts and build a fine reputation.

Keys to Success

You can dig yourself an early grave if you don't spend enough time preparing. Know that your competitors are out there, that they have just as many good candidates as you. All you have to do is set yourself apart by advertising the uniqueness of your service. A niche gives potential clients a way to pigeonhole you in a positive way, so that they associate your company name with whatever specific need they have (for example, Acme Personnel = engineering specialists).

EXPERT ADVICE

What sets your business apart from others like it?

"We have a personal approach and a high level of applicants to choose from; in that sense, we're a cut above the rest," says Fran Doll, President of Superior Staffing, Inc., in Akron, Ohio, and recognized Ohio Entrepreneur of the Year.

Things you couldn't do without

Doll says her business thrives on a telephone system, a computer, and fax machine. "If our phones go down, we're dead," she says.

Marketing tips

"You need to have worked in this industry for a while before embarking on your own. It's not as easy as it looks. Also, be sure you have enough capital or you'll have cash flow problems."

If you had to do it all over again . . .

"I would be more careful about the accountants I chose to work with. I had two accountants who really messed me up."

Ticket Broker

Start-up cost:	$15,000–$35,000
Potential earnings:	$25,000–$35,000+
Typical fees:	5 to 40 percent of each sale
Advertising:	Industry trade publications, newspapers, Web site with e-commerce capability via secure server
Qualifications:	Knowledge of state licensing requirements
Equipment needed:	Computer with specialized software program/hookup, toll-free phone number, e-commerce capability on Web site
Staff required:	No
Hidden costs:	Being liable for unsold tickets because contract didn't state otherwise

What You Do

How many times have you wanted to buy tickets for an event or a show only to find that they're all sold? For those who simply can't get to the big tickets, ticket brokers provide a welcome relief by offering tickets, often at a discounted rate, and the convenience of purchasing by phone or via the Internet. Organization and responsibility are key to this business. Your job includes assigning seat locations, providing ticket sales information, making recommendations about ticket pricing according to the area or event, soliciting group sales, and keeping a customer ticket list. You'll need to purchase specialized software that allows you to search online for ticket availability and accept credit card orders over the phone. Or, better yet, purchase an e-commerce Web site that allows you to make money while you sleep. An accounting or bookkeeping background would prove especially helpful, as there are a million little details that need to be managed on a daily basis to keep this one up and running.

What You Need

Computers are a way of life for this occupation. You have to be able to hook up to the ticket distribution center. Your fee will depend on the event and place. Typically your cut is between 5 and 40 percent of each sale, depending on whether you're selling locally or nationally.

Keys to Success

You may need to hire a staff to run this from your home; it all depends on how big you want to get. There may be some travel involved, and you'll want to attend all of the trade shows so the industry knows you are out there. Most of the big ticket brokers have been in business a long time and have a good reputation. Get to know them; you may need to network with them sometime.

Time-Management Specialist

Start-up cost:	$1,000–$6,500
Potential earnings:	$20,000–$40,000
Typical fees:	$75–$100 per hour or $100+ per person for classes
Advertising:	Free workshops/seminars and other public speaking, word-of-mouth, networking, news releases, written articles, Web site with some free tips
Qualifications:	High level of organization, analytical ability, punctuality, ability to deliver on your commitments, an open mind
Equipment needed:	Cell phone, computer with Internet access, fax, printer, time-management software, handouts
Staff required:	No
Hidden costs:	Preparation time if you are not already using a previously written program, licensing fees if you are

What You Do

Bringing relief to people under inordinate stress is just one of the many benefits of being a time-management specialist. In addition to making the workplace a little less of a sweatshop, you'll be assisting clients with setting goals, developing action plans, defining priorities, and scheduling/delegating tasks. You may decide to work as a consultant, identifying problems for harried company executives in pursuit of higher productivity. But you may also decide to add on additional services, such as seminars for large groups or individual personal productivity training. The opportunities to make money from time are there, you just need to send the message out to the many people in need of your services. Quick profitability is a definite possibility with this low overhead business, but you need to charge appropriately for your time and expertise. One last tip: Don't forget to offer periodic refresher courses to former clients; you'd be surprised how many of them would welcome the opportunity.

What You Need

Word-of-mouth advertising keeps initial costs low in this business, because it is based on credibility and trust of the specialist. To present a professional image, allow a minimum of $250 for business cards, letterhead, and brochures. Computer costs can range from $1,500 to $5,000. Remember that organizational dues will be necessary to continually network and prospect for clients; set aside at least $250 per year for this valuable lead-generator. Charge at least $75 per hour for corporate consulting and $1,000 per day for conducting seminars for groups of professionals.

Keys to Success

The art of managing time is relatively new to businesses. Hence, competition may not be a significant problem. If you enjoy leading others to dramatic results in a short period of time, this career can be extremely enjoyable. But you should be advised that this work demands a lot of your own time and energy to get started; are you able to practice what you preach? It may take as much as a year or two before you are able to make a full-time income.

EXPERT ADVICE

What sets your business apart from others like it?

Jennifer Annandono, Managing Partner of the Progressive Leadership Center in Kent, Ohio, says, "I greatly enjoy demonstrating to others how to have a more balanced work and personal life. My feeling is that time management is about setting goals and implementing new tools that will promote achievement."

Things you couldn't do without

Annandono says she could not do without a cell phone, voice mail, computer, and printer.

Marketing tips

"It is always more effective to market your service as the 'benefit' customers will receive rather than focusing on various features you might offer. Much of my marketing success is based in community interaction and word-of-mouth referral. The best advice is: always be a product of the service you provide!"

If you had to do it all over again . . .

"I would have spent the months preceding the opening of my business selecting centers of influence. If you are not already established in the community, it is never too early to identify and communicate with those individuals who know and trust you and clearly understand what service you provide."

Trademark Agent

Start-up cost:	$1,000–$1,500
Potential earnings:	$40,000–$65,000
Typical fees:	$175–$250 flat fee ($500–$10,000 for larger corporations)
Advertising:	Business publications, direct mail, referrals, networking, Web site

Qualifications:	Extensive experience in trademark or patent field, familiarity with specialized computer searches, law degree helpful
Equipment needed:	Cell phone, computer with Internet access, fax, business cards, letterhead, envelopes
Staff required:	No
Hidden costs:	Insurance, Internet service provider fees, subscription-only services

What You Do

The business cliché of today is that perception is reality. Whether you agree with that idea or not, the image of a product or service is undeniably a factor in its value. Since medieval times, a trademark has been a way of protecting an essential element of that image, the name. Since medieval times, however, an incredibly large number of names have been trademarked, and your clients need to know if they can call their stunt act Angelic Skydiving Service or if someone in Hawaii has already used that name. You will discover if the name has already been used by conducting a search of the paper records at the Trademark Office in Washington, D.C. Database information such as records from all 50 Secretaries of State is proprietary—owned by your giant competitors—so as a small business person, you must rely on detailed, cross-referenced searches in online databases. Many trademark agents specialize in a field they know well, such as tire names, for example.

What You Need

Costs are relatively low, especially if you already have a computer (add $1,000 if you don't). The outlay of your own labor will be high for each search. If you are an attorney, you'll likely use a computer database, but if you're not, you'll have to do it all manually or pay a researcher to do it for you. Charge $175–$250 per search/registry for small to medium-size businesses; by the project (typically $500–$10,000, depending on size and complexity) working for a large corporation, although some companies already have attorneys on the payroll who accomplish the same work.

Keys to Success

Skill and sometimes intuition are required to establish the validity of a given trademark. Finding the proper trademark files is an art. You can't simply look up a name, like "sword," in an index. Instead, you must consider all words with similar meanings, like "rapier" and "saber," as well as the words with similar sounds, like "sod" and "sore." Then you must consider designs that might include swords. It all becomes quite complicated, so be sure you enjoy minute details before embarking on this one.

Translation Services

Start-up cost:	$1,000–$2,000
Potential earnings:	$20,000–$30,000
Typical fees:	$25–$35 per hour
Advertising:	Trade journals, Yellow Pages, referrals, networking, Web site
Qualifications:	Proficiency in a foreign language, excellent writing and communications skills
Equipment needed:	Cell phone, computer with Internet access, fax, printer, translation software, office furniture, business cards, letterhead, envelopes
Staff required:	Yes, for languages you cannot translate yourself
Hidden costs:	Phone calls, marketing

What You Do

Thousands of languages are spoken across the globe, and even within the United States texts often need translation into other languages such as French or Spanish. For most business communications in the global marketplace, a translation service can be useful to develop, among other things, a glossary of terms to use in the translation process. Additional services can relate to development of icons and illustrations that are effective across cultures. You can specialize in a business field such as medical instrument sales or you can focus on one particular language. Producing effective, accurate results under deadline will enable you to build your translation business into a very successful enterprise.

What You Need

Reference materials and the normal office equipment are the major start-up costs. You'll need a printer that can produce all of the characters and accent marks used in your specialty language(s). A good translation software package would be helpful, too (although you shouldn't rely exclusively on it). Grand start-up total should be somewhere from $1,000 to $2,000. Earnings will come from hourly fees ranging from $25 to $35.

Keys to Success

The market for translation services is growing rapidly and will continue to do so in the future. English is by no means a universal language, and few Americans are fluent enough in a foreign language to produce their own translations. You'll be learning as you translate while providing a very significant service to your clients.

Translating is not a matter of simply plugging words into slots, one foreign word for one English term. It's a creative and challenging activity to communicate the total meaning of a sentence or paragraph accurately, and your pricing needs to reflect the time needed to do this.

⊨ Travel Agent

Start-up cost:	$2,000–$5,000
Potential earnings:	$25,000–$45,000
Typical fees:	10 percent commission on each sale
Advertising:	Travel, meeting/hotel magazines, Yellow Pages, direct mail, location, Web site with travel tips and special sales incentives
Qualifications:	Knowledge of the travel industry and particular destinations; often, certification is required through an accredited travel school; training on the customized computer systems most travel agencies use
Equipment needed:	A computer with Internet access, SABRE travel software, phone
Staff required:	No
Hidden costs:	Phone calls

What You Do

Would you find satisfaction helping others fly to exotic places? Have you always been a travel nut? If you answered yes to both questions, you could potentially succeed as a travel agent. As an outside travel agent, you would associate with a travel agency willing to work with you. You can refer business to them (for perhaps a 10 percent commission) or actually arrange travel bookings for which the agency will cut the tickets (because restrictions on ticketing won't allow you to do it). For the latter work, you can make as much as 60 to 70 percent of the commission. There are also networked travel agencies that rely almost solely on home-based agents. So your options are many if you decide to embark on this exciting and interesting business. The best part is, many travel companies offer incentives and special perks for agents like you. You could wind up doing some sightseeing yourself.

What You Need

You need a budget for advertising, the appropriate computer and office equipment, software, and phone. You may also have to pay small fees, such as $50, to use your associate's name and ticketing number.

Keys to Success

The travel business is huge and still growing by leaps and bounds. However, you are at the mercy of a highly competitive industry with low-cost travel options, so you'll need to price your services competitively in order to stay afloat. Despite this fact, many opportunities still exist to make money in this field. The cost of running a travel business is modest if you are working as an outside agent; little more than computer and office equipment are required. On the downside, opening your own agency can be an expensive proposition. It also takes time to get established, and competition from larger agencies capable of booking large corporate accounts can be daunting.

EXPERT ADVICE

What sets your business apart from others like it?

"My agents and I have traveled to almost every destination in the world, so I would say that personal experience sets us apart from other travel agents," says Helen Meek, owner of Helen Meek Travel in Fairlawn, Ohio.

Things you couldn't do without

Computers with specialized reservation programs leased from airline companies and telephones are the primary pieces of equipment needed to run this travel agency. "We also couldn't do without our experienced, wonderful staff," says Meek.

Marketing tips

"You need to look at location and market demographics. I knew my area would grow, and now I'm an established leader in my geographic location." Meek also advises entrepreneurs to get their names out there any way possible while building credibility.

If you had to do it all over again . . .

"Nothing. It's worked for thirteen years, and if you can get past those first five, you are probably going to make it."

Upholsterer

Start-up cost:	$150–$1,500
Potential earnings:	$45,000–$125,000+
Typical fees:	$75–$400 per upholstered piece

Advertising:	Community newspaper, direct mail or flyer, networking with staff at furniture stores and with interior designers
Qualifications:	Skills learned from the trade
Equipment needed:	Upholstery tool kit, vise and workbench, fabric swatch books
Staff required:	No
Hidden costs:	Additional materials and tools, membership in professional associations

What You Do

Furniture and fabric styles come and go. When it's time for a change, it's time to call in a professional. Maybe you're re-upholstering family heirlooms such as Grandma's Victorian recamier, breathing new life into tired old fabrics. Or perhaps you are recovering a series of chairs with the same fabric in order to provide your customer with a more unified look in their living room. As an upholsterer, you will remove old tacking and fabric from furniture and replace it with something new and spectacular. You may offer consultation services in which you advise your customers on their design options, or you could simply provide swatch books for your customers to locate their own new threads. You set your own hours and terms. You will always be able to find work if you live in a decent-sized market area and have the skills necessary to build a strong clientele.

What You Need

All you really need for a successful upholstery business is a decent set of upholstery tools and supplies, along with an eye for design detail. Of course, most upholsterers also share a love of great pieces of furniture. It may help you to buy a few books on antique furniture, in particular, so you can learn how to best preserve, restore, or re-upholster them.

Keys to Success

It would be a great idea to keep a portfolio of before and after photos of your recent upholstery projects. Pictures speak louder than words. If you decide to go high-tech and develop a Web site, be sure to include a photo gallery there as well. But really, when you launch this business, you would be wise to spend as little as possible until you've built up a clientele. Network with furniture stores and interior designers. Purchase classified ads in the "Services" heading. Go where you are likely to find those who are looking for upholstery services.

Used Computer Sales

Start-up cost:	$5,000–$15,000
Potential earnings:	$5,000–$100,000
Typical fees:	Used computers with appropriate software sell anywhere from $250–$3,000; your percentage could be a 50/50 split with the previous owner
Advertising:	Telephone marketing, word of mouth, networking, Web site with inventory listings
Qualifications:	Sales and negotiation skills, energy
Equipment needed:	Computer with Internet access, fax, printer, office furniture, business cards, letterhead, envelopes
Staff required:	No
Hidden costs:	Building inventory can be costly; be sure to figure in reconditioning costs if necessary

What You Do

There's definitely a market for used computers, but it's not an obvious one. To succeed in this business you will need to be the connection between buyer and seller. You will be advertising in both directions, as a buyer of used equipment and as a seller. Rapid changes in technology mean frequent upgrading of hardware by large organizations and even by many individuals. The "old" equipment may still function as well as it did when new, but need for a larger hard drive or more memory has made these machines seem obsolete. The previous generations of computers are very desirable to organizations that operate on a shoestring, to companies in developing countries, and to individuals who don't want to pay a lot to jump on the latest technology bandwagon. Your business opportunity arises from your ability to bring the used equipment together with its hidden market quickly and effectively. Operating this business entirely online is probably the best and most profitable option.

What You Need

A great deal of advertising is required, and this can cost you anywhere from $1,500 to $5,000 per year. Consider buying banner ads on general-interest and computer-related Web sites to gain some traffic to your Web site quickly. Inventory will be a variable but can lead to a considerable additional cost. Where are you planning to store all of these units? Add rent if you build up too much inventory for your basement. In this field, you could make a nice percentage of each sale. Your negotiation skills, however, will determine whether you can make a living doing this.

Keys to Success

If you love a bargain and can attract the attention of others who share that view, you can take advantage of the technology whirlwind that is costing the rest of us so much money. As businesses and individuals upgrade, they will appreciate the opportunity you present to sell their previous hardware rather than just junking it. And you will enable canny buyers to obtain the computers they need at a fraction of the price for the glitzy models hot off the retailers' shelves. Time and effort is needed to educate both sellers and buyers. Finding exactly the equipment a customer wants can be very time-consuming and require that you to have a network of sources. You will need to manage inventory costs carefully.

Vacation Rentals Broker

Start-up cost:	$500–$1,000
Potential earnings:	$45,000–$60,000
Typical fees:	10 to 15 percent commission
Advertising:	Advertising in real estate magazines and real estate section of newspaper, Yellow Pages, Web site with your listings, postings on other real estate Web sites
Qualifications:	Experience in real estate rentals, good organizational skills
Equipment needed:	A basic office setup for record keeping, computer with Internet access, cell phone
Staff required:	No
Hidden costs:	Insurance, vehicle maintenance

What You Do

A vacation rentals broker keeps track of all the details related to renting property for distant owners. Many people with second homes rent them for the better part of the year, reserving a week or two for themselves and their families. Renting helps with the costs of this additional residence, but it also creates a number of headaches and problems that are very difficult for someone who lives far away to deal with. Your service finds renters, writes the rental contract, and makes sure that the agreements are carried out. You collect the rent, check for any damage, answer the million and one questions renters always have, and generally keep an eye on things.

What You Need

Costs are minimal; you just need an effective way to keep track of information and money. Your income depends directly on how much time you put into the business. If you work hard and full time, expect to earn between $45,000 and $60,000 or more.

Keys to Success

Consider becoming a vacation rentals broker if you live in an area that has a high appeal for renters and a large stock of available summer (or winter) homes to rent. Once you develop a reputation for dependability, referrals will bring other home-owners to you. The amount of advertising you will need to do will vary depending on your area and the presence or absence of competing services.

Vacuum Cleaner Repair

Start-up cost:	$5,000–$15,000
Potential earnings:	$25,000–$40,000
Typical fees:	$45–$150 per repair, depending on complexity and parts availability
Advertising:	Yellow Pages, local newspapers, supermarket and community bulletin boards, direct mail
Qualifications:	Strong technical knowledge and hands-on ability
Equipment needed:	Parts, including central vacuum systems, from a variety of manufacturers (look for places that sell old vacuum cleaners for parts)
Staff required:	No
Hidden costs:	Shipping parts from overseas

What You Do

How many times has your beater bar been completely filled with animal hair to the point where it won't move anymore? The fact is, we've all experienced difficulty with our trusty vacuums from time to time. You'll have no shortage of customers. Every home has a vacuum cleaner, and all vacuum cleaners occasionally need service and parts. Market your business where most customers will look for you, such as the Yellow Pages or in coupon books. You could also offer a free six-month checkup for early problem diagnosis, and bring in instant business. Diversify as much as you can, too; by stocking replacement bags and commonly used parts you can make a tidy side profit.

What You Need

You'll need to set up shop in a comfortable place with adequate lighting and a sturdy workbench. You can do this in your home or spend $300 or more per month renting shop space. Regardless of which you choose, you'll need to advertise ($1,500–$3,000) and keep a fairly complete parts inventory. Charge at least $45 per job, plus parts, to be sure you're covering overhead and expenses.

Keys to Success

Supplement that business by installing and servicing central vacuum systems, a feature in many new homes. Cultivate contacts among local developers and builders. Build an inventory of new vacuums and offer them for sale as well. After all, if you own a $100 vacuum cleaner, would you want to spend $45 to fix it or would you just buy a new one? Offering solutions for your customers can ring up more sales for you.

Vending Machine Service

Start-up cost:	$1,000–$20,000
Potential earnings:	$20,000–$35,000, depending on the machine location and type
Typical fees:	$100–$500 per month, per machine
Advertising:	Direct mail, Yellow Pages
Qualifications:	Excellent sales ability
Equipment needed:	Vending machines and the products to fill them
Staff required:	No
Hidden costs:	Payment to the property owner of an average of 10 percent of earnings from each machine

What You Do

Although they seem to be everywhere, some research will be required to determine what type of vending machine is needed and exactly which spots might be most profitable for you. Without a doubt, you'll need good marketing and sales skills for this occupation. For example, solicit large factories to find out if they have round-the-clock shifts and need "real food" such as soup and sandwiches. Or, if it's a small firm, will only soda and candy machines do? Once you've obtained a client, that customer should be able to tell you what to stock, but ask to tour the facility so you can get a good idea of where to actually place the machine. If you go with soda and candy, make sure your client company will place your machine in a high-traffic area.

What You Need

Start-up costs depend on what type of vending machine you will want to use. Bubble gum machines cost as little as $100 and cappuccino machines can run as high as $1,000 or more. Whatever machine you decide to go with will be a winner if you market correctly, and you could earn $20,000–$35,000.

Keys to Success

Hit the big factories and large businesses. They usually pay you to come to them and don't require the 10 percent fee. You will also have to follow up on your machines; every day in a large business and a minimum of once a week for smaller-volume vending machines. This can pretty much be a five-day-a-week job, since most businesses close for the weekend.

⮒ Videographer

Start-up cost:	$5,000–$10,000
Potential earnings:	$30,000–$95,000
Typical fees:	$50–$75 per hour or $1,500 plus expenses per day for event coverage
Advertising:	Brochures, business cards, Web site (with streaming video samples of your work), wedding shows, direct mail to event planners and corporate marketing departments
Qualifications:	Cinematography and video editing background would be most helpful
Equipment needed:	High-end video camera, proper lighting and backgrounds, Mac-based computer with DVD creation package and/or video-editing software, DSL line, fax, printer, cell phone
Staff required:	No
Hidden costs:	Errors and omissions insurance, insurance for your equipment, maintaining equipment

What You Do

Whether it's a wedding or a cruise for top corporate sales producers, every meaningful event deserves to be preserved for posterity. As a videographer, you will capture the moments that people will most want to reflect upon in the days to come. You will take your expensive (and sometimes heavy) equipment with you everywhere, being very careful to plan for backup assistance in case it's needed. If you do primarily corporate work, creating sales or corporate capability videos, you can expect to travel a lot and to rely even more heavily on your editing and DVD creation software. You will also need to partner with a DVD or CD duplication house, if only as a source for mutual referral. Solicit new customers at bridal shows. And always bring lots of business cards to each event you cover, as referrals are key to your business.

What You Need

You'll need a high-quality video camera for sure, and this will likely cost at least $2,000. For your computer, a Mac with the right software packages ($3,000 or so, total) will best serve your need to edit and create DVDs or videos that can be burned to CDs. Get a cell phone if you don't already have one, since you'll be on the road 90% of your time. Spend the least you can on printed materials, as they are not as important as your Web site, which should include streaming video samples of your work.

Keys to Success

Stay current with the latest technology. Always be thinking about re-investing in newer equipment with enhanced capabilities. Remember to secure glowing testimonials about your work, and include these on your Web site. Most of all, since you're always taping other people having fun, don't forget to schedule some R&R for yourself. You'll need it, since this is a very physically challenging job.

Web Site Developer

Start-up cost:	$2,000–$3,000
Potential earnings:	$15,000–$150,000 or more
Typical fees:	$500+ per creation
Advertising:	Word of mouth, bulletin board services, trade journals, Web site as a showcase piece with dynamic links to your online portfolio
Qualifications:	Marketing skills, computer graphic skills, experience in cyberspace
Equipment needed:	Computer, high-speed Internet access, digital camera, scanner, and professional design software
Staff required:	No
Hidden costs:	Updating your own Web site

What You Do

Since they are so new and dynamic, Web sites are about as cutting edge as you can get in the world of marketing. Industries of almost all types are exploring the Internet; many have found that a home page connects them with their customers in new ways. An interactive full-color site works much better than a dull list of products with their specs. Producing an effective Web site is an art form that few can master effectively. If you can make the Web come alive for a client by designing a site that is visited often, you can be one of the busiest folks around in this ever-changing field. Businesses need to understand that surfers will spend time at a location on the Internet that offers something they want: an interesting, informative Web site that engages their imaginations and offers them products that they want or need.

What You Need

Internet service provider fees and design software will probably be your most significant costs, but you may be able to bundle cable TV, high-speed or wireless Internet access, and your phone service into one lower monthly cost through providers such as Comcast. You will want to advertise online as well; these rates will vary according to carrier but run $8–$10 a month for basic services and an average of $4 per hour on extended services. Set your fees according to what the market will bear. Check out what competitors are charging by visiting their Web sites.

Keys to Success

This business depends on several kinds of creativity at once. The process of making Web sites is challenging as well as compelling work. You're covering new ground each time you sit down to create. It will take creativity to market yourself as well, because the whole idea of computerized marketing is so competitive. Learning about your client companies so you can represent them creatively and effectively will keep you on your mental toes. Read up on the latest trends in cyberspace. Encourage daring creativity—and discourage "brochure-ware." Interactivity is king.

EXPERT ADVICE

What sets your business apart from others like it?

"We're based in the fundamentals of advertising and design," says Larry Rosenthal, Web designer in New York City. "We are also on the cutting edge; if it's new technology, it's been in here for an experimental run. Our clients appreciate the fact that we try everything out first."

Things you couldn't do without

Rosenthal says he couldn't do without a computer with high-speed Internet access, software tools, and external, peripheral equipment such as scanners.

Marketing tips

"Get yourself a Web site, and make it a well-constructed, easy-to-use one with a clear point of view. Also, use e-mail to market directly to those who might be interested in your services."

If you had to do it all over again . . .

"I would have started working on the Web even earlier. I would have also e-mailed Mark Andreeson from Netscape and asked to work with him!"

Window Treatment Specialist

Start-up cost:	$1,000–$5,000
Potential earnings:	$25,000–$35,000
Typical fees:	$20–$30 per hour or on a per-job basis
Advertising:	Personal contacts with interior decorators, fabric and drapery stores, Yellow Pages, local newspapers
Qualifications:	Basic sewing skills, ability to measure accurately
Equipment needed:	Commercial sewing machine
Staff required:	No
Hidden costs:	Materials can get costly; buy wholesale

What You Do

You can provide a year-round service with a heavy-duty sewing machine, space to create, and an interest in interior decorating. With the continuing influx of housing developments and condominium complexes, you should have no shortage for customers in need of fine window detail such as curtains, valances, or swags. Network with condo associations and apartment complex owners; they may provide you with regular referrals and a steady flow of business. Cultivate contacts with local fabric stores and interior designers. Remember, accuracy is a must because mistakes in measuring can get expensive if you have to replace fabric.

What You Need

Even with your equipment costs considered, you'll still be in the $1,000 to $5,000 start-up range with this business. The biggest cost, really, is your advertising. You'll need to get the word out through community newspapers, the Yellow Pages, and coupon books, so expect to spend $3,000 or more on advertising alone. Your hourly rate should be somewhere around $20 to $35 per hour.

Keys to Success

Make a portfolio with photographs of samples of your work to show prospective clients. Display some of them in fabric stores, and make business cards available to store owners and interior designers.

Word-Processing Service

Start-up cost:	$5,000–$15,000
Potential earnings:	$30,000–$45,000
Typical fees:	$5–$10 per page
Advertising:	Yellow Pages, focus advertising in a 5- to 10-mile radius of your business location, direct mail, university bulletin boards, networking with business and professional organizations, Web site
Qualifications:	Fast and accurate typing skills (at least 65 words per minute), customer-oriented attitude
Equipment needed:	Computer and software, high-speed Internet access, laser printer, copy machine, fax; optional: transcribing machine and scanner
Staff required:	No
Hidden costs:	Equipment and software upgrades

What You Do

Despite the abundance of personal computers, demand for off-site word-processing services has steadily increased. Essentially, word-processing is a fancier (and more technically correct) phrase for typing service. You'll be doing all the same kinds of work, only you'll be using a computer instead of the great typewriter dinosaur. Customers will come to you with everything from reports and term papers to resumes and technical documentation. The ability to produce an attractive product with quick turnaround will ensure your success in this fairly competitive field. Remember that just about any Joe with a basic computer system and printer thinks of getting into this type of business. You'll have to be able to set yourself apart from these folks as well as from the thousands of secretarial services out there (that perform services that go beyond your own). Position yourself close to a university or in a downtown area, and you'll increase your chances of success by at least 50 percent. Take it a step further and go after publishing companies for extra work.

What You Need

Your start-up costs are going to be quite reasonable if you already own a computer and laser printer. Most of your initial expense will result from advertising and appropriate software purchases, which will cost at least $3,000. Charge a per-page rate of $5–$10 or an hourly fee for the larger jobs. It may take you awhile to get a feel for which projects are more labor-intensive than others.

Keys to Success

Beware of underpricing your service. Consider adding a surcharge for handwritten or difficult-to-read documents and materials that include charts or tables. If you can stand the repetitive motion of using a keyboard, your income is limited only by your speed and the number of hours you want to work.

Workers' Compensation Consultant

Start-up cost:	$5,000–$7,000
Potential earnings:	$45,000–$60,000
Typical fees:	$1,500–$3,000 monthly retainer fee (depending on the size of the company)
Advertising:	Business periodicals, networking, referrals, Web site
Qualifications:	Ability to locate best rates for companies; experience in the field
Equipment needed:	Cell phone, computer, printer, office furniture, business cards, letterhead, envelopes
Staff required:	No
Hidden costs:	Insurance, membership dues

What You Do

A workers' compensation consultant is an outside contractor who works with companies to reduce the incidence of workers' compensation claims, find better rates, and discover innovative ways to save money. You will investigate the circumstances of the manner in which the employer deals with these problems. You might even administer the claims process for a period of time, instead of having a company employee do it. Typical strategies to reduce claims include: (1) investigating the claim thoroughly to determine whether it is indeed valid; (2) conducting regular reviews of workers' compensation benefits packages; and (3) recommending changes in the workplace to reduce injuries. The bottom line is, your nose for trouble can prevent a company from being taken advantage of—either by invalid claims or higher-than-ever rates.

What You Need

Investigative tools and the equipment to write reports are what you will need; spend at least $4,000 equipping your office with computer and printing equipment as well as a decent software package for all of your major communications. Your reports will need to be clear and easy to understand. (After all, they hired you to clear up the red tape, right?) Most disability consultants work on a retainer, typically $1,500 to $3,000 per month.

Keys to Success

This is quite a lively field. To establish your business you will probably need the experience gained from having been a workers' compensation specialist for an employer or at least another consulting firm. If you show that you can conduct excellent investigations, write effective reports, and make productive recommendations for improvements in processes, you can build a very successful enterprise. You will not be everyone's favorite person as you uncover cheaters, but you will be improving your clients' bottom line.

Index